SOCIOLOGY
of EDUCATION

SAGE was founded in 1965 by Sara Miller McCune to support the dissemination of usable knowledge by publishing innovative and high-quality research and teaching content. Today, we publish more than 850 journals, including those of more than 300 learned societies, more than 800 new books per year, and a growing range of library products including archives, data, case studies, reports, and video. SAGE remains majority-owned by our founder, and after Sara's lifetime will become owned by a charitable trust that secures our continued independence.

Los Angeles | London | New Delhi | Singapore | Washington DC

SOCIOLOGY
of EDUCATION

TOMAS BORONSKI AND NASIMA HASSAN

Los Angeles | London | New Delhi
Singapore | Washington DC

Los Angeles | London | New Delhi
Singapore | Washington DC

SAGE Publications Ltd
1 Oliver's Yard
55 City Road
London EC1Y 1SP

SAGE Publications Inc.
2455 Teller Road
Thousand Oaks, California 91320

SAGE Publications India Pvt Ltd
B 1/I 1 Mohan Cooperative Industrial Area
Mathura Road
New Delhi 110 044

SAGE Publications Asia-Pacific Pte Ltd
3 Church Street
#10-04 Samsung Hub
Singapore 049483

Editor: James Clark
Assistant editor: Rachael Plant
Production editor: Tom Bedford
Copyeditor: Camille Bramall
Proofreader: Derek Markham
Indexer: Avril Ehrlich
Marketing manager: Dilhara Attygalle
Cover design: Naomi Robinson
Typeset by: C&M Digitals (P) Ltd, Chennai, India
Printed in India at Replika Press Pvt Ltd

© Tomas Boronski and Nasima Hassan 2015

First published 2015

Library of Congress Control Number: 2014958339

British Library Cataloguing in Publication data

A catalogue record for this book is available from
the British Library

MIX
Paper from
responsible sources
FSC
www.fsc.org   FSC® C016779

ISBN 978-1-4462-7288-6
ISBN 978-1-4462-7289-3 (pbk)

At SAGE we take sustainability seriously. Most of our products are printed in the UK using FSC papers and boards.
When we print overseas we ensure sustainable papers are used as measured by the Egmont grading system.
We undertake an annual audit to monitor our sustainability.

CONTENTS

ABOUT THE AUTHORS

Tomas Boronski is Senior Lecturer and Programme Leader for Education Studies at the University of East London. He has worked in the primary, secondary and tertiary education sectors as well as in higher education. His publications include a book on the sociology of knowledge, articles on the family, inequality and multiculturalism as well as editing the UEL Reader in Education Studies.

Nasima Hassan, originally from Lancashire, has worked in secondary school teaching humanities, in teacher training and in strategic management in higher education. She has worked extensively overseas supporting teachers' professional development in India (Bangalore), South Africa (Kwazulu Natal) and most recently in conjunction with the United Nations High Commissioner for Refugees (UNHCR) in Malaysia. She has published chapters on the education system in South Africa, on Islamophobia and on the schooling experience of British Muslims. Her doctoral thesis explored the concept of 'Muslim consciousness' through a philosophical and political exploration of identity construction.

ACKNOWLEDGEMENTS

SAGE would like to thank the following reviewers, whose feedback at an early stage of this project helped to shape the final book:

Charlotte Barrow, University of Central Lancashire
Kevin Brain, Leeds Trinity University
Gill Forrester, Liverpool John Moores University
Yvonne Hill, Bishop Grosseteste University
Paul Wakeling, University of York
Sophie Ward, Durham University

The authors would like to thank all of those students at the University of East London (past and present) who provided their invaluable comments on the early drafts of this book and participated by reflecting on their own higher education experience.

Dedication

To Catherine and Josef
and
To Zulekha Abdul Latif Solkar

LIST OF TABLES

CHAPTER 1

SOCIOLOGY AND EDUCATION STUDIES

Chapter Aims

This chapter will examine sociology in the context of education studies and compare the sociological contribution to that of psychology and philosophy. It provides a brief introduction to the role of philosophy as both the mother and father of all modern academic disciplines including the foundation disciplines of education studies. However, it also offers a word of warning about the way such disciplines are used and the need to adopt a cautious and critical approach in our studies as students of education. Finally, there is a brief discussion of how disciplines such as psychology can be enhanced by a recognition of the social context and dimensions of education.

Key words: sociology, psychology, philosophy, educated, education, sociological imagination, disruptive experiment, inductive, deductive, theory formation, evidence, hypothesis, grand theory, middle range theory.

Introduction

This book is about education. More specifically, it examines education from a sociological perspective and provides you with an insight into the ways in which sociology can help us to understand some of the key debates in education today, as well as to challenge some of the things that are taken for granted and often go unquestioned. As students of education you can probably identify a variety of debates and trends in education that currently attract media and academic attention. However, it is just as important to identify those things we are so used to accepting that they go unnoticed or unchallenged but can, nonetheless, have a significant impact on society. For some critics of the education system there are a variety of generally accepted assumptions which they might question, such as the notion that our elected politicians should decide how our children need to be educated, that children should be tested on a regular basis and labelled with relevant degrees of success or failure, that schools are the best places to 'educate' children, that adults always know what is best for children or that children must acquire certain knowledge to be defined as 'educated'. These are just some of the issues that you, as education studies students, should be thinking about.

Thinking critically, however, does not necessarily mean thinking negatively, but it does mean challenging accepted wisdom and taken-for-granted assumptions that might seem, at first sight, to be unimpeachable. It also means being open-minded about conventional practices and being prepared to discuss them in a reasoned and academic way rather than on the basis of prejudice or merely personal opinion. Many of us find it very difficult and even stressful to do this because it may undermine our most strongly held views. Some social commentators and writers may seem to say things that sound eccentric or completely unacceptable. In the 1960s for example John Holt (1969) suggested that children should be able to choose what they wish to study rather than be told what they must know. In 1970 Ivan Illich (1971), a colleague of Holt's at the Centre for Intercultural Documentation (CIDOC) in Mexico, suggested that schools are places that inhibit learning and should be replaced by 'learning webs' and 'skill exchanges', which can be used by all freely and voluntarily. Schools, Illich claims, are places of control and forced learning that merely create social division and inequalities. More recently Richard Dawkins (2006) suggested that religious teaching in some faith schools amounts to 'child abuse'. This is a particularly contentious claim at a time when many faith communities are attempting to set up their own schools and both main parties have been supporting and encouraging faith schools in their schools policies.

Thinking point 1.1

Identify a value, belief or principle you hold very strongly. This might be religious, cultural or a common-sense assumption. Think of some of the challenges or opposing views to it. Is it easy to take these opposing views seriously or to be open-minded about them? Try to reflect on your feelings.

It may be a good idea to read Dawkins (2006) or Illich (1971), or at least discuss what you have read, with others on your course. Study groups are a good way to share ideas and reflect on the meaning and significance of new and challenging subjects.

A sociological imagination

The key question here is what sociology has to offer these debates and controversies? At a very basic level it could be said that such challenges to some of our most strongly held assumptions can act like a 'disruptive experiment' (Garfinkel, 1967) forcing us to re-examine the foundations of these beliefs and, perhaps, identifying some of their flaws and weaknesses. At a more academic level it is often said that to appreciate the full potential of sociology we must first develop a *sociological imagination*. This is a term coined by C. Wright Mills (1959), an American sociologist, who claimed that sociology encourages us to take a deeper look at every-day events and aspects of our society, and to make a point of challenging the familiar things we tend to take for granted.

In his introductory text on sociology Giddens (1989) uses the example of a cup of coffee to tease out the ways in which we can imagine a cup of coffee. For example, a cup of coffee is not merely a hot drink, it has a history: coffee is a product of colonial contact and (often unfair) international trade, and it is a legal drug; coffee can bring people together, 'Let's meet for a coffee', 'I'm having a coffee morning'; or it can denote a lifestyle – coffee table, coffee table book, skinny latte.

Thinking point 1.2

A sociological imagination is a distinct way of thinking but can take some practice. You might like to apply it to aspects of education. Try to focus on concepts such as gender, ethnicity, social norms and social class. Again, you might like to do this in your study group.

A key aspect of the sociological imagination according to Wright Mills is the interconnectedness between *individual problems* and *public issues*. Individuals experience particular troubles such as poverty, unemployment or educational failure. If an individual becomes unemployed, for example, we may expect them to use their skills and personal qualities to resolve the problem, such as by retraining and attempting to become more employable. However, when such private troubles become widespread and transcend the individual and the local by becoming aspects of the wider society, such as when there is a high level of unemployment, we have an institutional or social problem in that the individual's personal skills, character and qualities are no longer sufficient to resolve the situation. For Wright Mills sociology provides the insight that enables us to make the connection between the individual's situation and the wider social and historical conditions. However, Wright Mills argues that it is often the case that those in power – policy makers, politicians and business leaders – conceal these public issues by presenting them as private problems, suggesting that the problem lies primarily with the inadequacies of the individuals concerned rather than the structures within which these individuals exist and act. This can be seen in terms of the current debates in education such as why certain social groups or classes 'underperform'. Wright Mills' position on the role of professionals and policy makers is relevant here also because he suggests that many of those in positions of authority and power tend to focus on the 'pathological' traits of those who underachieve, rather than on the way politicians and policy makers organise the education system. The way working class boys are portrayed by politicians provides a good example of this. Responding to an Office for Standards in Education, Children's Services and Skills (Ofsted) report in 2003 on the 'underachievement' of boys, the then School Standards Minister, David Miliband said:

> We have to crack the lad culture that stops too many young boys doing well at school. This culture tells boys that it is fine to play around and not work hard. But this harms their chances of doing well, getting their exams and fulfilling their potential.

> (David Miliband quoted on the Department for Children, Schools and Families (DCSF) website (Department for Education, 2003).)

It could be argued that narrowing the issue of inequalities in educational achievement down to 'lad culture' seems to focus too much on the symptoms when much of the evidence shows that class factors and inequalities play a significant role in this process (Ball, 2008; Bolton, 2010; Dorling, 2011; Ipsos MORI, 2010; Jefferis et al., 2002).

A further dimension of the sociological imagination is that it does not merely accept what are often called common-sense beliefs about society; it encourages us to collect *evidence* in order to be able to look for patterns and trends and to be able to support our assertions. Evidence, no matter how convincing, rarely settles any issue because all evidence is subject to interpretation, but it is the basis upon which any credible claims are made. As a general principle sociology is about theory formation using evidence. Such theory formation can be either *inductive*, which involves collecting evidence and building a theory on the basis of this evidence, or *deductive*, developing a theory from which a hypothesis can be developed in order to test the theory against the evidence. Whichever approach is adopted, a logical and methodical procedure is expected and all claims and theories should be supported by the evidence or, at least, assessed and analysed in terms of the data collected. This enables others to check the evidence and any claims made for themselves. Theories are also believed to enable us to make generalisations about the world or specific aspects of it, which in itself is a worthy aim in terms of helping us to understand the world, and it may have implications for policy making.

The power of theory

A key issue in sociology is what constitutes a theory. Sociology in its classic phase during the late nineteenth century to the mid-twentieth century was characterised by attempts to develop *grand theories*. This means that sociology was seen as being able to explain how society works in one single overarching theory. In addition there was the belief that, by using modern scientific methods of research, the 'truth' could be 'discovered'. For example, Marx attempted to develop a theory of history that he believed was able to provide a comprehensive understanding of how society works and changes. Grand theory is also a term first used by Wright Mills (1959) to describe the systems theory of functionalist sociologists of the 1950s, such as Talcott Parsons, who, Wright Mills believes, were more concerned with abstract theorising and the function of systems and structures than with an understanding of the real world. What Wright Mills was identifying was a trend amongst sociologists at the time to develop highly detailed and abstract theories that made little attempt to consider what was really happening in society. More recently, postmodernists such as Lyotard ([1979] 1984) have pointed to the dated nature of grand theories that make great claims to have discovered the 'truth' about society. Lyotard suggests that the optimism of modernism, with its pursuit of progress, truth and objectivity, has given way to a postmodern condition characterised by a general decline in people's faith in science to bring about social progress and to solve the world's problems. In Chapter 3 we will examine the position of postmodernists on this issue in more detail.

In general, however, the initial optimism that sociology can act as a source of general 'truths' about society as a whole has given way to more modest ambitions. As Boudon (1991) suggests:

> it is hopeless and quixotic to try to determine the overarching independent variable that would operate in all social processes, or to determine the essential feature of the social structure, or to find out the two, three, or four couples of concepts ... that would be sufficient to analyse all social phenomena. (Boudon, 1991: 519)

Sociologists now tend to adopt a *middle range* approach to theorising (Merton, 1949), which consists of developing a theoretical understanding of a limited range of sociological problems through the examination of the evidence within specific contexts. The intention is to make connections between these different insights in order to build a more comprehensive understanding of society, rather than making extravagant claims to have discovered the 'answer to the ultimate question of life' (Adams, 1982).

However, even with these more modest ambitions, sociology has the conceptual power and methods to provide insights that common sense or, indeed, other disciplines are not able to provide. An excellent example of this is *labelling theory*, which was developed by Howard Becker (1963) to explain how the preconceptions we have of others can influence their behaviour. What Becker was attempting to challenge was the idea that all criminals and deviants are inherently bad and that deviance is essentially an individual act. Instead, he showed that deviance is as much to do with how situations are defined at a specific time, in particular, the power of certain groups of individuals to define these situations, and how certain groups are more likely to be defined as deviant than others. For example, in the late nineteenth century and early twentieth century, women who campaigned for the vote and for equal rights were seen as abnormal and even as 'unfeminine' and exposed to ridicule as well as criminalisation. The attempt to challenge male patriarchal power and authority was labelled as deviant. These labels can be seen to have effects that are independent of the motivations of the so-called deviant.

This is an extremely powerful idea which uses a number of conceptual tools that enable us to understand the spiral of deviance. However, rather than claiming that this is a total explanation for deviance in society, labelling theorists suggest that it helps us to understand how certain groups can become criminalised and may embark on a deviant career. Obviously, it cannot explain how extreme pathological behaviour occurs, nor does it purport to be able to do so. Moreover, labelling theorists do not claim to be able to explain how power is acquired and maintained. Nevertheless, the insights that labelling theory provides us in the field of crime and deviance clearly have relevance to the study of education, thus making the kinds of connections Merton was alluding to. For example, you might like to think about how the labels teachers use to define children can have an effect on their behaviour.

Thinking point 1.3

Think back to when you were at school. Were there other children who had particular identities or labels? Can you think of how they might have acquired those labels? Do you think that such labels may have affected the way they saw themselves and the way they acted?

A cautionary note

There is, however, a temptation to become seduced by the insights and revelations of a newly discovered discipline, and to see its novel ways of looking at the world as providing the answer to all of our questions. The reality is that no single discipline can do this. In the case of education, it should be borne in mind that in order to gain a fuller understanding of this subject, we must be able to apply the insights of a wide range of disciplines such as philosophy, psychology and social policy as well as sociology. This is essentially what education studies involves and this is one of its main strengths as it provides a multi-dimensional approach to education that enables us to see issues from a variety of perspectives. For example, a child's progress through the education system is affected by their social circumstances; they may have been born with a certain level of potential but, if this is inhibited by such things as a lack of opportunity and poor health caused by poverty or discrimination, then the child may have difficulties in maximising their potential. In addition, education and welfare policy will also have an impact on the child, and children in similar circumstances (Dorling, 2011; Jefferis et al., 2002; Wilkinson and Pickett, 2009). Indeed, the 'evidence based politics' of Wilkinson and Pickett (2009) takes just such an approach in its application of standardised World Health Organization (WHO) data on health and social progress to understand the effects of income inequality on the population.

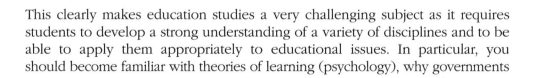

Thinking point 1.4

Think of the ways in which a child's educational progress in life might be affected by their social background, the historical and political circumstances they grow up in, as well as the psychological and philosophical ideas that prevail. A great place to start would be to view the Granada Television series *Seven Up* (2014). The series follows the fortunes of 20 children from a variety of social backgrounds born in 1957. You can find this on the following website: www.youtube.com/watch?v=CkNibRETzPc.

This clearly makes education studies a very challenging subject as it requires students to develop a strong understanding of a variety of disciplines and to be able to apply them appropriately to educational issues. In particular, you should become familiar with theories of learning (psychology), why governments choose to adopt particular education policies (political studies, social policy), how the education system has changed (history), how social and cultural factors influence educational attainment (sociology) and the purpose of education (philosophy). We will now examine two of the main foundation subjects of education studies – philosophy and psychology.

The foundation subjects of education studies

Philosophy

Philosophy is the mother and father of all existing academic disciplines; from physics to sociology, all are essentially the offspring of the philosophy of ancient times (generally agreed to have been located in Athens between the fifth century and the first century BCE). There were a number of fundamental questions which the Ancient Greek philosophers raised and which, to this day, remain key questions being addressed by writers, thinkers and academics: What exists? How do we know something exists? What are such things made of? Is there a purpose to life? What is the best way to live our lives? How can we discover truth? Clearly, such questions have links to education and the purpose of education. One of the most famous dialogues on matters relating to education from the classical period is Plato's *Republic* (circ. 380 BCE). A dialogue is a literary form in which the author creates hypothetical conversations between individual characters to explore an issue or a philosophical question. Socrates, for example, features as one of these characters in the *Republic*, which takes the form of conversations about the nature of the ideal society as well as an examination of the linked issues of justice and how education should be organised in such a society. It will probably come as no surprise to us that Plato suggests that philosophers should be the rulers of his ideal society – they should be 'philosopher kings'.

There is a clear link in the *Republic* between Plato's concept of justice, as voiced through Socrates, and his views about who should be educated and the form this education should take. He envisions a state in which justice involves everyone knowing their place and carrying out their roles without question. There are, he believed, clear natural distinctions between human beings; some have the qualities needed for leadership, and it is these 'golden' individuals who should be selected for philosophical training and ultimately they may, if successful in their studies, become 'guardians' or rulers. Through *dialectical debate* they come to see the connections between things and know the essence (forms) of fundamental concepts such as justice and truth. As a result of this training the talented few are expected to attain a condition of total knowledge. For Plato dialectic is the art of philosophical argument by which knowledge is achieved and this is essential for any ruler.

Those who are not chosen to become leaders – the common people such as traders, craftspeople and labourers, and soldiers – would be expected to receive training in their respective occupations. For such ordinary citizens it is the duty of the guardians to lead them to the light of truth. They would not have access to philosophical teaching, nor would they play any part in government but would be subject to the rule of the guardians. You may disagree with Plato's utopia and his definitions of justice; however, his ideas have had a great influence on generations of philosophers who have followed him. So great has been the influence of Plato on philosophy that the eminent twentieth-century philosopher W.N. Whitehead describes European philosophy as a 'series of footnotes' to Plato (Whitehead, 1979: 39). It was the Socratic Plato who stated that the 'unexamined life is not worth living', thereby urging us to think about life as more than just a series of physical experiences. Plato was, in particular, noted for his beliefs that knowledge can only be achieved through reason and that we should not rely on our physical senses alone to find it.

Thinking point 1.5

A good place to start an examination of philosophy is Bertrand Russell's *The History of Western Philosophy* (Russell, 1945). Russell provides a very accessible summary of the *Republic* and other dialogues.

You might like to read this section and discuss with your study group Plato's ideas about the ideal society, justice and the nature of knowledge. Why should we be concerned about such issues at all?

Aristotle (384–322 BCE), like his teacher Plato, was also concerned with asking fundamental questions about life as well as with finding the causes of all things and the links between them. Such an ambitious aim has been taken up by other philosophers over the past two millennia. However, with the huge growth in our knowledge about the world, both natural and social, philosophy began to branch out into fields such as theology, natural philosophy and political philosophy, philosophy of mind, aesthetics, ethics, logic and epistemology (theories of knowledge). Philosophers began to specialise and this eventually led to the establishment of separate disciplines as we know them today – physics, chemistry, biology, psychology, economics and sociology. Each has its own discrete body of knowledge and particular methods of investigation. With the separation of these disciplines from their parent discipline, philosophy was left to develop its own identity and fields of study.

A philosophy of education

The philosophy of education was one such branch of philosophy, which has continued to exercise the minds of philosophers ever since Plato's time, with questions such as how to define education, the purpose of education and how it should be delivered, figuring prominently over the years. However, if we were to enquire as to what constitutes the philosophy of education, we would be faced with a variety of answers. This is because there is no consensus amongst those who practice in this field as to what its subject matter should be, what its aims are and the methods that it should adopt (Carr, 2005). This is problematic for a discipline that aspires to be taken seriously but which tends to be recognised more for its divisions and disputes than its positive achievements. There are some practitioners who see the role of the philosophy of education as one of analysing and explaining the meanings of basic concepts in education: What is education? What is the difference between education and training? What is an educated person? Known variously as analytic philosophy (AP), ordinary language philosophy and linguistic philosophy, this branch of philosophy, which gained popularity in Britain during the 1960s and 1970s represented itself as being made up of second order practitioners concerned primarily with elucidating, defining and clarifying basic concepts for others who are able then to use such concepts to develop first order theories. Such first order accounts are likely to involve moral or political judgements about such things as the purpose of education or the fairness of the system. Philosophers in the AP tradition have made a specific commitment to avoid such tendentious positions and to be purely analytic (Hirst, 1965, 1974; Peters, 1966, 1973).

Nevertheless, what soon became clear is that AP is no more objective or value-free than any other discipline. Indeed, much of the work of AP has been criticised as being an ideologically biased philosophical tradition that supports and justifies the existing social order. Although analytic philosophers claim to be objective and value-free in their analysis of education, it has been suggested by some critics (McLaughlin, 2000) that AP is merely a source of justification for the prevailing education system of post-war Britain that has resulted in significant class inequalities in attainment and continuation rates into higher education. For example, what analytic philosophers such as Dearden et al. (1972) have claimed is that education is the transmission of fundamentally worthwhile activities as taught by the curriculum. The worthwhile activities Dearden et al. referred to was essentially the academic grammar school curriculum of the time (Carr, 2005). However, the evidence being collected during the 1960s and 1970s suggested that the liberal education system that analytic philosophers were advocating was, in fact, mainly being accessed by a minority of middle class and upper class pupils, and was being denied to most of the rest of the population, which tended to end up in secondary modern or technical high schools where the curricula were far less academic and few pupils progressed to university (Ministry of Education, 1954).

Tomlinson (2005) provides an excellent summary of the evidence collected during the three decades since the Second World War after the establishment of an education system in the UK which was supposed to be meritocratic, but which was turning out to be one characterised by a wastage of talent (Ministry of Education, 1959). Such patterns were already clearly discernible from the 1950s when, under the Tripartite System of education, evidence from government reports such as the Early Leaving Report (Ministry of Education, 1954) showed that working class pupils (Socio Economic Classes 4 and 5 of the Registrar General's scale) gained only half the number of grammar school places as might be expected in terms of their representation in the population. It seemed that the education system in Britain was far from being the fair and meritocratic system it was supposed to be.

Meritocracy

Meritocracy is a term first used by the social philosopher Michael Young in his book *The Rise of the Meritocracy 1870–2033* (1958), to describe a hypothetical society in which people are allocated to positions in terms of merit, which Young defines as ability (or intelligence as measured by such things as IQ tests), plus effort. Young was speculating about what was believed to be happening in Britain as a result of the policy of free education introduced after the Second World War. It was supposed to give equal opportunity to all members of society who could achieve their full potential, and bring an end to the pre-war system in which only the middle and upper classes had access to secondary and higher education, and hence all the best jobs. However, the evidence showed that this was not happening and that the class inequalities that characterised the pre-war period were merely being replicated under the new system. Analytic philosophers seemed to show little awareness of these historical and socially contingent factors in their analyses of education and as a consequence began to lack credibility. Their approach effectively amounted to an attempt to analyse education without taking account of the realities and context in which the education system was located.

Reading suggestion

You might read *The Rise of the Meritocracy* to examine Young's ideas as well as the problems he suggests might arise in such a meritocratic society.

Post-analytic philosophy of education

By the 1980s and 1990s analytic philosophers were starting to reflect on their position and there was an acceptance of the criticisms as well as an attempt by some to reconfigure AP to take account of these weaknesses in their approach (Carr, 2005). McLaughlin (2000) describes this second or 'later' phase of AP as a much broader approach to philosophy of education together with a consideration of educational practice, education policy and the wider social and political context of education. Others, such as Rorty (1979), developed what has come to be known as post-analytic philosophy of education. This focuses on providing a critique of modern philosophy and a challenge to its claim to be able to provide general principles and truths, something philosophers had long hoped to find. As we have seen, philosophers since ancient times have placed their faith in the ability of the philosophical method to reveal ultimate truths such as the meaning of life or what is the best way to live and organise our lives. Rorty proposes a more modest role for the philosophy of education as one of edification and pragmatism derived from the work of the American philosopher John Dewey. For Rorty, truth is essentially that which works in practice.

The challenge of postmodernism

For 2000 years a dominant theme in philosophy had been the desire to discover foundational knowledge. Foundationalism argues that certain beliefs act as the basis for other beliefs and do not depend on any other prior assumptions or justifications. Such knowledge, it is suggested, provides the foundations for 'truth'. So, the intention of analytic philosophy has been the identification of second order concepts on which to build first order theories in an attempt to create a true understanding of the world. The ideas of Rorty are very much in line with the more sceptical and challenging approaches to philosophy gaining ground during the 1980s and 1990s, in particular, the postmodern turn with its rejection of all truth claims and its critique of the modernist promises of progress and liberation through rational science. What post-analytic and postmodern philosophy were doing therefore was challenging the age-old mission of philosophy to discover the truth and certainty. Other philosophers of education have a more radical agenda and see their role as one of providing the means of bringing about social change through education.

Critical pedagogy

Pedagogy relates to the study of the aims and processes of education. In the relationship between teacher and learner there is a belief that some kind of exchange should occur, for example, skills or knowledge. Pedagogy attempts to examine this process in which, traditionally, the teacher gives and the learner receives such skills or knowledge. Critical pedagogy has its intellectual roots in critical theory, which is associated with the work of the Frankfurt School of Social Research. It is concerned with issues relating to the socialisation that takes place through family, school and the media. Each society has a dominant world view or ideology and it is from this point that critical pedagogy starts. In particular, it focuses on how, and in whose interest, knowledge is produced and passed on by schools and educators. Critical pedagogy is driven by the aims of critical theory, which are to investigate the role of social institutions such as schools and the practices that take place within them, with the intention of challenging the imposition of dominant ideologies and structures. Critical pedagogy, however, focuses primarily on the ways education can be employed to challenge the inequalities existing in the educational system. It examines issues of empowerment, and seeks more equitable and liberating educational experiences for those without a voice. The assumption is that a society that excludes groups from economic and political participation or that renders certain groups powerless is not just an unfair society but also an illogical society which needs to be changed. McLaren (2003) claims that critical pedagogy involves an examination of the relationships in schools, the way knowledge is produced and how schools are organised with the intention of altering them in the interest of the oppressed. The aim is effectively the transformation of society. This somewhat controversial role that is proposed for the philosophy of education is not necessarily shared by other philosophers, but the questions and claims made by critical pedagogy are certainly worthy of discussion and debate (see Chapter 4).

Thinking point 1.6

Think about the British education system: Are there oppressive power relations and inequalities?

The ambiguous status of philosophy

As we can see, the philosophy of education is a discipline with a variety of approaches and often incommensurable philosophical traditions (Carr, 2005). In addition, it has a very ambiguous status in the eyes of politicians and policy makers as well as philosophers themselves. Philosophy's potential value and relevance have been recognised since the ancients. Plato suggests that knowledge, as opposed to skills, can only come through the study of philosophy. It is a discipline that leads the ruler to the right decisions and to the greater good. Aristotle in his *Metaphysics* writes of the condition of 'man' as one of being in chains and that only philosophy can liberate him. However, for many, including Plato and Aristotle, philosophy should only be taught to the few.

The teaching of philosophy to a minority of the elite is a tradition that has been continued into the modern age in Britain, where platonic principles were adopted by the upper classes in the nineteenth century, and that, some might argue, persists to the present day. There developed a strong ideology supporting rule by a 'golden' elite over the masses and the maintenance of a highly disciplined and patriotic military caste. At the height of the British Empire in the nineteenth century and early twentieth century a gentleman who had aspirations to become a member of the ruling elite by becoming a Member of Parliament (MP), or of joining the civil service, generally attended the University of Oxford or the University of Cambridge first and studied philosophy rather than a vocational course. Practical subjects such as engineering were generally looked down upon. Teaching philosophy to the masses, or indeed anything that might cause them to reflect on their condition was strongly resisted. The emergence of radical social theories such as Marxism in the nineteenth century was even more of a reason for the ruling elite in Britain to be wary of the potential dangers of philosophy. Ideas such as 'universal suffrage', 'equality' and, of course, the agitation for socialist revolution caused great fear, especially as there were attempts to bring about socialist revolutionary change across the channel in France in 1871 during the short-lived Paris Commune, in the German states in 1848 and in Russia in 1905 and in 1917.

Eurocentric ideas

In July 2007 the then French President, Nicolas Sarkozy, addressed the students and staff at the University of Dakar in the former French colony of Senegal. In his speech Sarkozy spoke of the 'tragedy of Africa' (Purtschert, 2010: 1039) by which he meant the assumption amongst many politicians and academics that the relative lack of 'progress' in Africa in terms of her culture and economy was the result of something essentially African. Sarkozy stated that Africa has not yet 'entered into history' (Purtschert, 2010: 1039); she has not yet moved from a state of natural consciousness in which nature dominates her thought, to one where reflective thinking prevails. The President was actually parroting the ideas of Georg Wilhelm Friedrich Hegel (1770–1831) and the somewhat ethnocentric ideas contained in his *Philosophy of History* ([1824] 2001) in which nature is said to represent an unchanging system of beliefs and values that hold back progress. To be part of history, a society or culture needs to move from a natural consciousness to one based on spirit. Spirit represents the process of reflection on human ideas that leads to a restless desire for self-knowledge.

History for Hegel was driven by the dialectical process involving the conflict of ideas. Such conflicts result in a resolution (synthesis) leading to a new way of thinking. The ultimate direction of history he believed is towards truth. However, because Africa has not made the transition to spirit, Hegel claimed that the African consciousness was inherently natural and therefore likely to limit her progress.

Now we do not need to enter the debate about the merits of Hegel's philosophy, but clearly the views of one of the most respected western philosophers of the nineteenth century have had a great influence on the ideas and values of western civilisation. There is no doubt that his position was at the very least Eurocentric and at worst highly racist, but the legacy of Hegel is one of negativity regarding western attitudes towards African culture and civilisation, which clearly manifests itself in Sarkozy's speech. It could be said that contemporary views of Africa and African culture are still greatly influenced by Hegel's racist assumptions, which placed Black African people at the bottom of human development and evolution. As a consequence the achievements of African civilisation are often ignored or even denied.

When the first major European investigation was carried out on the ruined city of Great Zimbabwe by the German scientist Carl Mauch in 1871, he refused to accept that it was the work of Africans, instead claiming it must have been the product of the white settlers. We now know that it was part of the Bantu/Shona civilisation of the eleventh to fourteenth centuries. A similar view is evident with regard to African philosophy. Upon examining western academic tradition one would be hard pressed to find any reference to African philosophy unless it involved a specialised course in African culture. A cursory examination of some of the most popular education studies textbooks in the UK reveals little, if any, coverage of non-western or African philosophy (Bartlett and Burton, 2012; Blake et al., 2008; Sharp et al., 2009; Walkup, 2011; Warren, 2009). This is a strange anomaly given that the academy is supposed to be inclusive and open minded. In addition, given that we live in a multicultural society, the philosophical contributions of non-western philosophers are conspicuous by their absence in all but the most specialist centres of learning.

Verharen (2002) takes issue with the general assumption that philosophy was invented by the Ancient Greeks. He points out that all cultures have an intellectual tradition that includes philosophy – the love of wisdom – even if they do not use such explicit language. He goes on to argue that although he concurs with the aims of the ancients in relation to the purpose of philosophy in providing foundational knowledge – that is basic principles of truth that can be used to make connections between things to create an understanding of the whole – he does not agree with the approach of the ancients and modern educators to limit the study of philosophy to certain groups. A further claim which Verharen makes is that the ancient civilisations of Egypt and Nubia may have had a significant influence on the Ancient Greeks. If this is the case there is all the more reason for western philosophy to examine African philosophy and its influence on contemporary western thought. In addition, for Verharen, philosophy should be available to all, including children, who should be able to learn how to think critically and philosophically as soon as possible. It is rare in the UK as well as the USA for children below the age of 16 to be taught philosophy; it is not part of the National Curriculum in England and Wales. There are many justifications for this, including the claims by Plato and Aristotle that children lack the maturity to deal with complex philosophical questions. To this we may add the belief that teaching philosophy to children adds no clear benefit to the economy and is therefore a waste of time. However, one of the most telling reasons for their objection is that philosophy is potentially dangerous: knowledge is power. If we arm young people with the skills of the philosopher they may become too challenging to those in authority. Verharen suggests that such an approach has impoverished our education systems, claiming that 'public schools reinforce a slave mentality by refusing to include philosophy in their curricula' (Verharen, 2002: 304). Although he was referring primarily to the teaching of philosophy to Black school children in the USA, his ideas could just as well be applied to all children.

> **Reading suggestion**
>
> The debate about teaching philosophy to children is examined in Verharen (2002) as well as in Bleazby (2005) and Dawid (2006). They provide a useful starting point for students covering this issue in their course. (For references see the reference list at the end of this chapter.)

Psychology

Once again, we need look no further than the ancients such as Plato and Aristotle to find some of the first speculations about the workings of the mind; how we think and how we learn. However, while Aristotle located thought and emotion primarily in the heart, Plato identified the brain as the locus of such processes. He was one of the first *rationalists*, who suggested that although the brain is the centre of thinking, reflection, understanding and knowledge, we cannot rely on our senses alone for these processes. He stated that knowledge can only be acquired through the intellect, as opposed to through the human senses. Aristotle, on the other hand was an early empiricist who put more emphasis on the role of the senses; stating that knowledge of the world comes to us through our senses. These debates on the nature of the human mind and learning have continued ever since, and psychology emerged as a sub-discipline of philosophy, eventually becoming a highly respected academic discipline as well as professional practice in its own right, developing scientific theories of the mind and the brain based on experimental and analytic methods.

A word of caution

It is important to provide some words of caution about disciplines such as psychology, which potentially offer great practical and sometimes deceptively simple solutions to complex human problems. It is easy to be seduced by an elegant theory, often backed up by seemingly persuasive evidence, which purports to be able to explain the functioning of the mind or the measurement of human ability, the nature of our personality or the source of human language development. Students and even psychologists often take a theory that they have learnt or developed and apply it uncritically to specific situations. Psychology is a speculative discipline and it should be treated as such. Evidence needs to be examined and treated critically, yet we often accept certain psychological ideas as given, or accepted wisdom if not the truth.

Psychologists and geneticists have been involved in a variety of controversial debates and policies that highlight this point. A good example is the role of psychologists in the discredited theory of eugenics, which was a pseudo-scientific discipline devoted to the 'improvement' of the human race through the selective breeding of people with so-called desirable characteristics and of the 'control' of those with 'undesirable' traits. We can see an example of these ideas put into practice in Nazi Germany of the 1930s and 1940s, but it was also a popular discipline amongst policy makers in the USA and Britain for a time. In the USA two psychologists named Terman and Yerks were involved in advising the American government in the early twentieth century on how to control the number of individuals of 'inferior races' entering the USA. At the time there was a huge demand for labour in a burgeoning American economy and the fear was raised by some policy makers that uncontrolled immigration to the USA from all parts of the globe would weaken the nation in the long run due to the 'measured' inferior genetic quality of certain groups that included Poles, Russians and southern Europeans (Kamin, 1977). Despite the fact that eugenics has been discredited as a serious academic discipline, not least because of its association with the atrocities of the Nazi era, there is still a certain amount of academic activity that is sympathetic to the eugenics cause (see Chapter 5). A substantial number of eminent scientists and writers still subscribe to the view that we are not all the same – that some groups are less intelligent than others. James Watson who, together with his colleague Francis Crick, mapped the structure of DNA in the 1950s, is an advocate of 'positive eugenics', which involves, amongst other things, a policy of encouraging 'intelligent' people to have more children. The intelligent people Watson referred to did not include Black people about whom, it is alleged, Watson has some particularly offensive views (see Dorling, 2011: 68).

In the USA we also find support for such essentially racist attitudes. Herrnstein and Murray (1994) spoke of the new cognitive classes who reach the top of society due to their ability rather than because of any social advantage they may have had. The authors of *The Bell Curve: Intelligence and the Class Structure* suggest that a similar argument applies to the reasons why Black pupils in the USA perform less well in school and in social mobility generally. Psychologists, therefore, have been closely associated with the measurement of ability and intelligence, and in the sorting of individuals and groups into hierarchies. We can see within these psychological theories the influence of elitist educational philosophers such as Plato, where some groups are seen as superior to others and this is used as the justification for the creation of a hierarchical educational system.

There are, however, other philosophical positions that inform psychological theories and research on ability and intelligence, such as those which make the assumption that there are, in principle, no limits to what children can achieve. In practice, however, many children's abilities and talents are not effectively developed due to their social and physical environment (Dorling, 2011). Clearly we are not all the same, but many children are simply unable to develop to their full potential due to their basic needs not being met. A child who constantly goes to school hungry will not be able to develop or to study effectively and make progress (Campbell and Butler, 2012). Such experiences can also have long-term consequences for children's life chances. Maslow (1970) identifies a hierarchy of needs arguing that deficiency needs, such as the need for food and security, must be met before higher level needs such as intellectual achievement and, ultimately, self-actualisation can be effectively pursued. As we can see, there is much more to a child's education and development than innate ability. We will return to this issue later in Chapters 5 and 8.

The importance of the social

Moreover, we need to bear in mind the importance of the social environment in which children are born, live and develop. No psychological theory or research can be credible unless it includes these factors; children are social beings and the evidence collected by psychologists such as Vygotsky demonstrates this clearly. Vygotsky was one of the first psychologists to recognise the importance of the way cognitive development in children takes place through the medium of the child's culture (Vygotsky, 1978). Indeed, cultural factors including the values and language of a particular culture are believed to influence the nature and pace of cognitive development of children. If a society places high priority on particular cognitive skills or abilities, then the children in that society are likely to develop such skills sooner than they do in other societies where there is less emphasis on them (Woolfolk, 2013).

Despite these debates in which the role of psychologists has often been highly controversial, psychology has managed to establish its reputation in the field of education and now plays a key role in explaining how children learn and the cognitive processes involved in learning. Alexander (2009) in the very comprehensive *Cambridge Primary Review*, which presents a review of the main international and national research on the primary curriculum by psychologists, philosophers, sociologists, historians and policy experts over the past 50 years, identifies some of the key areas in which psychology has made important contributions:

- The role of play in children's development
- The age at which children should start school
- Effective teaching methods

In addition, educational psychologists occupy an important professional role in most education authorities advising and supporting head teachers, teachers and educational support workers in their day-to-day activities in schools.

Lessons from history

It would be reasonable to assume that education policy makers and experts have learnt a great deal from the mistakes of the past and from the accumulated knowledge of decades of research but, as with most politically charged issues, education is rarely left to the experts and some educationalists are quite scathing of the way governments have responded to the evidence gathered over the years:

> The lessons of past attempts at reform have not been learned. The lessons of past research and development have been treated as irrelevant not because they are genuinely inapplicable but merely because they are more than a few months old, or maybe because they challenge the preferred political agenda. (Alexander, 2009: 38)

So, we already know a good deal about what works and what constitutes good practice in education, however, politicians of whatever persuasion are usually driven by their own political ideologies and the next new idea, as well as the next election. What we actually get tends to be a compromise based on government priorities and limited by budgetary targets rather than pedagogically sound principles. In the following chapters these issues will be pursued in more detail.

References

Adams, D. (1982) *Life, the Universe and Everything*. London: Pan Books.

Alexander, R. (ed.) (2009) *Children, their World, their Education: Final Report and Recommendations of the Cambridge Primary Review*. London: Routledge.

Ball, S. (2008) *The Education Debate*. London: Policy Press.

Bartlett, S. and Burton, D. (2012) *An Introduction to Education Studies* (third edition). London: Paul Chapman.

Becker, H. (1963) *Outsiders: Studies in the Sociology of Deviance*. New York: Free Press.

Blake, N., Smeyers, P., Smith, R. and Standish, P. (2008) *The Blackwell Guide to the Philosophy of Education*. Oxford: Blackwell.

Bleazby, J. (2005) 'Reconstruction in philosophy for children', Inter-disciplinary.net Second Global Conference, 14 July. Available at: www.inter-disciplinary.net/at-the-interface/

education/creative-engagements-thinking-with-children/project-archives/2nd/#hide (accessed 7 January 2015).

Bolton, P. (2010) 'Higher education and social class'. Available at: www.parliament.uk/briefing-papers/SN00620.pdf (accessed 25 Jan 2015).

Boudon, R. (1991) 'What middle-range theories are', *Contemporary Sociology*, 20(4): 519–22.

Campbell, D. and Butler, P. (2012) 'Exclusive: Half of teachers forced to feed pupils going hungry at home', *The Guardian*. Available at: www.guardian.co.uk/society/2012/jun/19/breadline-britain-hungry-schoolchildren-breakfast (accessed 7 January 2015).

Carr, W. (2005) *The Routledge Falmer Reader in Philosophy of Education*. Oxford: Routledge.

Dawid, J. (2006) 'Communities of enquiry with younger children', LT Scotland Early Years and Citizenship Conference, July. Available at: www.docstoc.com/docs/26387812/Communities-of-Enquiry---Early-Years-Conference-notes (accessed 7 January 2015).

Dawkins, R. (2006) *The God Delusion*. Boston, MA: Houghton Mifflin.

Dearden, R.F., Hirst, P.H. and Peters, R.S. (eds) (1972) *Education and the Development of Reason*. London: Routledge and Kegan Paul.

Department for Education (2003) 'We can crack "lad culture" – Miliband', Wired-Gov. Available at: www.wiredgov.net/wg/wgnews1.nsf/54e6de9e0c383719802572b900514 1ed/d7e92417cfb856de802572ab004b802d?OpenDocument (accessed 14th June 2014).

Dorling, D. (2011) *Injustice: Why Social Inequalities Persist*. Bristol: The Policy Press.

Garfinkel, H. (1967) *Studies in Ethnomethodology*. Englewood Cliffs, NJ: Prentice-Hall.

Giddens, A. (1989) *Sociology*. Cambridge: Polity Press.

Hegel, G.W.F. [1824] (2001) *Philosophy of History* (with prefaces by Charles Hegel and the translator, J. Sibree, MA). Ontario: Batoche Books.

Herrnstein, R. and Murray, C. (1994) *The Bell Curve: Intelligence and the Class Structure*. New York: Free Press.

Hirst, P.H. (1965) 'Liberal education and the nature of knowledge', in R.D. Archambault (ed.), *Philosophical Analysis and Education*. London: Routledge and Kegan Paul.

Hirst, P.H. (1974) *Knowledge and the Curriculum*. London: Routledge.

Holt, J. (1969) *How Children Fail*. Harmondsworth: Penguin.

Illich, I. (1971) *Deschooling Society*. London: Marion Boyars Publishers.

Ipsos MORI (2010) 'Young People Omnibus 2010 (Wave16): A research study among 11–16 year olds on behalf of the Sutton Trust January to April 2010'. London: The Sutton Trust.

Jefferis, B., Power, C. and Hertzman, C. (2002) 'Birth weight, childhood socio-economic environment, and cognitive development in the 1958 British birth cohort study', *British Medical Journal*, 325(7359): 305.

Kamin, L.J. (1977) *The Science and Politics of IQ*. Harmondsworth: Penguin.

Lyotard, J.-F. [1979] (1984) *The Postmodern Condition: A Report on Knowledge*. Tr. G. Bennington and B. Massumi. Minneapolis, MN: University of Minnesota Press.

McLaren, P. (2003) 'The path of dissent', *Journal of Transformative Education*, 1(2): 141–9.

McLaughlin, T. (2000) 'Philosophy and educational policy: possibilities, tensions and tasks', *Journal of Education Policy*, 15(4): 441–57.

Maslow, A.H. (1970) *Motivation and Personality* (second edition). New York: Harper and Row.

Merton, R. [1949] (2007) 'On Sociological Theories of the Middle Range', in C. Calhoun, G. Gerteis, J. Moody, S. Pfaff and I. Virk (eds), *Classical Sociological Theory* (second edition). Oxford: Blackwell Publishing.

Ministry of Education (1954) 'Early Leaving Report. Report of the Central Advisory Council for Education (England)'. London: HMSO.

Ministry of Education (1959) 'Fifteen to Eighteen. Report of the Central Advisory Council for Education (England) (The Crowther Report)'. London: HMSO.

Peters, R.S. (1966) *Ethics and Education*. London: Allan and Unwin.

Peters, R.S. (ed.) (1973) *Philosophy of Education*. Oxford: Oxford University Press.

Plato (2007) [circ. 380 BCE] *The Republic*. Penguin Classics (second edition). Tr. Desmond Lee with an Introduction by Melissa Lane. London: Penguin.

Purtschert, P. (2010) 'On the limit of spirit: Hegel's racism revisited', *Philosophy and Social Criticism*, 36(9): 1039–51.

Rorty, R. (1979) *Philosophy and the Mirror of Nature*. Princeton, NJ: Princeton University Press.

Russell, B. (1945) *The History of Western Philosophy*. New York: Simon and Schuster.

Seven Up (1964) (2014) YouTube video, added by Trev Gibb [Online]. Available at www.youtube.com/watch?v=CkNibRETzPc (accessed 24th Jan 2015).

Sharp, J., Ward, S. and Hankin, L. (eds) (2009) *Education Studies: An Issues Based Approach* (second edition). Exeter: Learning Matters Publication.

Tomlinson, S. (2005) *Education in a Post Welfare Society*. London: Routledge.

Verharen, C.C. (2002) 'Philosophy's role in Afrocentric education', *Journal of Black Studies*, 32(3): 295–321.

Vygotsky, L. (1978) *Mind in Society: The Development of Higher Mental Processes*. Cambridge, MA: Harvard University Press.

Walkup, V. (ed.) (2011) *Exploring Education Studies*. Harlow: Pearson.

Warren, S. (ed.) (2009) *An Introduction to Education Studies*. London: Continuum.

Whitehead, R.N. (1979) *Process and Reality*. New York: The Free Press.

Wilkinson, R. and Pickett, K. (2009) *The Spirit Level: Why More Equal Societies Almost Always Do Better*. London: Penguin.

Woolfolk, A. (2013) *Educational Psychology* (twelfth edition). London: Pearson.

Wright Mills, C. (1959) *The Sociological Imagination*. New York: Oxford University Press.

Young, M. (1958) *The Rise of the Meritocracy 1870–2033: An Essay in Education and Equality*. London: Thames and Hudson.

CHAPTER 2

EARLY SOCIOLOGY OF EDUCATION

Chapter Aims

This chapter will examine sociology before it became recognised as a distinct field of study. The work of the eminent fourteenth-century Muslim scholar Ibn Khaldun will be discussed, as well as the claim that he was the founding father of sociology before it was properly developed in Europe during the nineteenth century. There will then be an examination of the emergence of modern European sociology focusing mainly on the work of Emile Durkheim, who is generally recognised as the first modern sociologist, and his sociology of education.

Key words: society, industrial society, social change, evolutionary change, revolutionary change, individualism, ideology, social solidarity, sociology, sociology of education, moral education.

Sociology before sociology

If, as we saw in Chapter 1, philosophy is the mother and father of all modern disciplines, then sociology is one of its children. It was conceived in the Enlightenment period of the eighteenth century, though some say this may actually have occurred as early as the fourteenth century (Alatas, 2006), and it was born in the nineteenth century. However, 'society' is something that philosophers have been writing about ever since ancient times in Asia (K'ung Futzu (Confucius) 551–497 BCE), in Ancient Greece (Plato and Aristotle) and in the Middle East (Ibn Khaldun, fourteenth century CE). In his discussion of the origins of sociology, Emile Durkheim, one of the founders of modern western sociology, claims that none of them applied a sociological approach to the study society, being concerned mainly with the idea of the 'perfect' society (Durkheim, [1918] 1960: 4). In the *Republic,* for example, Plato laid out his notion of the ideal city state in which social order and justice are the key themes. He claims that a just society is one in which everyone knows and accepts their roles in a strictly hierarchical system (Russell, 1945).

Plato had a very developed notion of such proto sociological ideas as *society,* which he saw as made up of a variety of parts all contributing to the unique character of the whole. In addition, he developed a distinct theory of social difference and stratification, the division of labour and the role of education in the socialisation and integration of society's members. However, if we define sociology as a discipline with its own specific area of study, a distinct body of knowledge using its own conceptual tools and methodology without recourse to non-social explanations such as divine mission or design, then according to Swingewood (1984) none of the earlier writers had applied a sociological approach to the study of society. They tended to be political philosophers concerned with defining or describing the ideal society rather than developing a theory of the functioning of social forces and laws.

However, Ibn Khaldun, the eminent Muslim scholar writing in the fourteenth century, produced a work that is believed by some scholars (Alatas, 2006; Dhaoudi, 1990) to be the first sociological work ever written. It is not known whether Durkheim or the other pioneers of modern sociology had come across or read this work, but in the *Muqaddimah* (2005) [1958] Ibn Khaldun claims to have developed a way of thinking (sociologically) that he had never come across before. It is, he suggests, a rational and evidence-based analysis of history in an attempt to develop a scientific understanding of how societies develop and change. Though a Muslim scholar, for Khaldun (2005) his religion was not an obstacle to this new science of society, for Islam, he claims, positively encourages observation-based knowledge and rational thinking. In addition, Ibn Khaldun (2005) emphasises the view that society is not governed by some divine plan, nor was it the result of individual motives and actions, but instead it is the result of social, cultural, environmental and political factors prevailing at the time.

> There is no hint of a divine purpose gradually unfolding in the course of history. The facts are observed, correlated and explained without any effort to fit them into a theistic interpretation to justify the way of God to man. (Schmidt, 1978: 24)

Such an approach to history and social change would not sound out of place today and yet it was written in the fourteenth century. From the start of the *Maqaddimah,* Ibn Khaldun proposes a rational philosophically based study of society. He identifies the ways in which the works of 'outstanding Muslim historians' (Ibn Khaldun, 2005: 5) have been distorted and rendered useless by their successors who he claims were merely interested in traditional and sensational accounts of history with no attempt to challenge or check the reliability of the evidence they reported. Ibn Khaldun's (2005) discussion of historical method reads like a modern manual for contemporary historians; he asserts that writing history requires the use of a variety of sources rather than a reliance on single traditional accounts and that there is a need to be guided by rational principles regarding the sources and credibility of historical evidence. In addition, he states that the historian needs to have a good knowledge and understanding of the cultural, religious, social and political conditions of the period under consideration.

Ibn Khaldun (2005) suggests that there are social laws that operate in societies, and societies with similar structures and modes of organisation tend to demonstrate similar patterns of development. This does not mean that history is predictable, as in the natural sciences, because he argues that environmental factors and human agency – the actions of people – play an important part in the historical process. Nevertheless, he claims that patterns are discernible that enable us to learn from history.

The basis for a sociological understanding of society

For Ibn Khaldun (2005) this is the key to his science of society: in order to develop a sound understanding of the social processes at work in society we must have a reliable source of evidence for our theories. Building scientific theories on tradition, hearsay or some external unexplained force is not the way to develop a scientific theory of social change. However, there is a clear tension in Ibn Khaldun's theory of history and social change, in that orthodox Islamic theology identifies a world unfolding according to God's plan. Ibn Khaldun seems to be attempting to reconcile the principles of rational philosophy with the teachings of the Quran by explaining how God has given humans the ability to think rationally, and by using this gift of rationality the social and physical worlds can be revealed to humans and more fully understood. We therefore need to place Ibn Khaldun's ideas in the context of the intellectual climate of the time; it was a period of a rapid growth of rational thought as well as one that demanded Islamic orthodoxy. The *Muqadimmah* is full of highly advanced philosophical insights that are regularly accompanied by affirmations of faith in the Quran and in God's wisdom.

Nevertheless, Ibn Khaldun (2005) presents a very modern approach to history and social change that effectively predates the work of more recognised sociologists such as Marx, Durkheim and the nineteenth-century German economist and sociologist Max Weber by several hundred years. The emergence of sociology is generally assumed to be a response to the effects of social change brought about by industrialisation. Ibn Khaldun (2005) was writing about the changes in Islamic societies but the changes were related to the effects of the transition from simple nomadic Bedouin societies to more settled urban/city societies which, at the time, had an impact that was almost as dramatic as that of the growth of industrialisation. In addition, Ibn Khaldun (2005) identifies the need for some form of social bonding, which would enable societies to unite their members together in a moral and social community. He calls this *asabiyah*, and it is a concept that anticipates the ideas relating to social solidarity which concerned Durkheim, Marx and Weber. These were the concerns of the earliest sociologist 400 years before the onset of industrialisation and the emergence of European sociology in the writings of the pioneers of modern sociology.

Ibn Khaldun and education

Ibn Khaldun's *Muqaddimah* (2005) was written as a response to the changing European and Arabic social, political and cultural conditions in the fourteenth century. Arabic scholars were concerned about the rapidly growing strength and intellectual flowering of European culture and the relative decline of Muslim civilisations, particularly in the Maghreb, which is the western part of the Arab world including Morocco, Algeria and Tunisia (Syed Agil, 2008). He attempts to provide a sociological account for the growth and quality of education as well as the reasons for its decline. Using his newly discovered historiography, Ibn Khaldun (2005) examines the patterns and evidence available and claims that the quality and nature of education in any society is closely related to economic growth, which is itself dependent on the nature of the society. Ibn Khaldun (2005) states that the level of intellectual and scientific progress has little to do with the intellectual ability of particular groups but is primarily related to the length of time a civilisation has existed, the size of its population and the amount of surplus labour. Where there is a large and growing surplus of labour the opportunity arises for greater numbers of individuals to engage in intellectual and scientific activities. This was the case in the more settled parts of the Arab world with large cities such as Baghdad and Cairo. However, in the nomadic societies of the Bedouins, which are less rooted, such intellectual achievements are much rarer due to their greater concern with meeting basic needs, thereby providing less time and opportunity to develop the intellectual disciplines. What we have in Ibn Khaldun's sociology of education is a clear recognition of the importance of social and economic growth in the development of education and its relationship to the division of labour, which was a key concern of Durkheim, as well as the amount of surplus labour, of which Marx wrote about in his political economy and his theory of class.

Reading suggestion

Examine a sample of introductory books on sociology such as Swingewood (1984), Macionis and Plummer (2008), Giddens and Sutton (2013) and Haralambos and Holborn (2013). How many contain a reference to the work of non-European sociologists such as Ibn Khaldun? How much space do they devote to such sociologists and their ideas?

The birth of modern sociology

Sociology as a distinctly modern discipline was born in the nineteenth century, a time of social, industrial and intellectual turmoil. Just as the first mass produced products were rolling off the furnaces and out of the factories of Europe, so too was there a flow of ideas and ways of thinking about the new industrial age as well as the potential dangers and benefits it might bring in its wake. In this strange, novel and, for many, confusing world there was clearly the need for an alternative vocabulary and language that would enable people to describe and to understand the processes involved in these changes. In the field of political economy Adam Smith, David Ricardo and Karl Marx examined the sources of wealth and profit in the new capitalist economy through concepts such as the *labour theory of value, surplus value* and *market competition*. Politicians, political reformers, trades unionists and political philosophers (such as Marx, again) debated the issue of enfranchising a growing and increasingly powerful industrial work force as well as of improving their employment rights and conditions of work. Natural philosophers such as Charles Darwin and Thomas Huxley proposed that humans had not been created in God's image, as most people believed at the time, but that they had *evolved* from more primitive forms of life.

The suspicion and confusion caused by such ideas and social changes are understandable given the degree of comfort the traditional certainties provided most of the population. However, Darwin's theory became very influential, not just in scientific circles, but also in the work of philosophers and the growing number of sociologists who saw in society a system that was subject to the same laws of evolution as any biological organism. In the words of Giddens

(1971: 66): 'It is difficult from the perspective of the modern age to recapture the extraordinary impact which Darwin's writings had upon social thought in the concluding decades of the nineteenth century'.

Thinking point 2.1

Reflect back on the first Thinking point you read in Chapter 1. Imagine how people in the eighteenth and nineteenth centuries might have reacted to such ideas as evolution or democratic rights for all, including women.

It is against this background that sociology was born. They were dramatic and exciting times that included the effects of the French Revolution of 1789 and the Industrial Revolution. The first person to coin the word 'sociology' was August Comte (1798–1857) in 1838, but he was only one of a number of philosophers who were concerned about the dramatic events taking place in Europe, such as the rapid change from agricultural to industrial societies, the shift from rural to urban living, and the changing ways of thinking, from traditional religious modes to rationally based principles; a process named by Max Weber (1864–1920), (Weber [1904–1905] 1958, Weber [1921] 1968) as 'rationalisation'. The response to these developments by philosophers at the time varied from the optimistic to the generally pessimistic; some saw such changes as a threat to the natural or divinely ordained social and hierarchical system and thereby to social stability.

Sociology emerged from this chaos as an attempt to understand such processes and events as well as predict what might happen. The immediate effects of rapid industrialisation and urbanisation were clear for all to see in the forms of poverty, disease, overcrowding, homelessness, crime and pollution. Such externalities associated with a rapidly growing industrial economy such as Britain were already being documented by social reformers and philanthropists including Charles Booth (1884–1903) and Seebohm Rowntree ([1901] 2000), whose studies of poverty in London and York, respectively, were groundbreaking not just in their methods of documenting poverty, but also because they found evidence to suggest that much of the poverty resulted not from the inadequacies of the poor, but from low wages. In other words, there were social forces beyond the control of the poor that caused their suffering. This ran counter to the prevailing view of the time and started a national debate about the need for a better fed and educated workforce.

Philosophical debates about the effects of industrialisation, the growth of democracy and urbanisation

The philosophers writing about these momentous changes during the nineteenth and early twentieth centuries had to develop a new lexicon in order to be able to describe and understand what they were witnessing. On a tour of the USA in the mid-nineteenth century the French philosopher Alexis de Tocqueville ([1853] 1969) believed that he had received a glimpse of the future of France and indeed the rest of Europe, which were experiencing the overthrow of, or decline in, the autocratic systems of government in which unelected aristocracies ruled. Tocqueville was impressed with the development of this new nation in which ordinary citizens – agricultural workers, tradesmen and the professional middle classes – were playing a part in the political process. This was something the ruling elites of Europe generally looked upon with horror. However, Tocqueville, although himself an aristocrat, was one of many thinkers who regarded this as an inevitable development that had to be managed rather than halted, unlike many of his French contemporaries such as the conservative romantics Maistre (1754–1840), Bonald (1754–1840) and Lamennaise (1782–1854), who were committed to defending traditional rule by divinely appointed monarchs and who harked back to a golden past when everyone knew their place in society. In *Democracy in America*, however, Tocqueville ([1853] 1969: 12) acknowledges that the movement towards greater equality and democracy was 'too strong to be halted'.

Despite Tocqueville's acknowledgement of the inevitability of such developments, he was mindful of the potential problems that they posed, in particular the threat of excessive individualism. Whereas American writers such as Ralph Waldo Emerson (1803–1882) saw the self-reliance and self-containment associated with extreme individualism as virtues to be encouraged, Tocqueville viewed such a trend as contrary to 'individualism properly understood', by which he means one that promotes the common good and the welfare of society. In Emerson's individualism Tocqueville sees the potential for individuals to lose their connections with others leading to 'egoism', which he refers to as 'exaggerated self-love' (Tocqueville [1853] 1969: 506). In such cases self-love becomes a barrier to citizenship and the fulfilment of one's obligations to one's neighbours and nation.

However, Tocqueville saw in American society the signs of social mores and behaviour, which he believed helped to promote the common good. For example, he saw the role that religion plays in the public and social life of Americans as an important means of regulating behaviour in family and domestic affairs, as well as being the basis of laws and of social behaviour generally. In addition,

Tocqueville identified the popularity of civic and political associations in America as an important means of bringing individuals together and reminding them of their membership of 'society'. He uses the term 'self-interest rightly understood' to describe the way in which citizens help one another in such organisations thereby combating the natural tendency to serve one's own self-interest.

As we can see, the importance of developing new types of social bonds to replace the declining traditional ones was a focus of Tocqueville's writing. In looking to the future and new ways of dealing with these potential problems he can be described as a progressive when his opinions are compared to the reactionary ideas of Bonald, Maistre and Lamennaise, who were advocating a return to pre-revolutionary times of aristocratic and clerical rule, in which a rigid social hierarchy was thought to be divinely ordained. Nevertheless, Tocqueville does show a certain degree of concern at the prospect of mass democracy and the need for those who govern to 'educate democracy' (Tocqueville [1853] 1969: 12). Here we see the signs of a growing recognition of the key role education would play in these new and modern societies.

The ideas of Ferdinand Toennies: Gemeinschaft and Gesellschaft

Clearly there was a great deal of division about how to interpret the social changes being experienced as well as how to deal with them. Even progressive thinkers such as Tocqueville showed a qualified approval for the growth of democracy and the individualism associated with it. This ambivalence on the part of many philosophers is understandable given the fact that no society had experienced such phenomena before and there was nothing to compare them with. One device used by the early sociologists as a means of distinguishing between traditional and modern societies was to devise typologies that would identify the key characteristics of each and to highlight the main differences as well as the similarities between them. It should be added that no society will fit the typologies exactly; they are ideal types and act primarily as heuristic devices in academic analysis. A heuristic device is a commonly used way of helping to identify the key aspects of a process or a phenomenon. It tends to distil an idea to its simplest elements and acts as the basis for developing a deeper understanding rather than providing an explanation. For example, in examining the process of social change, it is possible to identify the key characteristics of a society before the process of change has taken place and then compare them after the change has occurred.

The German sociologist, Ferdinand Toennies, is noted for one of the more memorable typologies of this kind. His work displays the kind of ambivalence to the changes of the time mentioned earlier but, as with Tocqueville, Toennies realised that there was no possibility of turning back the clock; the genie had been released from the bottle and it could not be put back. The move towards democracy, individualism and increasing rights was seen as too powerful to restrain and, for Toennies ([1857] 1957) the question was not how to stop them but how to create a new type of society that contained the best aspects of community living of the past, which he called *gemeinschaft*, and minimised the potential dangers associated with the more individualistic and impersonal type of society that was emerging, which he called *gesellschaft*.

In his analysis of the changes in German society, Toennies developed a set of concepts with which to describe and understand them. As a starting point he suggests that social action is generally directed by two sorts of will or motivation; one is based on traditional ideas that usually require little in the way of conscious deliberation due to their habitual nature. For example, in feudal societies rituals of deference and obedience to authority were usually performed without prompting; everyone knew their place. Toennies calls this *wesenwille*. Traditional bonds of family, community, church and with the feudal lord were seen as natural. The second type of will is one that is driven more by rational and instrumental motivations. It requires thought and reflection rather than a habitual response.

Toennies associates these two categories of motivation with the two types of society, one of which is based primarily on *wesenwille*, where social bonds are based on traditional family, religious and ancient customs (*gemeinschaft*), and the other in which there is more emphasis on individual contractually based interactions negotiated on merit and rational principles rather than ritual or tradition (*gesellschaft*). Although elements of both *gemeinschaft* and *gesellschaft* may exist in any society to varying degrees, Toennies suggests that with the growth of industrialisation, commerce and increasing social and political freedom, there is a move towards *gesellschaft*. In line with many theories of the time, Toennies took an evolutionary approach to social change and employed biological or organic analogies in order to develop his ideas. In distinguishing between *gemeinschaft* and *gesellschaft*, for example, he suggests that the former has the characteristics of a 'living organism' (Toennies [1857] 1957: 35), whereas *gesellschaft* displays the qualities of something manufactured or created. Moreover, he suggests that there was a progression from community-based societies to ones based more loosely on contract, business, rationality and self-interest.

There seems to be a tone in Toennies's writing that displays a sense of despair at the decline of what he believes are the more natural and spontaneous kinds of social relationships in *gemeinschaft* and the growth of individualism, which he believes results in the loss of community bonds and the emergence of atomised individuals motivated only by self-interest. This is a view he shared with the utilitarianism of Spencer (1820–1903), who claimed that there is a growth of atomised individuals resulting from the spread of industry and the production of goods and services. However, while the utilitarians argued that such developments enabled these individuals to use their self-interest to maximise their happiness through a greater ability to meet their individual needs and thereby their degree of social cohesion, for Toennies such spontaneous harmony was unlikely to occur. He believed that it was necessary for the state to intervene in the form of institutions designed to achieve this (Swingewood, 1984). Toennies did not seem to think that modern societies could spontaneously develop their own new forms of social solidarity. He suggested that they had to be imposed by the state. This is where Durkheim's total sociological approach differs from that of Toennies, for he believed that the basis for social solidarity in industrial societies could be found within society itself rather than having to be imposed from above.

Durkheim

It was in response to the writings of philosophers such as Tocqueville, Toennies and Spencer, as well as more radical writers such as Marx, that Durkheim entered the debate on the effects of industrialisation, urbanisation and the growth of democracy. He was also much exercised about the consequent spread of individualism and its impact on social solidarity. Durkheim was not only the first 'proper' sociologist – he was the first academic ever to become a professor of sociology – but he was also the first to attempt to provide a fully sociological account of how societies function and cohere. He sought the answers to these questions within society, and asked how each society was able to create its own moral order from within rather than externally through the political system. In Paris where he taught, students and intellectuals discussed the ideas of Marx, whose work was being translated into French. They pondered the possibilities of socialism as a means of creating a society where extremes of poverty and inequality could be abolished. Paris in the late nineteenth century was the place to be for philosophers, radicals and revolutionaries from all parts of Europe and beyond. Durkheim, however, attempted to stand outside the political debates and events of the time. He was more concerned with the effects of industrialisation *per se* rather than the effects of a particular type of industrialisation known as capitalism. He therefore saw the main problems as arising from the processes involved in industrialisation and not, as Marx suggested, in the class inequalities and the conflict of economic interests. Moreover, whereas Marx saw such conflict as inevitable in industrial capitalist society, Durkheim believed that the conflict being experienced at the time was abnormal and could be ended through the establishment of a new social and moral order in which excessive individualism would be controlled by such things as occupational associations (Durkheim, 1947) and a system of education that instilled in young people a sense of community and belonging to the wider society (1961).

Consensus versus conflict

The debate at the time between Marxists and Durkheim had fundamental political consequences as well as theoretical implications for sociology, for while Marx (Marx and Engels [1846] 1964) saw conflict in capitalist societies as inevitable, Durkheim was much less pessimistic and believed in the possibility of creating a new and harmonious social order, claiming that class conflict was not unavoidable. Marx's conflict theory was based on the assumption that all *modes of production* that have existed are based on a conflict of interests between a *dominant class* and a *subordinate class*. Marx defined a mode of production as a historical epoch characterised by a specific set of *productive relations*, such as slave labour or wage labour, and *forces of production*, comprising the materials, tools and technological means of producing goods. This was part of Marx's general theory of historical development in which he saw the evolution of these modes of production towards socialism, the only socio-economic system he believed capable of resolving these conflicts.

In the slave systems that existed in Ancient Greece and Rome most of the work (labour) was performed by slaves (the subordinate class). Citizens (the dominant class) were able to own and use slaves as they wished and, without such a mode of production, Ancient Athens and Rome could not have existed and prospered. Indeed, it is arguable that Plato and Aristotle would not have been able to spend so much time thinking and writing, or, in the case of Socrates, 'philosophising' had they not lived and prospered in a slave society. Similarly, in capitalist society Marx saw a conflict of interests between the workers (the *proletariat*) and the dominant capitalist class (the *bourgeoisie*) in that the latter, Marx claimed, wish to make as much profit from the former by making them work as hard as possible for the minimum pay possible.

The role of ideology

Marx suggested that any such systems of exploitation could not last for long unless the dominant class has control over the way people think. He claimed that in all modes of production those who control the means of production;

that is, the way the economy functions, impose their 'ruling class ideology' on the rest of society. In other words, they are able to convince all other members of society that the way society is organised is fair and just.

Ideology is a very important concept in Marxist theory as it helps to explain how societies, no matter how unfair or unequal, are able to exist and cohere by making the system appear normal or natural.

The search for a new moral order

Like Marx, as well as Ibn Khaldun and Tocqueville before him, Durkheim was concerned with the effects of the transition from one type of socioeconomic system to another and in particular the effects of industrialisation on social cohesion and solidarity. In his analysis of these issues we can see clear signs of Tocqueville's influence. Durkheim saw in industrial society many benefits and certainly did not suggest that there was a golden age which was being lost and needed to be recaptured. However, he did believe that the transitional phase in which he lived at the time was likely to experience conflict and upheaval as a consequence of the problems caused by excessive individualism. Durkheim did not see the growth of individualism as problematic *per se* but distinguished between moral individualism, which he claimed was the basis of a new form of social solidarity that he called organic solidarity, and egoism, which he described as self-love in which individuals place their biological desires and impulses above those of others.

His examination of individualism led Durkheim in a direction that seems to have run counter to his earlier work, which sought an essentially sociological account of social change and social solidarity. Nevertheless, he seems to have felt the need to develop a theory of human nature in order to explain the positive aspects of individualism, which result in increased social solidarity, and the negative aspects of individualism, which result in egoism. Human nature is, according to Durkheim, made up of two 'states of consciousness' (Durkheim, [1914] 1973); one which originates from our biological being and satisfies our basic desires, and the other which originates from and is instilled by society. Durkheim asserts that these states of human consciousness are constantly at odds with each other; one striving to satisfy selfish needs and the other striving to meet social ends. He suggests that these two parts of ourselves become more manifest with the growing division of labour in society (Durkheim, 1947). In modern societies work becomes more specialised and individuals come to see themselves as separate and more important as others become more reliant on their skills or knowledge. As a consequence there is the need for a new type of solidarity to ensure that the egoistical state of consciousness does not prevail. This is where Durkheim sees the role of occupational groups and education as playing crucial roles. The former would help to morally regulate individuals and ensure that members operated in the collective interest, and the latter would help to inculcate a moral individualism in the young.

The importance of education in Durkheim's theory

Not only was Durkheim the first official sociologist, but he was also the first sociologist to produce a sociology of education. The discipline of sociology was seen by Durkheim as essentially a sociology of morals that would provide the foundations for the new industrial society. He suggested that the transition crisis was not one of a conflict of material and class interests, as Marx proposed, which could only be resolved through a revolutionary change of society into a state imposed socialism. Nor did he agree with the views of the utilitarians such as Spencer, who suggested that social cohesion would spontaneously arise out of the economic contacts formed between individuals through the daily exchange of goods and services. He believed that individual economic interests alone were not sufficient to promote social solidarity. Toennies' notion of state-imposed institutions for the promotion of solidarity were likewise rejected by Durkheim as he believed that social solidarity in modern society should be established through social institutions in which individuals submit voluntarily to something morally superior to themselves, rather than having it imposed by external sources. He calls such notions or symbols of things standing above or superior to the individual and which motivate human action 'collective representations' (Durkheim, [1897] 1951). It is the collective representation of society as being exterior to as well as superior to the individual that Durkheim saw as the basis of a moral education and the creation of a new moral order.

Sociology as a profession

Durkheim saw sociology as a profession that had a role in helping to bring about social reform, setting it apart from any other academic discipline. For him education is the means by which we gain the physical, mental and, above all, the moral ability to function effectively in society. Durkheim did not have a single definition of what education is but thought that it should serve the needs of society. Each society is different so the form it takes will differ from society to society. He disagreed with the ideas of Kant who claimed that 'the end of education is to develop, in each individual, all the perfections of which he is capable' (Kant, cited in Durkheim, 1956: 62). He saw such ideas as too vague and lacking in social context. In modern industrial society, for example, he suggested that there is a need for the division of labour and for individuals to develop the potential they have in particular skills and abilities, which will equip them for their role in society; we all have particular talents and it is these we should develop rather than all possible skills, which he saw as an unrealistic ambition.

For Durkheim though the main task of education in modern societies is the effective teaching of moral education. Because he believed that the sources of morality and social cohesion lay within society and could not be imposed externally, Durkheim assumed that sociology is uniquely positioned to provide the means of bringing about a new moral order with which to stimulate social solidarity. He did not assign the task of the moral education of children to the family or to the church as he believed that in the modern age this should take place within the context of the school, which would prepare young people for the demands of society. In addition, he was quite clear that education should be devoid of all religious content. It is here that we can see some of the principles and ideals upon which the French education system rests: that of a secular organisation devoted to promoting the ideal of loyalty to the French nation.

The family is the appropriate institution for developing within the child 'homely sentiments basic to morality' and indeed for guiding children in their development of 'the simplest personal relationships' (Durkheim, 1961: 19), but, in terms of preparing children for the demands of the wider society, Durkheim saw the family as wholly unsuited and inappropriate due to its limited range of social relations. Regarding religion, Durkheim was concerned that there was a danger of religious organisations diverting or dividing the loyalty of individuals who he believed should be devoted only to the nation. In addition, a moral society as envisioned by Durkheim would be one based on rational scientific principles whose ideals are supported by reason and not, as in the case of most religions, based primarily on faith. As Durkheim (1961: 19) states: 'a rational morality cannot have the same content as one that depends upon some authority other than reason'.

The dimensions of a moral education

Durkheim's primary intention was to create a new secular curriculum that focuses on the three dimensions of morality he thought essential for children to learn and internalise. The first aspect of morality that Durkheim identifies is discipline, or self-discipline, which he believes is necessary if children are to learn to be able to control their egoistic states of consciousness. By accepting the necessary limits to our desires we acknowledge our obligations to society.

In addition, Durkheim suggests that limiting our desires is a means of achieving individual happiness, for having unrealistic expectations can only lead to disappointment. A further point Durkheim makes is that discipline is essential for the development of individuals, particularly if they are to be able to use their will in reflective and responsible ways: by restricting our desires we are able to more responsibly use our freedom.

Enforcing discipline

In enforcing discipline Durkheim does not advocate physical or corporal punishment. In fact, he believes that if moral education is to promote the idea of the dignity of 'man' then corporal punishment can only be seen as an affront to that principle:

> In beating, in brutality of all kinds, there is something we find repugnant, something that revolts our conscience – in a word something immoral. Now, defending morality through means repudiated by it, is a remarkable way of protecting morality. It weakens on the one hand the sentiments one wishes to strengthen on the other. One of the chief aims of moral education is to inspire in the child a feeling for the dignity of man. Corporal punishment is a continual offence to this sentiment. (Durkheim, 1961: 183)

Durkheim's position on this matter can only be viewed as progressive at a time when in countries such as Britain corporal punishment was widely justified and practised at all levels and in all sectors of the education system from the public schools to the elementary schools. However, although he did not approve of any form of physical punishment in schools in enforcing discipline, Durkheim was in favour of the judicious use of other forms of punishment. The purpose of punishment for Durkheim is not to cause suffering to the child or exact retribution for an unacceptable act or behaviour, but instead to highlight the act and its unacceptable nature, as well as to show how it offends against the community of the school. Children are expected to develop a notion of the school as something above them and as having a sacred quality that elicits respect and submission to its authority. As a consequence the offender is expected to acknowledge the harm caused to the community. Ideally, any punishment would entail some element of rehabilitation or compensation and should be seen by the pupil as worthwhile rather than eliciting resentment: 'Denying participation in games, extra tasks, as well as reproaches and reprimands are the chief elements of school punishment' (Durkheim, 1961: 198).

The importance of attachment

Though Durkheim believed that discipline is an important element in ensuring the acceptance by children of moral principles and values of the school, he did not think that conformity brought about by a fear of punishment was sufficient in itself to promote moral development in a child; there needs to be a sense of attachment to the community. In this respect the school acts as a miniature society in which children can develop an understanding of the wider society and its rules as well as a love for their nation. Moral development can only take place in the context of a wider loyalty and interest than just to one's self.

> There are no genuinely moral ends except collective ones. There is no truly moral force save that involved in attachment to the group. However, when one is committed to that society of which he is a member, it is psychologically impossible not to be bound to the people who compose it and through whom it comes into being. (Durkheim, 1961: 82)

Autonomy

Durkheim has often been criticised for presenting a picture of individuals as essentially the products of society with little in the way of autonomy. Indeed, in attempting to provide a totally sociological account of education he ran the risk of developing an 'over-socialised conception of man' (Wrong, 1961). Morality clearly has personal and psychological dimensions and individuals are not totally controlled by external social factors: they are thinking, meaning makers who interpret the world around them and act accordingly. However, Durkheim does not seem to take such an extreme position. As we have seen already, he had a view of human nature that informed his ideas about the development of individualism.

In addition, in his third dimension of teaching moral education, Durkheim includes the importance of individual autonomy. He suggests that conformity to morality can only be effective if it is performed freely and autonomously, but this is dependent on a rational understanding of the rules and values being taught. However, none of us is completely rational and sociology does not have a completely rational explanation for all moral principles, nevertheless Durkheim argues that it is not necessary for us to fully understand what it is we are being asked to accept, or the reasons why we should accept them, we merely have to understand that the basis for such rules is rational. In the process, the more we learn and understand, the more autonomous we become.

In his theory of moral education Durkheim is clearly attempting to create a morally unifying education that would help to develop the necessary social solidarity for a new age at the same time as promoting a moral individualism guided by the ability to show self-discipline, a sense of attachment to the community and a rationally based acceptance of the need for conformity to a moral system in the interest of society.

Chapter summary and comment

Most sociology textbooks suggest that the term 'sociology' was coined by August Comte in 1839 and that Durkheim was the first to develop a new science of society, which, as far as he was concerned, did not yet exist. He started to develop a set of conceptual tools and methods of research that were distinct from other disciplines such as psychology. His focus of study was 'social facts', which he claimed had an influence on how individuals behave and which were distinct from the internal psychological drives that influence human behaviour.

However, evidence suggests that sociology as a distinct discipline had already been devised by the Arab scholar Ibn Khaldun in the fourteenth century in his seminal work the *Muqaddimah* (1377) approximately 500 years before Durkheim. Ibn Khaldun clearly identifies the focus of this new science and outlines the method by which it should be studied. He claims to have discovered the laws that govern society and the process of social change. While Ibn Khaldun studied the social changes occurring in the Maghreb in the fourteenth century, such as the decline of the powerful city states, Durkheim attempted to provide an understanding of the effects of industrialisation on societies such as France, and to develop the means of ensuring a peaceful and non-revolutionary transition from pre-industrial society based on mechanical solidarity, to a modern industrial society based on organic solidarity. They were two pioneering sociologists writing about their own times but also attempting to provide practical advice to the rulers of their day, and both identified the importance of education in the social and economic development of society. Unfortunately, Ibn Khaldun's work seems to have been unknown or unacknowledged in the nineteenth century and, as a consequence, Durkheim and other European sociologists such as Weber and Marx take much of the credit for being the founding fathers of sociology.

Durkheim saw his ideas as forming a distinct alternative to the more radical ideas of Marx whose works were being discussed in the cafes and streets of France and Europe at the time. Durkheim did not see sociology's role as a purely academic one but envisioned a discipline that would have a role in policy making as well as in education, where sociology would act as a moral science guiding the nation's children in the acquisition of a morality that would curb the effects of excessive individualism resulting from the transition from pre-industrial to industrial society.

In developing the new science of sociology Durkheim was determined to base his theories on purely social factors and explanations that are external to the individual, as opposed to internal ones such as human instinct or human nature. However, despite this intention Durkheim did resort to ideas of human nature, which formed the basis of much of his sociology – particularly his sociology of education. In *The Dualism of Human Nature and its Social Condition*, Durkheim (1914) writes of the dual aspects of human beings, one in which we are driven by our individual bodily needs and the other which represents our social being. In addition, Durkheim claims that as individuals we have a limitless desire for self-gratification. As a consequence, education and, more specifically, moral education is seen as an essential means of limiting those desires and teaching children the need for discipline and commitment to society. Nevertheless, Durkheim denies that his sociology is based on theories of human nature, instead claiming that it was sociology which provided such insights into the human condition, a claim that does not seem entirely consistent with his writings (Ritzer and Goodman, 2003).

Whatever is the case, it illustrates the difficulty in developing a totally sociological understanding of society and the need for sociologists to use the ideas of other disciplines such as psychology and philosophy. Indeed this applies to the other disciplines also: a psychology that ignores the sociological dimensions of children's learning and development will be of limited validity. As education studies students we should be mindful of this.

References

Alatas, S.H. (2006) 'The autonomous, the universal and the future of sociology', *Current Sociology*, 54(7): 7–23.

Booth, C. (1884–1903) *Life and Labour of the People in London*. London: Macmillan.

Dhaoudi, M. (1990) 'Ibn Khaldun: the founding father of eastern sociology', *International Sociology*, 5(3): 319–35.

Durkheim, E. [1897] (1951) *Suicide*. New York: Free Press.

Durkheim, E. [1914] (1973) 'The dualism of human nature and its social condition', in R. Bellah (ed.), *Emile Durkheim: On Morality and Society*. Chicago, IL: University of Chicago Press.

Durkheim, E. [1918] (1960) *Montesquieu and Rousseau: Forerunners of Sociology*. Tr. Ralph Manheim. Ann Arbor, MI: University of Michigan.

Durkheim, E. (1947) *The Division of Labour in Society*. New York: The Free Press.

Durkheim, E. (1956) *Education and Sociology*. New York: The Free Press.

Durkheim, E. (1961) *Moral Education*. Glencoe: The Free Press.

Giddens, A. (1971) *Capitalism and Modern Social Theory: An Analysis of the Works of Marx, Durkheim and Max Weber*. Cambridge: Cambridge University Press.

Giddens, A. and Sutton, P.W. (2013) *Sociology* (seventh edition). Cambridge: Polity Press.

Haralambos, M. and Holborn, M. (2013) *Sociology: Themes and Perspectives* (eighth edition). London: Collins.

Khaldun, I. [1958] (2005) *The Muqaddimah: An Introduction to History*. Tr. Franz Rosental. Princeton, NJ: Princeton/Bollingen Paperbacks.

Macionis, J.J. and Plummer, K. (2008) *Sociology: A Global Introduction*. London: Pearson, Prentice Hall.

Marx, K. and Engels, F. [1846] (1964) *The German Ideology*. London: Lawrence and Wishart.

Ritzer, G. and Goodman, D.J. (2003) *Sociological Theory*. New York: McGraw Hill.

Rowntree, S. [1901] (2000) *Poverty: A Study of Town Life*. Bristol: The Policy Press.

Russell, B. (1945) *The History of Western Philosophy*. New York: Simon and Schuster.

Schmidt, N. (1978) *Ibn Khaldun: Historian, Sociologist and Philosopher*. Lahore: Universal Books.

Swingewood, A. (1984) *A Short History of Sociological Thought*. London: Macmillan.

Syed Agil, S. (2008) 'Philosophy of education in the prolegomena of Ibn Khaldun', *UNITAR-EJOURNAL*, 4(5): 57–76.

Tocqueville, A. de [1853] (1969) *Democracy in America*. J.P. Mayer (ed.). Garden City, NY: Doubleday.

Toennies, F. [1857] (1957) *Community and Society*. Edited and translated by C.P. Loomis. New York: Harper and Row.

Weber, M. [1904–1905] (1958) *The Protestant Ethic and the Spirit of Capitalism*. New York: Scribner's.

Weber, M. [1921] (1968) *Economy and Society*. Totowa, NJ: Bedminster Press.

Wrong, D. (1961) 'The oversocialised conception of man', *American Sociological Review*, 26: 183–93.

CHAPTER 3

DEVELOPMENTS IN SOCIOLOGY OF EDUCATION

Chapter Aims

This chapter will cover the key developments in sociology of education since the Second World War. It identifies the key political and intellectual influences on the discipline.

Key words: functionalism, Marxism, feminism, postmodernism, critical pedagogy, grand theories, epistemology, teleology, relativism, empiricism, rationalism, Fabianism, Sociology of Knowledge.

Introduction

As we saw in Chapter 2, sociology has a long heritage stretching back centuries and, though it was not called sociology, philosophers such as Ibn Khaldun [1958] (2005) were effectively writing sociology long before August Comte coined the term in 1839. In the nineteenth century, however, European sociology experienced a rapid development when philosophers such as Comte (1896), Toennies ([1857] 1957) and Spencer (1896) found it necessary to explain and understand the effects of social change resulting from industrialisation, urbanisation and modernisation on something they identified as 'society'. Durkheim, however, took the credit for being the first 'proper' sociologist due to his aim to provide a totally sociological understanding of human societies and for developing methods sociologists might use in this new discipline (Durkheim, [1897] 1951, 1938). As the first academic to be appointed professor of sociology he saw in sociology the potential means of creating a new moral order in France, which was rapidly developing into a modern industrial society, and sociology of education was seen as something to be taken seriously by both academia and policy makers.

Sociology in England

In England things were not quite so straightforward. Up until the mid-twentieth century there was no English sociology to speak of, let alone sociology of education. No academic discipline can be said to be politically neutral or unaffected by political and cultural traditions (Ball, 2004), and it is necessary to understand how these factors have affected its progress and development. In line with the approach suggested in our opening chapter, it is important to examine educational issues, including theories, from a variety of positions in order to gain a better understanding of the situation.

Sociology in England was particularly slow to take off and this could be partly attributable to the English distrust of academic theorising and a preference for factual and empirical research. This empiricism is a key feature of English and Scottish academic culture originating in the Enlightenment of the seventeenth and eighteenth centuries through the work of philosophers such as John Locke and David Hume, who promoted the idea that the world can only be understood by testing our ideas through the collection of observable phenomena (see Thinking point 3.1 on p. 56). As a result continental styles of philosophical thinking have been seen more as forms of intellectual posturing than as providing any relevant understanding or insights. This is aptly illustrated by George Orwell's reference to the French Marxist philosopher Jean-Paul Sartre as a 'bag of wind' (Garton Ash, 2010: 354) on account of the latter's often impenetrable existentialist writings. While the French revere their intellectuals including their sociologists, radical or otherwise, in England there is no comparable degree of respect. Moreover, the further you look to the right of the political spectrum, the greater the suspicion there is of philosophers and intellectuals such as sociologists (Garton Ash, 2010). We can see examples in Chapter 10 of this book with regard to the views of New Right thinkers and politicians such as Sir Keith Joseph and Margaret Thatcher. Indeed, so great was Thatcher's distrust of sociology in particular, that in her first term as prime minister during the early 1980s she ordered a change in the name of the Social Science Research Council (SSRC), a key higher education funding body, to the Economic and Social Research Council (ESRC), insisting that sociology was neither a science nor a proper subject. Nevertheless, Thatcher is known for her sociological 'insights' such as when, in an interview for *Woman's Own* magazine in 1987, she stated that there is no such thing as society, there are only individuals and families.

English sociology of education

Early sociology of education in England during the mid-twentieth century was associated with the Fabian Society (2014), an English social reform movement founded in the late nineteenth century by, amongst others, the playwright George Bernard Shaw and the social reformers Beatrice and Sidney Webb, dedicated to the creation of a democratic socialist society through a Welfare State based on the collective ownership of key sectors of the economy including energy, transport, natural resources and communications. As you will see in Chapter 10, the election of a Labour government in 1945 was seen as an opportunity to create a democratic socialist society with the provision of a 'cradle to grave' system of welfare into which everyone paid through general taxation and National Insurance contributions. Free education for all was seen as a key policy in this programme of promoting greater equality of opportunity and an increasingly meritocratic society where roles would be allocated on the basis of achievement rather than privilege or tradition.

Reading suggestion

The Origins of Fabianism

The Fabian Society derives its name from the Roman general Quintus Fabius, known as Cunctator from his strategy of delaying his attacks on the invading Carthaginians until the right moment. The name Fabian Society was explained in the first Fabian pamphlet which carried the note:

> For the right moment you must wait, as Fabius did most patiently, when warring against Hannibal, though many censured his delays; but when the time comes you must strike hard, as Fabius did, or your waiting will be in vain, and fruitless. (www.fabians.org.uk/about/the-fabian-story/)

Browse the Fabian Society website and identify some of the eminent English sociologists and social reformers who were Fabians and were also associated with the London School of Economics, which was founded by the Fabians in 1895. What kinds of research did they do in relation to education?

If English sociology of education can be said to have a political foundation, then Fabian democratic socialism is it. However, though underpinned by notions of equality, community and fairness, Fabian research was associated less with developing a theoretical critique of British society, and more with collecting empirical data relating to how fair England was becoming under the new Welfare State (Banks, 1955; Glass, 1954). In short, there was an examination of the effectiveness of education in the creation of a more meritocratic society. This approach to educational research has sometimes been called 'political arithmetic' and has provided a great deal of empirical data on the state of the nation.

In terms of its intellectual and sociological foundations, English sociology of education at this time was influenced by what Bernstein (1974: 149) calls a 'weak structural functionalism'. Structural functionalism was the theoretical perspective underpinning most sociology in England and the United States during the 1950s, which focused on the role of education as part of a wider systems theory that emphasised consensus and evolutionary, rather than revolutionary or rapid, social change. This perspective had significant influence in America, and Britain, at a time of Cold War politics and increasing tension between the Soviet Union and the west, and when the Marxist prediction of the inevitability of class conflict was considered to be a genuine threat to western democratic societies. By the 1950s American structural functionalism became the dominant sociological perspective and Kingsley Davis (1959) goes so far as to suggest that all sociology is functionalist in that the main concern of sociologists is to examine the way all parts of society are linked to each other.

The American connection

The work of American functionalists, such as Talcott Parsons, emphasises the notion that the affluence of American democracy had created a system in which social conflict had become obsolete and that violent social change is now abnormal or deviant, in contrast with the way the Soviet Union had come about as a social and political system. Sociological theory was, in effect, an academic weapon in the American arsenal against communism and much of Parsons' work alludes to white middle class American society and institutions. As we saw in Chapter 1, structural functionalism was also part of an intellectual movement to create *grand theories* (Wright Mills, 1959) of society that attempt to provide a comprehensive explanation of how societies cohere, function and develop. For structural functionalism each part of a society, such as the education system and the family can only be understood in terms of their relationship with other institutions and of the reciprocity of such relationships.

This systemic functionalism, as it is sometimes referred to, which is associated with the work of Parsons (1951) and Davis (1949), focuses on observable social phenomena rather than unobservable and subjective motives of individuals in society. They adopted Durkheim's approach to sociology by seeing it as a positive science of society in which social facts, such as statistical data about social trends and patterns are collected, rather than examining individual and personal motives for action. They believed that each society has its own levels of integration and patterns of behaviour that exist *sui generis* and are the result of the ways the key institutions of society such as the family, the moral and religious institutions, and the education system work together to bring about social cohesion. For example, Durkheim ([1897] 1951) claims that the level of suicide in any society tends to show a consistent pattern, which is not the result of individual motives, but is rather the product of the degree and types of social integration which prevail in that society.

Functional prerequisites

A further assumption is that all societies have functional needs or prerequisites that relate to the general conditions needed to maintain and reproduce themselves. These include the requirement each society has for the allocation of roles and for satisfying the affective or emotional needs of its members. They also include the regulation of deviant behaviour through the socialisation of members of society into the accepted norms and values, and the use of sanctions through the justice system.

The role of education in systemic functionalism is very clear in terms of its integrative function, which relates to the socialisation of younger members of society and preparation for their roles in society through appropriate training in the skills required by the economic system. For functionalists such as Parsons and Shils (1962) the tendency towards equilibrium is based on the assumption that institutions such as schools effectively socialise pupils according to the norms and values of society and allocate them to the roles most suited to their abilities. This again closely follows Durkheim's view of education as a morally unifying process that helps to develop the necessary social solidarity for a modern industrial age, and how, in such a modern rational society, education is seen as a key mechanism for efficient role allocation.

Structural differentiation

In Parsons' evolutionary theory social institutions are subject to a process known as *structural differentiation*, which means that their roles become less generalised and more focused on a limited range of specialised functions. For example, Parsons (Parsons, 1959, 1965; Parsons and Bales, 1955) suggests that industrialisation has led to changes in the role of the family from a cumbersome extended pre-industrial domestic unit of production, in which all family members are engaged in the production of goods and services and the socialisation and education of children, to a geographically mobile and specialised nuclear family ideally suited to the needs of modern society. With the growth of urbanisation and factory production education, food production and welfare provision are gradually taken over by specialist institutions and the family focuses more on the roles of reproduction, primary socialisation and the stabilisation of adult personalities through the expressive mother, or housewife.

In addition, role allocation, in terms of occupations and other status-related positions, is expected to be increasingly determined by achievement and universal standards against which everyone is judged rather than on the basis of custom or inheritance. While in traditional societies children were generally destined to enter occupations similar to their parents, modern industrial society requires roles to be allocated on merit and on the basis of universally agreed and understood criteria.

Education and stratification

We can see in early English sociology of education a general acceptance and adoption of a functionalist approach, particularly the idea of evolutionary social and political progress towards a more meritocratic society based on the rational allocation of roles. There lies within the theory an inherently *teleological* assumption about society which assumes that social systems have an in-built mechanism guiding them in a particular direction or towards a particular end state. The most comprehensive functionalist explanation of stratification in industrial societies is provided by Kingsley Davis and Wilbert Moore (1969) in their paper 'Some Principles of Stratification' first published in 1945. They suggest that there are no societies in which complete equality exists without social classes or stratification of any kind because, they claim, inequality is a normal, universal social phenomenon.

Moreover, they argue that if a society is to thrive and progress then it must apply the most efficient means of allocating roles, otherwise the most important positions in society may be occupied by those least suited to them. For Davis and Moore the education system is the most effective means of allocating roles due to its supposed objective methods of assessing pupils' talents and abilities, which enable employers to take on the best candidates for occupations considered functionally most important and to reward them the most. The higher rewards commanded by those individuals occupying the most important jobs incentivise everyone to try their utmost to achieve their full potential. In terms of Davis and Moore's theory, stratification based on ability will inevitably mean inequality but this is justifiable on the grounds of efficiency and merit.

The problem remains, however, as to how society decides which jobs are functionally the most important. For Davis and Moore the method of measuring this is to identify the degree to which the training and expertise required for one occupation would enable an individual to do the work of someone from another occupation and vice versa. So, for example, an electrical engineer could do the job of an electrician, but an electrician could not do the job of an electrical engineer. The latter job requires intensive higher education, whereas the former only requires a tertiary education. Whether this is the best way of measuring the functional importance of an occupation is debatable in that it is quite clear that many highly rewarded occupations in contemporary society, for example, fashion modelling or acting, require very little in the way of extensive training or expertise, whereas others that require long periods of study and training such as teaching and nursing may be rewarded much more modestly (Tumin, 1967). Clearly, there is more to occupational rewards than merely rational or educational criteria.

Critiquing structural functionalism

Davis does concede in a later paper (1949) that stratification by talent and educational achievement is not the only mechanism that seems to operate in the allocation of roles in industrial societies – he also recognises that roles are often acquired through privileged access as well as inherited wealth. Nevertheless, he believes that ultimately, due to the development of industrial society and the growing rationality of such a system, traditional methods of role allocation become less common. This point is significant as it recognises the weakness of the structural functionalist position on the role of the stratification systems in industrial societies, such as the USA and Britain, in that it is often a theory of *what ought to be* rather than *what is* (Sadovnik, 2007). Indeed, critics of structural functionalism challenge the picture of society presented in American textbooks, which were generally devoid of political and social context. They suggest that it tends to be highly theoretical and makes claims that cannot be supported by the evidence (Sadovnik, 2007). Moreover, functionalist theory of institutions such as education and the family is so limited in its scope of analysis that there is little, if any, recognition of race, ethnicity or class (Morgan, 1975).

American society in the mid-twentieth century

From the images of America presented by academics and popular culture, one could be forgiven for believing that all American households were white, middle class and made up of nuclear families, living in pleasant ranch-style houses in the suburbs with facilities and appliances that most people in Europe and the rest of the world could only dream of. It was an image promoted not just by academics such as Parsons, but also by American popular culture such as film and television (Coontz, 2001).

Coontz (2001), however, points out that reality in America was not quite so white or comfortable for all. If, as she states, one-third of white families could not survive on the income of the main breadwinner in early 1960s, then the plight of minority ethnic groups was much worse. In the post-war period the ethnic composition of the USA was affected by large scale migration to America from Mexico and Puerto Rico. These groups as well as the Native Americans and Black population were denied many of the rights enjoyed by white Americans. Low wages, poor housing and a lack of basic civil rights created second class citizens of these groups. Coontz (2001) states that over 40 per cent of Black mothers with small children did paid work, and a quarter of these were single mothers.

Three-quarters of Black Americans lived in the south where they were denied the protection of the Constitution. Moreover, the practice of 'redlining' in the fields of education, rented housing, mortgages, bank loans and employment had a serious impact on Black households. Redlining involved local authorities, insurance companies and banks drawing red lines on maps identifying communities, usually Black, which were seen as unfit to be provided with proper financial and other services. Fifty per cent of Black families in the early 1960s lived in poverty (Coontz, 2001). Clearly, for many, the American Dream would remain just that, a dream in which the opportunity to obtain a decent education, a well-paid job and a mortgage for a home was open mainly to white Americans. Those who dared to speak out and point to the absence of so-called American democracy, free speech and equal opportunities, risked being branded unpatriotic or communists. This was merely one aspect of the Truman doctrine, which involved creating fear and suspicion among the population as a means of combating the spread of Soviet communism. One of the most sinister forms this took was in the House Un-American Activities Committee hearings during the 1940s and 1950s, in which prominent Americans, such as the playwright Arthur Miller (1987), were invited to confess their communist allegiances, and to name other communists, or face prison.

It is quite significant that although there has been a great deal of change in the USA since that time which has given minority groups more rights, this was the result of considerable violence and loss of life by those involved in the civil rights movement, rather than through consensual agreement. The civil rights movement revealed that there was a distinct change of mood in popular and political culture in some parts of America and Europe. This was symbolised by a growing consciousness of injustice amongst the Black population and certain sections of white educated youth, the emergence of the counter culture and the growth of the women's movement, all of which included highly vocal groups that were challenging US domestic and foreign policy and pointing to the perceived hypocrisy of their political leaders. This took the form of university occupations and the Free Speech Movement (FSM), which started at Berkeley in 1964 in response to the university administration's ban on political activity on campus. Many students had spent the summers of the 1960s marching with the civil rights movement and on their return to campus demonstrated against their government's involvement in Vietnam. It was a time of growing interest in politics and challenge to convention. The counter culture was experimenting with everything including drugs, sexuality, economic and domestic relations as well as education. Communes sprang up along the west coast and the US government became very concerned about the potential effect of these 'radicals' on the youth of America.

The shift to the left among youth, which also spread to Europe, was reflected in the intellectual shift among writers and academics. Gouldner (1970: 404) refers to this as a change in the 'infrastructure' of social theory, by which he means a change in the general assumptions about what is considered to be real and relevant in the existing social conditions. In response to his own question: 'Whose side are we on?', Howard Becker (1967) states that we should be on the side of the 'underdog', those groups whose voices are rarely heard such as the poor, the deviant, the marginalised and other minorities. This was clearly a time of growing scepticism among the new generation of students and academics about the adequacy of existing theory to deal with a newly identified reality. The 'New Left' perceived the consensus theory of functionalism as incapable of identifying and explaining conflicts within western society relating to race, gender, class and power. C. Wright Mills, one of this new breed of New Left theorists, carried out a highly effective critique of functionalist sociology, particularly its abstract theorising, which he claimed limited rather than enhanced our understanding of everyday social life. In his book *The Sociological Imagination* (1959) Wright Mills encourages us to examine the private problems of life and to place them in their wider social and historical context. In *The Power Elite* (1956) he mounts an effective assault on the traditional assumption that America is a land of equal opportunity and political democracy when he reveals that most of the political and economic power is held by a small group of families he calls the 'power elite'. Their education, wealth and access to power enable them to manipulate the political agenda in their own interests rather than those of ordinary people, particularly members of minority groups.

Political arithmetic in England

Sociologists and policy makers in England between the 1940s and the 1970s were quite closely linked, and their relationship with their 'clients' was very 'top down' (Shain and Ozga, 2001). This involved sociologists identifying deficits, or problems, believed to be inherent in so-called 'failing groups', which were primarily made up of the working class. Researchers such as Bernstein (1961) claimed to have identified a deficiency in working class speech codes that, he suggested, affected the ability of these children to engage effectively with the curriculum. In terms of 'family climate', sociologists were pointing to such things as the poorer levels of support for children in working class homes compared to those of the middle classes as the reason for the gap in the levels of educational achievement between the two groups (Douglas, 1964), or to the inappropriate values held by working class families, such as excessive levels of fatalism and an inability to defer gratification, all of which run counter to those values needed to succeed in education (Sugarman, 1970). The problem, in effect, was seen to lie with those groups that were unable to make best use of the opportunities available to them in the new welfare system. There was still a great deal of optimism that the Welfare State could be used to help equalise society and that the education system, particularly the new comprehensive system, was a key means of doing this.

A good example of the use of welfare mechanisms, which were a feature of the consensus politics of the day in which both main parties tacitly agreed to use the Welfare State to improve the lot of all citizens and to help create a fairer society, was the establishment of Educational Priority Areas (EPAs) by the Labour government in the late 1960s in some of the most deprived areas of the country. Anthony Crosland, the Education Minister at the time, enlisted the support of the eminent sociologist A.H. Halsey (1972) to oversee the scheme, which involved the provision of extra resources to families in those areas deemed to be suffering from multiple deprivations that were believed to be affecting their children's educational progress (see Chapter 10 for further discussion of this scheme).

The shift to the left in English sociology

The failure of the scheme triggered a debate within academic sociology over the continuing differences in educational attainment and social mobility between the working class and the middle class. A new and more critical generation of English sociologists was emerging who were focusing on the nature of the welfare system and capitalist society in general as reasons for these class differences in attainment. They focused on perceived low levels of social mobility, rather than continuing to identify the problem as being located within the working class itself (Boronski, 1987). The New Sociology of Education (NSOE) adopted an altogether more radical approach compared to the 'old sociology of education', which had essentially been part of the political establishment and had displayed a degree of optimism about the potential for a modern welfare-based social democratic system to create a more meritocratic and socially just society.

This is a significant point because, while English sociology of education was moving to the left, the general direction of movement in party politics was to the right. In the late 1970s there was a breakdown in the political consensus in which first the Conservatives and eventually Labour, began to adopt neoliberal ideas that were less concerned with inequality and social justice and increasingly focused on the need for a more competitive economy, and an education system that would prepare young people for their role in the labour market (see Chapter 10). Margaret Thatcher's policy of promoting market principles as the basis for policy making, for example, led to a move away from state welfare as a means of helping those at the bottom of society, to the promotion of competition and self-help as a means of bringing about social and economic progress (Tomlinson, 2005).

The fact that these two groups were heading in different directions was a factor that made conflict a distinct probability. Terms such as *Marxism, class conflict, class inequality* and *capitalist exploitation*, which were becoming increasingly common in sociology textbooks, raised the concern and suspicion of politicians such as Margaret Thatcher and Keith Joseph who saw in them a clear association with Soviet communism. This was a period of intense Cold War politics in which the Soviet Union was described in 1983 by the then US President, Ronald Reagan as the 'evil empire'. The radical tone of much sociology of education raised questions regarding the patriotism and 'academic objectivity' of such academics.

Reading suggestion

In 1983 the US President Ronald Reagan made a speech about the American way of life and the threat to it posed by Soviet communism. The extract below gives some idea of the tone of the speech. Have a look at the full text at http://voicesofdemocracy.umd.edu/reagan-evil-empire-speech-text/.

> I, a number of years ago, I heard a young father, a very prominent young man in the entertainment world, addressing a tremendous gathering in California. It was during the time of the cold war, and communism and our own way of life were very much on people's minds. And he was speaking to that subject. And suddenly, though, I heard him saying, 'I love my little girls more than anything.' And I said to myself, 'Oh, no, don't. You can't – don't say that.' But I had underestimated him. He went on: 'I would rather see my little girls die now; still believing in God, than have them grow up under communism and one day die no longer believing in God'. (http://voicesofdemocracy.umd.edu/reagan-evil-empire-speech-text/)

The gulf between sociology and policy making widened as sociology of education was moving away from working within officially approved frameworks of advising governments within the context of the existing economic, political and educational system, to becoming a critique of both education and the capitalist system in which it was located. This type of research was becoming increasingly seen as irrelevant by policy makers who were seeking within educational research a direct contribution to classroom practice, school management and education policy rather than radical critiques, Marxist or otherwise (Shain and Ozga, 2001).

The New Sociology of Education

What we see emerging in England during the 1970s and 1980s was not a single sociology of education, but several, which have been collectively referred to as the New Sociology of Education (NSOE) (Young, 1971). Although NSOE encompassed a variety of approaches to education, it was united in the common assumption that the education system works to the disadvantage of working class pupils and, as it exists, is part of the problem rather than the solution to what they described as the continuing class inequalities in Britain. This was a period in which, according to Saunders (1996, 2010) sociology became dominated by left-wing sociologists who subscribed to what he calls the SAD thesis. This theorised that people's destinies are determined by the levels of social advantage and disadvantage (SAD) that prevails in society, rather than by such things as innate ability and effort.

Ball (2004) identifies three main strands of the NSOE, one of which focuses on neo-Marxist theories of capitalist reproduction of labour and class relations (Bowles and Gintis, 1976), a second strand that conducts a critique of the curriculum and the form which classroom knowledge takes, as well as how this disadvantages working class pupils (Keddie, 1973; Vulliamy, 1972; Young, 1971), and thirdly, the use of ethnographic research to explore the processes at work in the school that result in the educational 'failure' of working class pupils (Willis, 1977).

The key assumption behind the NSOE is that working class pupils are likely to end up with working class jobs because there is a tendency for the education system under capitalism to reproduce itself (Althusser, 1971; Bowles and Gintis, 1976). This does not necessarily occur in a simple and mechanical way, because working class pupils are often complicit in the process as they are able to partially 'penetrate' the myth of meritocracy (Willis, 1977). They fully expect to end up in factories like their fathers and therefore try to make the period of schooling as tolerable as they can by having as much fun as possible through acts of defiance and disruption, often at the expense of girls and minority ethnic groups (Willis, 1977). During their schooling they experience a process of symbolic violence (Bourdieu and Passeron, 1977) in which their own culture and language are defined as inferior to that of the dominant class (Keddie, 1973; Young, 1971). There is in NSOE a general position of pessimism about the prospects of bringing about change and greater equality in society through education: working class children seem destined to remain at the bottom of the class system with little prospect of improving themselves. This is particularly evident in the work of structural Marxists such as Althusser (1971) and Bowles and Gintis (1976) who see all institutions in capitalist society, including the education system, as being determined in the last instance by the economy and ultimately serving the interests of capitalism.

Whose knowledge?

In an attempt to challenge conventional deficit approaches to working class educational underachievement, Young (1971) presents an interpretivist analysis of knowledge and the curriculum, which takes from Berger and Luckmann (1966) the notion that all reality, including all knowledge, including the scientific and educational, is socially constructed. On the basis of this assumption Young believes that some forms of knowledge tend to be valued more than others and the role of the sociology of education is to establish how a hierarchy of such knowledge comes about with some ideas and beliefs having the status of 'official knowledge'. In Britain, for example, we have a clear academic and vocational divide with traditional academic subjects such as mathematics, history and English literature taking precedence over practical subjects such as woodwork and domestic science. In their definition of an 'educated person' analytic philosophers such as Dearden et al. (1972) tended to point to someone who is the product of an academic grammar school education (see Chapter 1).

This hierarchy is relevant to the way in which teachers define and assess pupils such as through IQ tests and official exams. Young states that because an academic grammar school curriculum is viewed as superior to other curricula, an 'intelligent' child is one who has passed the 11-plus and does well in their GCEs, or GCSEs. As most of the pupils who attend grammar or selective schools tend to be middle class it is these pupils who are most likely to be defined as intelligent rather than working class pupils who tend to follow a vocational curriculum. Bourdieu and Passeron (1977) claim that in every society there is one group which is able to impose its definition of reality on the rest, thereby committing acts of *symbolic violence* against those whose culture does not fit the dominant form. They suggest that this is how societies reproduce the patterns of inequality between social classes. They further claim that the knowledge of the dominant class is not actually better or superior; it is just that it has become defined as such by those with the power to do so.

A good illustration of this is Vulliamy's (1972) examination of music education in England. In *Music in Secondary Schools* he traces the origins of music in the English curriculum and how it was originally introduced to teach religious and moral values. With the proliferation of different genres of music there was an attempt by educators during the early twentieth century to classify it in a hierarchical way. For example, 'good' music was identified as that associated with the classical European tradition such as Bach, Beethoven, Mozart and Chopin, usually involving large orchestral pieces. Vulliamy claims that despite the African-American influence on western music of the twentieth century, genres such as jazz, blues, rock and reggae have not been properly acknowledged as serious music, because African-American culture has been identified as low status and non-classical music has not been seen as representing serious musical forms. He concludes that this hierarchy in music represents an example of the symbolic violence inflicted by the dominant white culture on African-Americans.

The issue of relativism

In suggesting that all knowledge is of equal value the NSOE takes what is called a *relativist* position, which means that it lacks any means whereby we can judge the merit of truth claims because it treats all knowledge as being of equal value. The only difference, according to this position, is that some groups have the power to define their knowledge as superior, as more valid or truthful. Many philosophers however point to the importance of an *epistemological* approach to knowledge, which relates to specific criteria by which we can assess the validity and merits of a truth claim (Gellner, 1992; Harre and Krousz, 1996; Moore and Muller, 1999).

Thinking point 3.1

The meaning of epistemology

Since ancient times, philosophers have tried to develop ways of discovering foundational knowledge. Foundationalism argues that certain beliefs act as the basis for others. Foundational claims do not depend on any other prior assumptions or justifications. Such knowledge is believed to provide the foundations for 'truth'. In ancient philosophy, rationalists such as Plato argued that certain types of pure knowledge could be gained, but not through our senses. This foundational knowledge, he claimed, could only be obtained through reasoning and rational thought. The sophists, on the other hand, were sceptical about any attempts to discover 'truth'. All we can hope to do, they claimed, is be more convincing in our argument than others. Pure knowledge is unattainable, so we should not waste our time pursuing it. This approach did not satisfy many philosophers who saw it as their duty to discover the truth. It is in this spirit of the search for truth and certainty that the European Enlightenment arose in the seventeenth and eighteenth centuries. This involved a belief in the power of reason over blind faith and superstition in an attempt to free the human mind, and to liberate the individual and humanity from traditional authorities such as superstition and religion. The pursuit of the truth by the rationalists was matched by the growth of empiricism, which, like rationalism, was also concerned with discovering strong foundations for knowledge. The key difference being that, for empiricists, knowledge must be based on sensory experience, or what could be called the doubting Thomas principle: the refusal to believe something is true unless there is (sensory) evidence to support it.

The Enlightenment was, therefore, driven by both rationalist and empiricist ideas. In the nineteenth and twentieth centuries the seeds sown in the Enlightenment seemed to have come to fruition, with the emergence of theories that were believed to provide comprehensive accounts of the social, economic, psychological and natural world. Each of these claimed to be able to provide foundational knowledge within their respective fields. For example, within the field of economics it was claimed that there is a 'hidden hand' that controls the market and economic behaviour. In biology the unstoppable force of 'evolution' is believed to be at work. In society 'social forces' are seen to be regulating human action. These grand theories, as Wright Mills (1959) calls them, are part of an optimistic and progressive (teleological) vision of history that was emerging about the modern world: with greater knowledge and understanding we can solve our human and material problems and create a 'better' world. We can certainly see this notion in functionalist theory mentioned above.

(Continued)

(Continued)

- Do you think there is such a thing as truth? If so, what is the basis upon which you would make such a claim?
- Do you think that with greater scientific knowledge and understanding the world is becoming a better place?

For writers such as Moore and Muller (1999) knowledge must have more secure foundations than merely claiming that all knowledge is socially created and therefore must be of equal value. To take such a position implies that not only are the views of silent groups such as the poor, the disabled and minority ethnic groups just as valid as those of the powerful and wealthy, but those of extremists of any kind with offensive views, such as racists, are equally valid. In addition, such relativism has little practical value to those with the task of deciding what to include in the curriculum as there is no standard by which to judge the worth of knowledge that we might teach to our children. This issue of relativism, as we will see below, is also a problem faced by post-modernist theory.

The growth of feminist classroom research

The interactionist approach of Willis (1977) inspired a new wave of feminist and standpoint theorists to give voices to women and other marginalised groups who had been virtually ignored in previous sociological research. Feminists were already making an impact on family sociology (Oakley, 1974) and gender studies (Sharpe, 1976) generally, developing both a theory of sexual oppression as well as challenging essentialist notions of gender differences. This means they were providing an alternative to the biological explanations for gender inequality and showing how gender differences are socially constructed through gender role socialisation and patriarchal relations.

The classroom observations of Dale Spender (1983), for example, revealed the disproportionate amount of attention given to boys in the classroom; the interviews carried out by Stanworth (1983) suggest that teachers and indeed girls themselves hold stereotypical views about which occupations are suitable for young women, which limits their ambitions; and Judy Samuel (1981) shows how the language of science in textbooks reinforces the traditional view that science is a boys' subject. Much of this evidence might not have been revealed by using the traditional methods of research adopted by the old sociology of education with its focus on collecting large amounts of summative data relating to such things as the outcomes of examinations, staying on rates and social mobility. Arguably the work of feminist researchers has played an important part in providing vital evidence for the women's movement in its campaigns for greater gender equality in education and employment in the form of anti-discriminatory and equal opportunities legislation that we now take for granted (Mitsos and Browne, 1998).

The postmodern turn

As we have seen, philosophers have for centuries been driven by a desire to discover truth in the form of foundational knowledge upon which we can place absolute trust and confidence in its reliability and dependability. The Enlightenment, in particular, saw a move away from traditional and superstitious explanations of the world to a place in which rational and empirical or evidence-based knowledge became more influential as the bases for understanding the social, as well as the physical, world.

Philosophers and scientists of the Enlightenment developed grand theories that provided comprehensive explanations of the world based on reason and logical argument. There is an assumption that this form of knowledge brings progress and liberation. Durkheim, for example (see Chapter 2), saw in sociology the means of creating a positive science of society that would help governments to make effective decisions enabling the newly industrialising European societies to function more rationally and effectively, thereby eliminating the prospect of social conflict. This is a moment of history and knowledge that postmodernists define as *modernity* and it is based on the idea of human betterment through epistemological certainty.

Despite its theme of liberation and freedom, according to Adorno and Horkheimer (1972) there lies within the Enlightenment the potential for domination and oppression. For example, a core theme was the control of nature for the benefit of humanity. Scientific and instrumental rationality can also be seen as leading to the domination of humanity through the development of bureaucratic state systems in which officials wield knowledge, power and surveillance over their citizens. Indeed, this has been one of the key themes of the postmodernist critiques of the Enlightenment.

However, a distinction needs to be made between the terms *postmodern* and *postmodernism*. The former is a term coined by a group of philosophers who refer to it as a moment or period in advanced capitalist societies which, according to Lyotard (1979), has existed at least since the early 1960s, and which involves a change in cultural, social and economic relations and conditions, and an end to modernist assumptions of certainty as well as the rejection of a teleological belief in progress, as represented in the grand theories that arose from the Enlightenment. Postmodernism is a theoretical critique of all these alleged changes and involves the analysis and description of the postmodern condition. This includes a focus on the dissolution of conventional relations of class and other forms of collective identity, to one in which there is an emphasis on individual difference and consumption as a means of identity creation (Pakulski and Waters, 1996), and an examination of the different forms of knowledge and power used by modern states and their institutions to classify, discipline and regulate populations as part of their attempt to order the world (Foucault, 1967, 1973, 1981).

Postmodernism and education

In their seminal work entitled *Postmodernism and Education*, Usher and Edwards (1994) state that there is no single postmodern position on education, however, there is a common critique, running through postmodern discourse, of Enlightenment notions of education as a means of creating a rational and informed population that finds itself liberated and able to maximise each individual's potential.

They identify Foucault, who is generally associated with the poststructuralist tradition that focuses on language structure and discourse analysis, as having made a particularly significant contribution to a postmodern understanding of education. Usher and Edwards (1994) suggest that because Foucault examines the role of discourse in the use of power and knowledge and because he presents a challenge to modernist ideas about knowledge, progress and the alleged liberatory nature of education, he also falls within the postmodernist tradition. For Usher and Edwards this may explain Foucault's approach to the difference between the modern and postmodern. Whereas most postmodernists such as Lyotard ([1979] 1984), Bauman (1992) or Baudrillard (1988) see a clear qualitative difference between the modern and postmodern moments, Foucault (1986) sees much continuity between them as well as many differences. However, it is significant that some prominent interpreters of Foucault's work such as Stephen Ball (2013) make little reference to him as a postmodernist.

Foucault, truth and education

In common with most postmodernist approaches to knowledge, Foucault (1970) does not employ epistemologies, or ways of finding truth, instead he uses the term *episteme*, which refers to any statement being 'within the true' rules of discourse regarding a particular problem and its possible solutions (Foucault, 1970: 31). Epistemes are based on rules created by experts, or what Foucault calls 'discursive police' (Foucault, 1970: 3), and the parameters relating to the way we are able legitimately to think about and understand something. Such forms of discourse create power relations that act as a means of controlling groups defined by governments as 'problems'.

For Foucault, state institutions such as asylums, prisons and indeed schools have become places of control through the power that is validated and supported by systems of knowledge held by experts such as psychologists, teachers and academics. The knowledge of these experts creates classes of people who are compared to the notional 'normal' person. Foucault wrote a *genealogy*, or history, of knowledge and practice that attempts to show why the behaviour of certain groups has become 'problematised' and that of others has not (Foucault, 1983). In the modern state professionals are used as means of creating knowledge with which to identify and control such groups as well as to silence them. The discourse of knowledge and power that results from this relationship 'creates truth'. Anyone who speaks outside this accepted framework of knowledge is dismissed as lacking in credibility. Groups defined as dangerous, including 'racial' groups, those with impairments, those defined as mad, sexually deviant or educationally subnormal, have all at one time or another been deemed to be in need of control, segregation or worse. In the case of those with physical or other impairments we can see how they have been classified as both a burden to society and as a threat to humanity due to their 'undesirable' characteristics, which psychologists such as Cyril Burt feared would 'contaminate' the rest of the 'normal' population (see Chapter 8). For Foucault (1983: 75) 'The problematisation is an "answer" to a concrete situation which is real'.

The issue of relativism

The tone of Foucault's work reflects a postmodernist scepticism about the role of institutions such as education as a means of creating the conditions for enlightened tolerance, individual autonomy and personal freedom. It is also clear that Foucault is less interested in developing an epistemological understanding of knowledge and more concerned with the way knowledge and power combine to create truth and reality. In education this takes the form of problematising issues relating to the management of populations through the identification of certain groups and behaviour patterns and assessing their levels of threat, ability, performance and usefulness.

This raises the nebulous issue of relativism, which Moore and Muller (1999) are so critical of. However, Usher and Edwards (1994) suggest that while postmodernists tend to adhere to the view that there is a multiplicity of truths that are dependent on specific standpoints of particular groups, such epistemic relativity does not imply a position of moral relativism. This means that post-modernists are not neutral on such issues but are at the forefront of identifying and analysing problems of injustice and oppression, as we can see in the work of Foucault. They therefore reject accusations that for postmodernism 'anything goes' (Usher and Edwards, 1994: 27).

Critical Pedagogy

No survey of developments in sociology of education would be complete without reference to critical pedagogy. As a theory of education it combines Marxist theory with interactionism, as well as a critical position on 'official knowledge' as represented by the NSOE, to create both a critique of education in contemporary capitalism and an alternative to the existing system of school knowledge and classroom practice. In the case of Paulo Freire (1996) there are even Christian notions of love and justice woven into his writings.

Paulo Freire

Any analysis of critical pedagogy must start with Paulo Freire, who first came to prominence as a result of his work on adult literacy programmes in Brazil during the 1960s. His subsequent work focused on a wide range of issues, and inspired a large number of writers working in the field of critical theory (Darder et al., 2009). There are five key aspects to Freire's work. The first is his emphasis on *dialogue*. Freire claims that education should be a dialogue between teacher and learner rather than the teacher being the one who 'deposits' knowledge into the pupil. Second, is his idea of *praxis*. This is action informed by reflection. Dialogue is not just about deeper understanding but also about changing the world. Dialogue is a cooperative activity involving individuals showing respect for each other. For Freire this process enhances a community and helps to build social capital that is about people making links with each other. This, he suggests, will lead us to act in ways that help to create a more just and humanising society.

A third theme running through Freire's work is his concern that the poor and oppressed be given the powers to *name* the world. The idea of 'a pedagogy of the oppressed' is about developing consciousness (*conscientisation*). This consciousness will enable the oppressed to transform the world. Fourth, by locating education within the lived experience of students he believes they are provided with new ways of *naming* and defining the world, rather than allowing teachers to define the world for them.

Finally, Freire has drawn on a number of Christian sources with which to communicate his ideas. These have had special significance in Latin America, Africa and Asia where Christianity still has a strong influence. In *Pedagogy of the Oppressed* Freire refers to concepts such as 'loving' the people and having 'faith' in them (Freire, 1996: 68–70). He also refers to God and the teachings of religious leaders (Freire, 1996: 124). Freire seems to have tapped into a popular theme of liberatory politics on a global scale using education as a means of changing the world. However, Freire's work, though influential, has not been immune to criticism. In particular, his use of inaccessible and complex language can be seen as being contrary to his desire to communicate with ordinary and uneducated people (Hendricks, n.d.).

Recent developments in critical pedagogy

The theorist best known today for keeping the Freirean torch burning is the Canadian academic Peter McLaren (2003), who writes very fervently in favour of a revolutionary pedagogy as opposed to a 'domesticated' or watered-down version of Freire. By 'revolutionary' McLaren means a humanist Marxist approach to educational struggle, which includes an analysis of the class relations in a capitalist society that lead to the oppression of the working class. It is about the means by which the working class can be liberated, creating a socialist alternative to capitalism. McLaren describes the influence of Marxism on his work, in all its diverse forms, though he was initially attracted to postmodernism and its critique of power relations in a global capitalist system. However, while accepting that identity politics, as advocated through postmodernism, has played a key role in promoting the dignity and respect for different sexual, racial or religious groups, Moraes (2003) argues that class relations are the source of all inequalities that exist in capitalist society and postmodernists have reached a political and intellectual dead end by denying the importance of class in advanced capitalist societies. As a consequence he sees postmodernism as lacking the intellectual means with which to expose global capitalism, and the political and economic processes involved in exploiting the poor, as well as lacking the methods needed to end such exploitation.

Marxism and the collapse of communism

In 1992 Francis Fukuyama (1992) declared 'the end of history', by which he means that with the collapse of the Soviet Union and the rejection of socialism by its Eastern European satellites, everybody now accepts that there was no alternative to liberal capitalism. Marxist theory had indeed been associated with the repressive regimes of Stalin and his successors. McLaren admits that Marxism and socialism may seem anachronistic in this post-Cold War world, but he believes that Marxism has never been more relevant in a world dominated by 'rampant' global capitalism (Moraes, 2003).

Indeed, he claims that only Marxism contains within it the possibility of challenging this 'oppressive' system and of providing hope for the oppressed to be liberated. However, McLaren acknowledges that, although Marxism offers the method for achieving liberation, it does not have a ready-made blueprint for an alternative to capitalism. This is where McLaren proposes the use of revolutionary praxis and critical pedagogy as a means of transforming the world. Together he sees them as enabling us to know the world and therefore to change it.

McLaren and critical pedagogy

For McLaren radical educationalists must participate with the oppressed in the process of discovering alternatives to the exploitative system of capitalism. He believes that the education system plays a crucial part in this process as it helps to reproduce labour for the capitalist system. McLaren is highly influenced by the Italian communist Antonio Gramsci (1971), who locates the education system in what he calls 'civil society' as opposed to the political or economic arena. As such it works through ideological control and by manipulation through *hegemony*. Hegemony is a broad term that is used by Gramsci (1971) to denote domination in its widest sense. It is based on the voluntary acceptance of the ideology of the dominant class by the working class and becomes even more effective when the dominant class is able to incorporate its ideas into the common-sense view of the world possessed by the working class such as through the education system. This usually involves the notion that there is such a thing as a 'natural order' and that things can't be changed.

Gramsci (1971) does not see ideologies in terms of their truth value, but according to their power to bind together the members of social classes and to put into practice particular views of how society should be organised. He also recognises the importance of an ideological apparatus that helps to secure the consent of the oppressed. In capitalist societies this involves institutions such as the family and the education system, which help to spread and maintain the dominance of ruling class ideology.

The role of organic intellectuals

Such control and dominance Gramsci suggests is not complete, as radical elements such as working class organic intellectuals have set themselves the task of developing a socialist class consciousness among the working class. According to Gramsci (1971), this can be done by educating them and making them aware of the possibilities of an alternative society. To this end he was concerned with developing a *historical bloc*, made up of workers and 'organic intellectuals', coordinated by a revolutionary party to assist the working class to become a class for itself, in active pursuit of its own interests. Just as intellectuals emerge naturally (organically) among the members of the ruling class through their exposure to higher and professional education, Gramsci believed it was possible to nurture intellectuals from amongst the working class whose knowledge and understanding of their own class condition could be used to lead the rest of the working class in challenging the hegemony of ruling class ideology. For Gramsci it was essential for the working class to be led by their own members rather than by an elite group of party leaders and intellectuals from the existing ruling class. He saw it as his role to help nurture these working class intellectuals through informal education such as through debates and articles in the socialist journal *L'Ordine Nuovo*. By such means he hoped that a new and revolutionary consciousness could be developed that would be passed on to the rest of the working class through these organic intellectuals.

McLaren recognises that things have moved on since Gramsci wrote his *Prison Notebooks* between 1929 and 1935. Indeed, he claims that global capitalism has meant that organic intellectuals today must develop strategies to forge international alliances with anti-capitalist and workers' movements worldwide. He suggests campaigning against the agencies of international capital such as The World Bank and the International Monetary Fund, which are believed to cause the underdevelopment of countries in Africa, Asia and Latin America.

In order to develop a global strategy, McLaren identifies critical intellectuals as playing a crucial role. This is a term developed by James Petras (1999) to describe militant intellectuals who shun the attractions of collaboration with global capitalism, or the pessimism of some intellectuals who have given up the struggle for a socialist alternative to capitalism. These militant intellectuals instead accompany their writings and teaching of liberation with revolutionary practice. McLaren proposes also that the leaders of the revolutionary struggle today must be mindful of the need to develop environmental policies which ensure that the working class has a viable planet to inherit.

Obstacles

McLaren identifies what he sees as the main obstacles to the class struggle. In particular he is concerned about the liberal left which he accuses of uttering many of the concepts of liberation politics but being more concerned with making capitalism more 'compassionate' by arguing for more welfare rather than promoting the idea of transforming society. He points to the capitalist class as being very adept at dividing the working class in terms of promoting racism, homophobia, xenophobia and sexism. Freire was also very mindful of such tactics. The key to dealing with this for McLaren is for the militant intellectuals to show, through critical pedagogy, that exploitative class relations are the source of all these divisions.

The work of writers such as Freire and McLaren as well as that of postmodernists present very challenging and often radical approaches to education, and it is easy to dismiss them as far too abstract and elusive; however, as suggested in Chapter 1, philosophers and sociologists are involved in challenging our common-sense assumptions about the world and asking what might seem strange or unusual questions. This is a feature of any intellectual endeavour: without asking such questions new ways of thinking and doing things will not occur. Nevertheless, in a world in which neoliberal ideas dominate all areas of policy making including the education system, sociology of education, just as any other academic discipline, is expected to prove its usefulness in immediate, measurable and practical ways, but without challenging the nature of existing economic relations.

Chapter summary

This chapter has made a broad sweep of developments in sociology of education since the Second World War. It has shown how sociology in general, and sociology of education in particular, were slow to take off in England and how there was an emphasis on political arithmetic as a means of describing and measuring the degree to which Britain was becoming a more meritocratic society as a result of the introduction of the Welfare State in 1945. The prevailing sociological perspective was based on American structural functionalism, which tended to present an idealised picture rather than what was actually happening in the education system. The disillusionment of many sociologists with the perceived inability of the Welfare State to reduce class inequalities in England led to a new and more radical sociology of education that was at odds with the move to the right in British politics. The result was an end to the close links sociologists had with British governments in the immediate post-war period. Sociology has continued in a more critical and radical direction ever since, though it could be said that there are many sociologies of education rather than just one, some of which challenge traditional sociological claims to provide a valid and truthful picture of society.

References

Adorno, T. and Horkheimer, M. (1972) *The Dialectic of the Enlightenment*. London: Verso.

Althusser, L. (1971) 'Ideology and ideological apparatuses: Notes towards an investigation', in L. Althusser (ed.), *Lenin and Philosophy and Other Essays*. New York: Monthly Review Press.

Ball, S. (ed.) (2004) *The Routledge Falmer Reader in Sociology of Education*. London: Routledge Falmer.

Ball, S. (2013) *Foucault, Power and Education*. London: Routledge.

Banks, O. (1955) *Parity and Prestige in English Secondary Education*. London: Routledge and Kegan Paul.

Baudrillard, J. (1988) *Selected Works*. Edited by M. Poster. Cambridge: Polity Press.

Bauman, Z. (1992) *Intimations of Postmodernity*. London: Routledge.

Becker, H. (1967) 'Whose side are we on?' *Social Problems*, 14: 239–47.

Berger, P. and Luckmann, T. (1966) *The Social Construction of Reality*. Garden City, NY: Doubleday.

Bernstein, B. (1961) 'Social class and linguistic development: A theory of social learning', in A.J. Halsey, J. Floud and C.A. Anderson (eds), *Education, Economy and Society*. New York: Free Press.

Bernstein, B. (1974) 'Sociology and the sociology of education: A brief account', in J. Rex (ed.), *Approaches to Sociology: An Introduction to Major Trends in British Sociology*. London: Routledge.

Boronski, T. (1987) *Sociology in Focus: Knowledge*. Harlow: Longman.

Bourdieu, P. and Passeron, J. (1977) *Reproduction in Education, Society and Culture*. London: Sage.

Bowles, C. and Gintis, H. (1976) *Schooling in Capitalist America: Educational Reform and the Contradictions of Economic Life*. New York, NY: Basic Books.

Comte, A. (1896) *Positive Philosophy*. London: Bell and Sons.

Coontz, S. (2001) '"Leave it to Beaver" and "Ozzie and Harriet": American families in the 1950s', in B.J. Fox (ed.), *Family Patterns: Gender: Relations* (second edition). Ontario: Oxford University Press.

Darder, A., Baltodano, M.P. and Torres, R.D. (2009) *The Critical Pedagogy Reader* (second edition). London: Routledge.

Davis, K. (1949) *Human Society*. London: Routledge and Kegan Paul.

Davis, K. (1959) 'The myth of functional analysis as special method in sociology and anthropology', *American Sociological Review*, 24:757–72.

Davis, K. and Moore, W. (1969) 'Some principles of stratification', in C. Heller (ed.), *Structured Social Inequality*. London: Collier-Macmillan.

Dearden, R.F., Hirst, P.H. and Peters, R.S. (eds) (1972) *Education and the Development of Reason*. London: Routledge and Kegan Paul.

Douglas, J.W.B. (1964) *The Home and the School*. London: MacGibbon and Gee.

Durkheim, E. [1897] (1951) *Suicide*. New York: Free Press.

Durkheim, E. (1938) *The Rules of Sociological Method*. New York: Free Press.

Fabian Society (2014) 'The Fabian story'. Available at: www.fabians.org.uk/about/the-fabian-story (accessed: 8 January 2015).

Foucault, M. (1967) *Madness and Civilization*. London: Routledge.

Foucault, M. (1970) *The Order of Things*. New York: Pantheon.

Foucault, M. (1973) *The Birth of the Clinic: An Archaeology of Medical Perception*. London: Tavistock.

Foucault, M. (1981) *The History of Sexuality: An introduction*. Harmondsworth: Penguin.

Foucault, M. (1983) 'Discourse and truth: The problematization of parrhesia'. Six lectures given by Michel Foucault at the University of California at Berkeley, October–November 1983. Available at: http://foucault.info/documents/parrhesia/foucault.dt6.conclusion.en.html (accessed 8 January 2015).

Foucault, M. (1986) 'What is Enlightenment?', in P. Rabinow (ed.) *The Foucault Reader*. Harmondsworth: Peregrine Books.

Freire, P. (1996) *Pedagogy of the Oppressed*. London: Penguin.

Fukuyama, F. (1992) *The End of History and the Last Man*. New York: The Free Press.

Garton Ash, T. (2010) *Facts Are Subversive: Political Writing from a Decade Without a Name*. New Haven, CT: Yale University Press.

Gellner, E. (1992) *Postmodernism, Reason and Religion*. London: Routledge.

Glass, D.V. (ed.) (1954) *Social Mobility in Britain*. London: Routledge and Kegan Paul.

Gouldner, A. (1970) *The Coming Crisis of Western Sociology*. Heineman: London.

Gramsci, A. (1971) *Selections from Prison Notebooks*. London: Lawrence and Wishart.

Halsey, A.H. (1972) 'Educational priority, vol. 1'. London: HMSO.

Harre, R. and Krousz, M. (1996) *Varieties of Relativism*. Oxford: Blackwell.

Hendricks, S. (n.d.) 'Freire, Paulo (1994)'. *Pedagogy of Hope: Reliving Pedagogy of the Oppressed*. New York: Continuum Publishing Company. Review by Sarah Hendricks (OISE/UT). Available at: http://fcis.oise.utoronto.ca/~daniel_sc/freire/sh.html (accessed 8 January 2015).

Keddie, N. (1973) 'Classroom Knowledge', in M. Young (ed.) *Tinker, Taylor – The Myth of Classroom Deprivation*. Harmondsworth: Penguin.

Khaldun, I. [1958] (2005) *The Muqaddimah: An Introduction to History*. Tr. Franz Rosental. Princeton, NJ: Princeton/Bollingen Paperbacks.

Lyotard, J.-F. [1979] (1984) *The Postmodern Condition: A Report on Knowledge*. Tr. G. Bennington and B. Massumi. Minneapolis, MN: University of Minnesota Press.

Miller, A. (1987) *Timebends: A Life*. London: Methuen.

Mitsos, E. and Browne, K. (1998) 'Gender differences in education: the underachievement of boys', *Sociology Review*, 8(1): 27–31.

Moore, R. and Muller, J. (1999) 'The discourse of "voice" and the problem of knowledge and identity in the sociology of education', *British Journal of Sociology*, 20(2): 189–205.

Moraes, M. (2003) 'The Path of Dissent: An Interview With Peter McLaren', *Journal of Transformative Education*, 1(2): 117–34.

Morgan, D.H.J. (1975) *Social Theory and the Family*. London: Routledge and Kegan Paul.

Oakley, A. (1974) *The Sociology of Housework*. Oxford: Martin Robertson.

Pakulski, J. and Waters, M. (1996) *The Death of Class*. London: Sage.

Parsons, T. (1951) *The Social System*. New York: Free Press.

Parsons, T. (1959) 'The social structure of the family', in R.N. Anshen (ed.), *The Family: Its Functions and Destiny*. New York: Harper and Row.

Parsons, T. (1965) 'The normal American family', in S.M. Farber (ed.), *Man and Civilization: The Family's Search for Survival*. New York: McGraw-Hill.

Parsons, T. and Bales, R.F. (eds) (1955) *Family, Socialization and Interaction Process*. New York: Free Press.

Parsons, T. and Shils, E. (1962) *Towards a General Theory of Action*. New York: Harper.

Petras, J. (1999) 'NGOs: In the service of imperialism', *Journal of Contemporary Asia*, 29(4): 429–40.

Sadovnik, A.R. (ed.) (2007) *Sociology of Education: A Critical Reader* (second edition). New York: Routledge.

Samuel, J. (1981) 'Feminism and science teaching: Some classroom observations', in A. Kelly (ed.), *The Missing Half*. Manchester: Manchester University Press.

Saunders, P. (1996) *Unequal But Fair? A Study of Class Barriers in Britain*. London: Civitas.

Saunders, P. (2010) *Social Mobility Myths*. London: Civitas.

Shain, F. and Ozga, J. (2001) 'Identity crisis? Problems in the sociology of education', *British Journal of Sociology of Education*, 22(1): 109–20.

Sharpe, S. (1976) *Just Like a Girl: How Girls Learn to be Women*. Harmondsworth: Penguin.

Spencer, H. (1896) *The Study of Sociology*. New York: D. Appleton.

Spender, D. (1983) *Invisible Women: Schooling Scandal*. London: Women's Press.

Stanworth, M. (1983) *Gender and Schooling; A Study of Sexual Divisions in the Classroom*, London: Hutchinson.

Sugarman, B. (1970) 'Social class, values and behaviour in schools', in M. Craft (ed.), *Family, Class and Education*. London: Longman.

Thatcher, M. (1987) Interview for *Woman's Own*, 31 October.

Toennies, F. ([1857] 1957) *Community and Society*. Edited and translated by C.P. Loomis. New York: Harper and Row.

Tomlinson, S. (2005) *Education in a Post Welfare Society*. London: Routledge.

Tumin, M. (1967) 'Some principles of stratification: A critical analysis', in R. Bendix and S.M. Lipset, *Class, Status and Power* (second edition). London: Routledge and Kegan Paul.

Usher, R. and Edwards, R. (1994) *Postmodernism and Education: Different Voices, Different Worlds*. London: Routledge.

Vulliamy, G. (1972) 'Music in secondary schools – some sociological observations', unpublished MA dissertation, University of London, Institute of Education.

Willis, P. (1977) *Learning to Labour: How Working Class Kids Get Working Class Jobs*. New York: Columbia University Press.

Wright Mills, C. (1959) *The Sociological Imagination*, New York: Oxford University Press.

Young, M.F.D. (ed.) (1971) *Knowledge and Control: New Directions for the Sociology of Education*. London: Collier-Macmillan.

CHAPTER 4

CRITICAL AND RADICAL PEDAGOGIES

Chapter Aims

This chapter will address the work of key theorists in critical and radical pedagogies in response to twenty-first-century challenges in education including
social justice, inequality and schools as transformational spaces of possibility.
In addition, the notion of teachers as transformative intellectuals is considered
as a potential catalyst for the revolutionary change critical and radical pedagogies demand. This chapter will consider the work of global theorists including
Paulo Freire (Método Paulo Freire), Henry Giroux (transformative pedagogy)
and Peter McLaren (the three Rs: Reflection, Resistance and Revolution on
teacher education reform). Finally, a consideration of hip hop as a community-
based alternative radical pedagogy, as implemented in America and Brazil but
gaining global momentum, will conclude this chapter.

Key words: social justice, transformation, critical consciousness, social exclusion,
banking concept.

Introduction

Critical and radical pedagogies are embedded in a creative range of academic
disciplines including politics, history and philosophy of education, and com-
prise social movements that combine education with critical theory. The basic
tenet of critical pedagogy is that there is an unequal social stratification in
society based on class, race and gender; in response, critical and radical pedagogies provide cultural, political and ethical guidance for those in education
who are open to change and seek liberation as an authentic goal in a radically

different world based on equality. Key principles such as democracy and free-dom from oppression are recognised as the cornerstones of critical and radical pedagogy, as illustrated in the American context in the work of Apple (1995) and Giroux (1983), who have applied the works of Marcuse ([1937] 1968) and Freire (1970b), arguing that a movement of raising consciousness in society is the first step for attaining the necessary change and subsequent freedom. Critical pedagogy is therefore preoccupied with challenging social injustice via revolutionary transformation within society. Critical and radical pedagogies aim to create new forms of knowledge by challenging the relationships between who occupies the centre and who occupies the margins of power in schools; this new knowledge is concerned with providing a way of reading history as part of a larger project of reclaiming power and identity, particularly as these are shaped around the categories of race, gender, class and ethnicity. The func-tion of critical and radical pedagogy is to raise consciousness in society and to motivate the critical person to seek social justice; to seek emancipation. Therefore critical and radical pedagogies are engaged with bringing about change and it is here that Marx's Thesis XI on Feuerbach comes to life: 'The philosophers have only interpreted the world, in various ways; the point, how-ever, is to change it' (Marx [1845] 1977: 158).

Twenty-first-century challenges in education

A postmodern example of a radical pedagogy demanding transformative change in schools is the work of Tait Coles, a former science teacher and author of *Never Mind the Inspectors: Here's Punk Learning*. Coles applies the revolutionary passion of the punk movement as a catalyst to change classroom pedagogy via creativity, independent learning and student ownership. Punk learning (Coles, 2014a) positions students at the centre of their learning, cham-pioning ownership as opposed to imposed curriculum, and allows them to take control of how and what they are learning. For Coles, punk learning is about reclaiming teaching as a profession from the control of central government and the destruction of the inspectorate process while at the same time engaging students in ways that he feels currently they are disengaged. Rooted in the anarchy of the punk movement and classical sociology, Coles presents a man-ifesto, almost a call to arms; he demands that teachers should challenge the control of school structures and draw pupils in from the margins to the centre of curriculum design and delivery and as such he claims transformation of schooling in the UK will take place. An example of how this vision might appear on a practical level is evident in the BAFTA award winning Channel 4 series *Educating Yorkshire*, which is based on the pupils and teachers of

Thornhill Community Academy. Set in a socially and economically deprived setting the school is notable for its acute focus on nurturing leadership skills, social justice and moral citizenship alongside the all-important academic attainment. The transformation of 'Musharaf', a shy young man with a stammer, into a formidable role model was the highlight of the series. However, the real story is the transformation of a schooling culture where pupils are active in their own transformation; how the entire school is invested in this process; how an alternative curriculum can champion change and finally how the commitment and care of teaching staff can act as a catalyst towards such a transformation – as it was in the case of 'Musharaf'.

Critical and radical pedagogies are embedded in the notion that education has the power to bring about change. In other words a vision of education is one that locates the moral purpose of education. As a result, critical and radical pedagogies are not centred on a prescriptive set of practices but on a continuous moral project that enables students to develop a social awareness and their role as active citizens in a society based on equality.

Paulo Freire

Freire's critical pedagogy has two central themes: critical consciousness and literacy, both of which are deeply rooted in the critical concept of power, making his ideology relevant beyond the historical period and geographical setting of the original application in late twentieth-century Brazil. Freire's work is concerned with the development of *'conscienticizao'*, which is translated as critical consciousness (Freire, 1970a, 1970b), a process by which the student is made aware of their ability to participate in their own learning and in the transformation of society. Freedom, for Freire, begins with a consciousness-raising movement (McLaren and Leonard, 1993), which is noted as a beginning point of the liberatory praxis; this means the bringing about of social change through reflection and action. Change, in consciousness and concrete action, are linked for Freire (Freire, 1985; McLaren and Lankshear, 1993), therefore a momentum- and goal-orientated focus is noted in Freirian thought, change is the outcome. Freire draws attention to and challenges what he calls 'the banking concept of education' (Friere, 1970a), which regards students as empty bank accounts waiting to be filled by the school teacher or the imposed curriculum. Freire argues that the student must not be perceived as a *tabula rasa* (a Latin term meaning 'blank slate') but must be included as an active participant in their own transformation arguing that 'The oppressed must be their own example in the struggle for their redemption' (Freire, 1970b: 54). In a later publication and linked to adult literacy Freire reinforces this point, which is the keystone to the radical postmodern pedagogy 'punk learning'. 'Education makes sense because women and men learn that through learning they can make and remake themselves; because women and men are able to take responsibility for themselves as beings capable of knowing' (Freire, 2004: 15). Freire's critical pedagogy demonstrates change via literacy and the potential to escape the prison-like state of being trapped and dependent on others, and the sense of powerlessness (Freire, 1973) caused by the lack of ability in reading and writing. For Freire, the development of a sense of self-esteem and collective self-confidence, coupled with the desire to change, not only one's self, but the circumstances of one's social group bring together the overarching principles of freedom, democracy and equality in a critical pedagogy which acknowledges that a literate population is a stepping stone to active participation in democratic society.

Thinking point 4.1

Many critical theorists and important figures have championed revolution in the modern era with the added aim of restructuring global education systems, including Peter McLaren (Marxist educationalist), Malala Yousafzai (Nobel Peace Prize winner, 2014) Owen Jones (historian, journalist), Asmaa Mahfouz (Egyptian blogger), Che Guevara (Marxist revolutionary) and Russell Brand (celebrity). Are there any similarities in the varied radical pedagogies mentioned above and what would the schooling system look like if such a revolution were to take place?

Not all radical pedagogies are linked to charismatic figures and political rhetoric. To illustrate, the reader by Bragg and Manchester (2012) explores, from the British context, the flagship 'creative learning' programme as part of the Creative Partnerships pedagogy that sets out to ensure young people are at the centre (as opposed to the margins) of its work. This research is particularly relevant because it explores student voice as a factor in the power relations that are evident in schools. In considering this radical pedagogy review your response to the previous question: What would the schooling system look like if such a revolution were to take place?

Peter McLaren

McLaren is a teacher, a poet and a researcher whose work has been influenced by key figures in classical sociology and philosophy including Marx, Guevara, Althusser, Bourdieu, Fromm, Hegel, Dewey and Gramsci. He was also a close friend and associate of the late Paulo Freire who inspired his commitment to social justice. This has infused his writing on critical pedagogy, which is referred to as Marxist humanism. Like Freire, McLaren's body of work details how western educational systems work in tandem with an 'imperial ideology' (Eryaman, 2009: 188) to maintain inequities, thus making the space for a radical pedagogy all the more imperative. To clarify, for McLaren the aim of critical and radical pedagogy depends not on the abolition of private property, which is the classical Marxist position, but on the enlightenment or raised consciousness of the alienated and oppressed labour force; for critical pedagogy to be realised it must help those engaged in the pedagogical encounter to transcend their own exclusion. This aspect illustrates the centrality of resistance in McLaren's vision.

McLaren writes from the American perspective and defends the position that public schools (the equivalent of state schools in the UK) are legitimate sites for democratic advancement concentrating predominantly on the reform of teacher education in his Reflection, Resistance, Revolution pedagogy. Building on the revelations in Jonathan Kozol's (1991) classic book *Savage Inequalities*, which expose the unequal conditions in American public schools based on his personal reflections of racial segregation using terms such as 'educational apartheid' (Scherer, 1993) and 'ghetto education' (Michalove, 1993), McLaren confidently calls for revolutionary change in teacher education in order to challenge the status quo.

McLaren's radical pedagogy is shared by his contemporaries including Ira Shor and Henry Giroux, and is referred to as social reconstructionism; a pedagogy where teachers are active in the process of bringing about social change via a range of strategies including cross cultural communication and cultural literacy. In this way, a regeneration of teachers takes place, moving away from the traditional authoritarian transmission of a dominant culture to 'transformative intellectuals' who embody a commitment to social justice and equality. It is important to articulate that McLaren's rally call is not a new pedagogy, but based on a number of very influential publications and theorists. First, he is influenced by the reconstructionist position set out by Counts (1932) in *Dare the School Build a New Social Order*, which included a manifesto for socialist reform and collectivism. Second, he captures the spirit of Dewey, who criticised traditional forms of teacher education and called for a new social and educational philosophy which motivated 'a zeal for the betterment of our common civilization' (Dewey, 1933: 270). Third, he was influenced by a historic movement of 'frontier educators' (Grant and Secada, 1990) who emphasised a focus on an understanding of the conditions under which learners live in order to offer intellectual and practical guidance for progression. Finally, McLaren takes note of the work of Kilpatrick (1933), writing at a time of immense social unrest and change:

The socially unenlightened teaching too often found in the ordinary college or normal school can hardly have any other result than turning out teachers ignorant of our social situation and with no intelligent concern about it. Each staff member should be encouraged to know first-hand how the less favoured among us live and feel. First-hand contacts carry greater potency. We can easily disregard the needs of those we do not know. Without this, we can hardly hope for socially prepared teachers. (Kilpatrick, 1933: 266)

So, what are the characteristics of the teacher who reflects McLaren's radical pedagogy? A comprehensive list is offered including a demonstrated commitment to developing an ethical dimension of critical reflection; application of data on racism, sexism and social class inequality linked to special educational needs; an understanding of global educational practices beyond white, middle class and heterosexual educational norms that perpetuate fixed ideas about minority groups and indigenous groups; and enabling student teachers to develop the skills to critically examine the ideological nature of teachers' work including the concept of the negotiated curriculum as opposed to the predetermined, imposed curriculum. Fundamentally, McLaren, who makes thoughtful reference to the work of Hill (2001) and the British context, purports 'a model of a teacher as a transformative intellectual who does not instruct students what to think but who learns to think dialectically and who develops a critical consciousness aimed at social transformation' (McLaren, 2001: 16). In conclusion, the radical nature of McLaren's pedagogy is that the elements discussed above are simply the tip of the iceberg; in reality the reform of teacher education is more about the bigger societal injustices (Cole, 1998) that exist and, in order to dismantle the structures that maintain such injustices, an intellectually transformative teaching profession can facilitate social reform on a wider scale.

Henry Giroux

A close friend of Paulo Freire, Henry Giroux is one of the founding theorists of critical pedagogy in the USA and is currently captivating new audiences on Facebook and social media in order to secure his goal of a more socially and economically just society that not only eliminates oppressive inequalities of wealth, power and privilege, but does so with the creation of an 'open, self-critical community of inquiring citizens' (Giroux, 1983: 190). Giroux has been influenced by the Frankfurt School, Bourdieu, Willis, Gramsci, Apple and Marcuse, who argued that the structures of schooling are a barrier for students to developing their own goals, and essentially serve to de-skill students (Giroux, 1992); as a result he has made consequential contributions to many disciplines including critical theory, youth studies, cultural studies, higher education and public pedagogy. Giroux is a formidable postmodern theorist whose work is based on his honest and transparent insights into his own lower working class upbringing including experiences of food shortages, exclusion in school and feeling an outsider at college, all of which led to the formulation of his own critical consciousness. His personal story of transformation is an important facet of his writing as he is able to capture the acute injustice of invisibility (Hassan, 2014; Hollander and Howard, 2000) as well as the stigma, social markings and structural inequalities (Heller, 2011) of the white academic as captured in the extract below taken from an interview:

> When I first started teaching at Boston University I did not have the knowledge, theoretical tools or the experience to move into a world largely dominated by middle- and ruling-class cultural capital. I was constantly confronted with faculty and students who assumed a god-given right of privilege and power, especially with regards to their academic credentials, middle-class language skills and lifelong experience in which people like myself were defined through our deficits, and largely as outsiders. All of these requisite changes were brought home to me during my second semester. My father had just died of a heart attack, and I had returned to the campus after attending his funeral. My Dean at the time was a guy named Bob Dentler, an Ivy-League educated scholar. I ran into him on the street shortly after my father's death and he said to me, 'I am sorry to hear about your father. It must have been difficult settling his estate?' Estate? My father left a hundred dollars in an envelope taped behind a mirror. That was his estate. I was immediately struck by how out of touch so many academics are with respect to those others who are not replicas of themselves. (Peters, 2011)

It is important to reflect momentarily on the power of a personal story of transformation as a catalyst for a radical pedagogy – the impact of oppressive structures on an individual, and the criticality of resistance (Kincheloe, 2004) cannot be underestimated, and it is based on this rationale that it is important to reflect on Giroux's lived experiences *in his own* words in order to fully appreciate and understand his pedagogical standpoint.

Giroux's vast canon of academic literature has an overwhelming radical edge and explores the notion of schools as sites of struggle; institutional sites and cultural sites of contestation where the oppressed and economically marginalised are further disempowered, hence the call for a radical pedagogy of reform. For Giroux, pedagogy is defined as follows:

> Pedagogy is not simply about the social construction of knowledge, values, and experiences; it is also a performative practice embodied in the lived interactions among educators, audiences, texts, and institutional formations. Pedagogy, at its best, implies that learning takes place across a spectrum of social practices and settings. (Giroux, 2004: 61)

The focus on 'sites of learning' (these can be multiple, shifting and overlapping) is significant as this draws on the notion of the production and distribution of power, which has political, economic and educational impacts. Schools are clearly key sites of radical pedagogy; however, the concept of 'permanent education' (Williams, 1967) extends the focus to lifelong education and a holistic environmental conceptualisation of education, which Giroux links to cultural reproduction – the idea that knowledge is produced under certain conditions. To summarise, Giroux's radical pedagogy is rooted in democratic values and practices that build on the histories and struggles of excluded and marginalised groups based on class, race, gender, age or disability. It is not a road map to overcoming these societal challenges but a powerful lens that focuses in on the unequal distribution of power and calls for teachers to consider this alternative lens in order to better understand the world and to transform it when necessary. In common with Thornhill Community Academy, Giroux argues that schools should explore the creative curriculum (Dirlik, 2002), which involves building a curriculum around the varied histories, experiences, literacies and values of the diverse school community in order to consolidate their identity and encourage their participation in not only their own transformation but also in becoming engaged global citizens who have the capacity to bring about social change.

Keepin' it real: Hip Hop Pedagogy

> I may not change the world but I guarantee that I will spark the mind that will.
>
> Tupac Shakur rapper, activist (1971–1996)

Since its birth on the streets of New York in the 1970s, hip hop has been transformed from a youth movement to an international phenomenon (Emdin, 2010; DeHanas, 2013; Lamont Hill, 2009) translating globally into education pedagogy

(Aponte, 2013). Hip hop pedagogy is presented as a holistic community-based educational approach that aims to meet the needs of minority students by providing them with space for an emancipatory learning experience and celebrates sociology in the form of Giroux who calls for us to 'reconsider education, to engage in understanding it as a way of life in which learning is a collective activity' (Giroux, 1992: 14).

In acknowledging the intersections of race, power, identity, history and politics in hip hop music as a reflection of the exclusion, economic disadvantage and inferiority experienced by Afro-American, Latin and Caribbean young people in America and Brazil (Marcyliena and Bennett, 2011), it is clear to see how a movement entrenched in a collective consciousness and a powerful urban culture that nurtures young people can translate into a restructuring of the classroom. The Brazilian context differs slightly in that hip hop is rooted in street dance and reflects a striking similarity to Brazil's traditional martial art, capoeira (Dowdy, 2012). Both forms of cultural expression emerged from African diasporic roots and are associated with disaffected young people (the majority of whom are male), often unemployed and with limited education who began to occupy public spaces and form a strong sense of group organisation, cohesion and consciousness. Academics have noted that it is the potential for channelling this consciousness that transports hip hop from a culture into an educational pedagogy 'the term hip-hop *culture*; it's the *culture* that gets us in touch with each other. We create community and we discover ourselves in the process. This reality is our *consciousness*' (Pardue, 2008: 29). Similarly, politicians who advocate hip hop pedagogy in both America and Brazil focus on the capacity for inclusion, self-esteem and collective support as elements that can enhance the educational life chances of young people, offering a positive counter narrative to social exclusion and educational failure (Rohter, 2007).

To illustrate the pragmatic implications of hip hop pedagogy in the classroom, the work of an urban school teacher, Sam Seidel (www.hiphop-genius.org), is captured in his book *Hip Hop Genius: Remixing High School Education*, providing an innovative insight into how a school curriculum can be devised with the students at the centre and with liberatory outcomes. The school, High School for Recording Arts (HSRA) in St. Paul, Minnesota, provides a space for young people to explore their artistic skills while learning about computing, digital media and business. Working mainly with high school 'dropouts' and incorporating hip hop culture as a tool to include, motivate, inspire and maintain retention the school emphasises 'respect for the brilliance and resilience of young people' (Seidel, 2011: 54) at the heart of its delivery. Hip hop pedagogy is championed as an educational strategy through the Hip-Hop Education Centre in New York, a joint project with the

Schomburg Center for Research in Black Culture and New York University, who proudly boast that the President talks of listening to Jay-Z on his iPod. In an educational system preoccupied with transferrable employability skills, scholars of all kinds, but especially those who use hip hop culture as their lens of critical enquiry, must guide students to think about society beyond employability targets. Gosa (2013) argues that hip hop scholarship has much to offer wider society beyond the social issues that contributed to hip hop's origins and its continuing relevance as a cultural force as a culturally relevant pedagogy. Hip hop, like all popular culture, has to wrestle with many challenges. First, the close associations with celebrity, explosive record sales, a burgeoning economy and the acute contradictions of role models such as Carlos Coy a.k.a. South Park Mexican (sexual assault of a child), Tab Virgil Jr, a.k.a. Turk (attempted murder) and Reminisce Smith a.k.a. Remy Ma (illegal weapon possession and attempted coercion) to name just three. Second, from within the academy questions remain unanswered such as are professional hip hop practitioners the best equipped to teach hip hop studies? Can hip hop be adapted in a multidisciplinary manner or must it exist as a discrete subject? Third, as the second generation of hip hop adherents enter higher education, has its identity evolved and how true to its origins can it remain? Finally, beyond building academic resilience and literacy, can hip hop be taken seriously in higher education (Tinson, 2013)?

Reading suggestion

The following academic paper engages the reader in a critique of hip hop based education (HHBE). In addition to considering a range of perspectives, the authors pose questions for the reader, samples of which are captured below:

Gosa, T.L. and Fields, T.G. (2012) 'Is hip hop education another hustle? The (ir) responsible use of hip hop as pedagogy', in B.J. Porfilio and J. Viola (eds), *Hip Hop(e): The Cultural Practices and Critical Pedagogy of International Hip Hop*. New York: Peter Lang, pp. 195–210.

1. An important part of HHBE involves using rap lyrics in classroom activities. Pretend you are going to use lyrics in a high school history class. What songs and artists would you use?
2. What impact could HHBE have on the quality of the nation's teaching force? Do you think the inclusion of hip hop will help diversify the teaching pool?

Chapter summary

This chapter considered the work of key theorists in critical and radical pedagogies in response to twenty-first-century challenges in education including the work of global theorists Paulo Freire, Henry Giroux and Peter McLaren. In addition, the discussion captured a postmodern radical pedagogy in the form of hip hop, a cultural identity incorporating DJing, breakdancing, graffiti and knowledge with a mass global following, burgeoning economy and cult celebrity endorsement, which has been subject to critical enquiry in order to effect the transfer into pedagogy for educational advancement.

References

Aponte, C.A. (2013) 'When hip-hop and education converge: A look into hip-hop based education programs in the United States and Brazil', Master's Thesis, Carnegie Mellon University, Dietrich College of Humanities and Social Sciences.

Apple, M.W. (1995) *Education and Power*. New York: Routledge.

Bragg, S. and Manchester, H. (2012) 'Pedagogies of student voice', *Revista de Educaci'on*, 359: 143–63. Available at: http://oro.open.ac.uk/31331/6/RevistaFINAL090412.pdf. (accessed 9 January 2015).

Cole, M. (1998) 'Globalization, modernisation and competitiveness: A critique of the New Labour project in education', *International Studies in Sociology of Education*, 8(3): 315–32.

Coles, T. (2014a) *Never Mind the Inspectors: Here's Punk Learning*. Carmarthen: Crown House Publisher.

Coles, T. (2014b) 'Critical pedagogy: schools must equip students to challenge the status quo', Teacher Network, *The Guardian*, February 2014. Available at: www.theguardian.com/teacher-network/teacher-blog/2014/feb/25/critical-pedagogy-schools-students-challenge (accessed 9 January 2015).

Counts, G. (1932) *Dare the Schools Build a New Social Order?* New York: The John Day Co.

DeHanas, D.N. (2013) 'Keepin' it real: London youth hip hop as an authentic performance of belief', *Journal of Contemporary Religion*, 28(2): 295–308.

Dewey, J. (1933) *How We Think*. Chicago, IL: Henry Regnery.

Dirlik, A. (2002) 'Literature/identity: Transnationalism, narrative, and representation', *Review of Education/Pedagogy/Cultural Studies*, 24(3): 29–38.

Dowdy, C.S. (2012) 'Youth, music, and agency: Undoing race, poverty and violence in Rio de Janeiro, Brazil', Master's Thesis, American University, Department of Cultural Studies.

Emdin, C. (2010) *Urban Science Education for the Hip-Hop Generation*. Rotterdam: Sense Publishers.

Eryaman, M.Y. (ed.) (2009) *Peter McLaren, Education, and the Struggle for Liberation*. Cresskill, NJ: Hampton Press, Inc.

Freire, P. (1970a) *Cultural Action for Freedom*. Cambridge, MA: Harvard Educational Review.

Freire, P. (1970b) *Pedagogy of the Oppressed*. New York: Seabury Press.

Freire, P. (1973) *Education for Critical Consciousness*. New York: Seabury.

Freire, P. (1985) *The Politics of Education: Culture, Power, and Liberation*. South Hadley, MA: Bergin Garvey.

Freire, P. (2004) *Pedagogy of Indignation*. Boulder, CO: Paradigm.

Giroux, H.A. (1983) *Theory and Resistance in Education*. South Hadley, MA: Bergin Garvey.

Giroux, H.A. (1992) 'Resisting difference: Cultural studies and the discourse of critical pedagogy', in L. Grossberg, C. Nelson and P. Treichler (eds), *Cultural Studies*. New York: Routledge, pp. 199–212.

Giroux, H.A. (2004) 'Cultural studies, public pedagogy, and the responsibility of intellectuals', *Communication and Critical/Cultural Studies*, 1(1): 59–79.

Gosa, T. (2013) 'Colleges love hip hop, but do they love black men too?' *Chronicle of Higher Education*, 15 February. Available at: http://chronicle.com/blogs/conversation/2013/02/15/colleges-love-hip-hop-but-do-they-love-black-men-too/ (accessed 30 April 2014).

Grant, C. and Secada, W. (1990) 'Preparing teachers for diversity', in W.R. Houston (ed.), *Handbook of Research on Teacher Education*. New York: Macmillan.

Hassan, N. (2014) 'Muslim consciousness in the narratives of British Muslim women in east London', PhD Thesis, University of East London.

Heller, J.L. (2011) 'Enduring problem of social class stigma experienced by upwardly mobile white academics', *McGill Sociological Review*, 2: 19–38.

Hill, D. (2001) 'State theory and the neo-liberal reconstruction of schooling and teacher education: A structuralist neo-Marxist critique of postmodernist, quasi-postmodernist, and culturalist neo-Marxist theory', *British Journal of Sociology of Education*, 22(1): 137–57.

Hollander, J.A. and Howard, J.A. (2000) 'Social psychological theories on social inequalities', *Social Psychology Quarterly*, 63: 338–51.

Kilpatrick, W. (ed.) (1933) *The Educational Frontier*. New York: The Century Co.

Kincheloe, J.L. (2004) *Critical Pedagogy*. New York: Peter Lang.

Kozol, J. (1991) *Savage Inequalities*. New York: Crown Publishers.

Lamont Hill, M. (2009) *Beats, Rhymes, and Classroom Life: Hip-Hop Pedagogy and the Politics of Identity*. New York: Teachers College Press.

McLaren, P. and Lankshear, C. (1993) *Politics of Liberation: Paths from Freire*. New York: Routledge.

McLaren, P. and Leonard, P. (1993) *Paulo Freire: A Critical Encounter*. New York: Routledge.

Marcuse, H. [1937] (1968) 'Philosophy and critical theory', in J. Habermas (ed.), *Negotiations, Essays in Critical Theory*. Boston, MA: Beacon Press.

Marcyliena, M. and Bennett, D. (2011) *Hip-Hop and the Global Imprint of a Black Cultural Form*. American Academy of Art and Sciences. Available at: www.mitpress-journals.org/doi/pdf/10.1162/DAED_a_00086 (accessed September 2014).

Marx, K. [1845] (1977) 'Theses on Feuerbach', in D. McLellan (ed.), *Karl Marx: Selected Writings*. New York: Oxford University Press, p. 158.

Michalove, S. (1993) 'The educational crusade of Jonathan Kozol', *Educational Forum* 57: 300–11.

Pardue, D. (2008) *Ideologies of Marginality in Brazilian Hip Hop.* New York: Palgrave Macmillan.

Pardue, D. (2011) 'Brazil taking stock of the state: Hip-hoppers' evaluation of the cultural points program in Brazil', *Latin American Perspectives*, 23: 93–112.

Peters, M.A. (2011) 'Henry Giroux on democracy unsettled: From critical pedagogy to the war on youth', Truthout interview. Available at: www.truth-out.org/opinion/item/2753:henry-giroux-on-democracy-unsettled-from-critical-pedagogy-to-the-war-on-youth (accessed 9 January 2015).

Rohter, L. (2007) 'Brazilian government invests in culture of hip-hop', *The New York Times*, 14 March.

Scherer, M. (1993) 'On *Savage Inequalities*: A conversation with Jonathan Kozol', *Educational Leadership*, 50(4): 4–9.

Seidel, S. (2011) *Hip Hop Genius: Remixing High School Education.* Lanham, MD: Rowman & Littlefield Education.

Tinson, C. (2013) 'Introduction to Special Issue: Hip hop, critical pedagogy, and radical education in a time of crisis', *Radical Teacher*, 97 (Fall).

Williams, R. (1967) 'Preface to second edition', *Communications.* New York: Barnes and Noble.

CHAPTER 5

DIFFERENTIAL EDUCATIONAL ATTAINMENT AND THE DEBATE ABOUT INTELLIGENCE

Chapter Aims

The aim of this chapter is to examine the key areas of debate relating to inequalities in educational attainment including theories of intelligence, social and cultural explanations as well as the role of schools. Government policies and attempts to address these inequalities will be assessed.

Key words: meritocracy, social mobility, equality of opportunity, intelligence, IQ, eugenics, genetic determinism, social capital, cultural capital.

Introduction

One of the longest running and most controversial debates in sociology of education relates to the issue of differential educational attainment; that is, the debate about why some groups in society perform better than others usually in relation to *social class, gender* or *ethnicity*, but here we will focus primarily on social class differences. These differences in attainment affect the degree of social mobility and relate to how open our society is. In England this debate takes place against a background of post-war welfare reforms and education policy in which there was to be a new era of equality of opportunity and *meritocracy*. This is a term that we now take for granted, but it was coined by Michael Young in his 1958 book, *The Rise of the Meritocracy 1870–2033,* and refers to a society in which all roles and positions are allocated on the basis of effort and merit as opposed to tradition or inheritance. In such a society those who govern are alleged to be the most able and have gained their positions through the greatest *effort* and the highest *ability* as measured by such supposedly objective criteria as intelligence and educational achievement.

From negative to positive

Although the idea of meritocracy tends to be seen in positive terms nowadays, Young wrote this work as a dystopian vision of Britain in which inequality based on merit gradually replaces a society based on social class inequalities. He suggests that this brings with it its own problems in that, while there was once educational injustice due to class inequality and class privilege during which those at the bottom of society could explain their lack of upward social mobility and educational success as something beyond their control and in need of change, in a meritocratic society the unfairness is justified as being based on a fair system. This leaves little opportunity for those at the bottom to progress further in life, regardless of effort, once they have been designated as having limited ability.

Young was writing at a time of great optimism in the prospect for social democracy and the desire to create a new and fairer society based on rational and efficient systems of role allocation that would replace unfair and inefficient traditional ones. However, he was pointing out the potential problems that he envisaged arising from the tripartite system of education in which ability is believed to be measurable by means of intelligence tests that can predict the performance potential of all children. Meritocracy is inherently bound up with the principle of selection and that is why the Norwood Committee of 1943 recommended a system of secondary education involving the separation of children at age 11 on the basis of the '11-plus'. This age was chosen on the grounds that according to government psychologists such as Cyril Burt (see Chapters 8 and 10) intelligence in children is essentially inherited at birth and fixed by that age. Such testing was seen as the best means of allocating them to the type of education most suited to their talents: a grammar school for the academically gifted, a secondary modern school for the non-academic child and a technical high school for those with practical talents. Those parents with independent means were still able to send their children to private schools, which remained relatively untouched during the post-war reforms despite the recommendation of the 1944 Fleming Report that the public schools, the most prestigious private schools that are members of the Headmasters' Conference, be integrated into the state system.

The increasing amount of evidence (Early Leaving Report; Ministry of Education, 1954; Crowther Report; Ministry of Education, 1959) which showed that the tripartite system was not benefiting working class pupils and was leading to 'a wastage of ability' led some politicians in the 1960s to propose a comprehensive system of education in which all children should be educated together in order to achieve more equality of opportunity. *Comprehensivisation* had been Labour Party policy since 1952, but the Labour government's half-hearted approach meant that it was only in 1965 that Local Education Authorities (LEAs) were 'requested' to start planning for the introduction of a comprehensive system (Green, 1991). However, no sooner had a comprehensive system been introduced, than it became branded as the cause of all the alleged problems within the education system, including falling standards and deteriorating discipline in schools (Tomlinson, 2005). The *Black Papers* (Cox and Dyson, 1969) suggested that selection was essential because it was the only way to ensure that pupils received the education most suited to their talents.

The evidence produced during the 1950s and 1960s revealing that working class children were not performing as well as middle class children in terms of gaining access to grammar schools and thereby university (Banks, 1955; Floud et al., 1956) confirmed the views of many at the time that ability and intelligence are inherited and that, on average, middle class parents are more intelligent than working class parents (Saunders, 1996, 2010). There are still sociologists, psychologists and educationalists who argue that levels of educational attainment and patterns of social mobility are the result primarily of inherited intelligence in the population (Herrnstein and Murray, 1994; Jensen, 1969; Saunders, 1996, 2010, 2012; Shakeshaft et al., 2013).

The rise of a meritocracy?

According to Peter Saunders (1996, 2010) we live in an age of meritocracy almost as envisaged by Michael Young. The problem, Saunders suggests, is that British sociology is, and has long been, a profession dominated by left-wing academics who are obsessed with class divisions and are driven by what he calls the 'SAD thesis' (Saunders, 2010); that is, the belief that people's destinies are determined by the levels of social advantage and disadvantage (SAD) that prevail in society rather than by such things as innate ability or intelligence. In effect, he states that sociologists tend to focus on social causes for differences in educational attainment and levels of social mobility, and find it difficult to accept that natural phenomena such as genes might play a part. Due to a reluctance to consider non-sociological explanations, Saunders claims that most sociologists automatically leap to the conclusion that it is the system that is to blame for the poorer educational achievements and lower levels of occupational mobility of the working class.

Clearly, there is some validity in Saunders' claim that sociology experienced a shift to the left in thinking and writing during the 1960s and 1970s in response to the perceived failure of the Welfare State to make an impact on class inequalities and the continuing class segregation of the education system (see Chapter 3). However, his arguments relating to intelligence are highly contentious and controversial. In his examination of a wide range of British evidence on educational attainment and social mobility, Saunders (2010, 2012) claims confidently that it is a myth to describe Britain as a closed society as is suggested by politicians such as Nick Clegg (Her Majesty's Government, 2011) and Alan Milburn (Her Majesty's Government, 2009), asserting that the evidence confirms what he had suspected: the key elements influencing a person's class position are intelligence and effort. He agrees with the ideas of the American psychologists such as Richard Herrnstein (Herrnstein and Murray, 1994) who argue that countries such as the USA are now much more meritocratic, pointing to systems in place, examinations, IQ testing, competitive application systems and interviews, which make it much more likely that those with the most 'ability' get the best jobs. Herrnstein and Murray talk of the new 'cognitive classes' in the USA who have gained their positions not because of their family status or inherited wealth, but because of their ability. For Herrnstein and Murray there has clearly been a decline in the power elite referred to by C. Wright Mills in the 1950s.

Yet most of Saunders' assumptions are based on a somewhat partial analysis of the data, often pointing to statistical anomalies if the evidence challenges his beliefs, or taking a very uncritical approach to the reliability of theories of intelligence and the evidence that supports it. In fact, despite the general lack of consensus amongst psychologists and geneticists (Sternberg, 1977; Gardner, 1983; Hart and Drummond, 2014; Rose et al., 1984) about what intelligence is and whether it can be rendered in the form of a single and fixed aggregate, Saunders feels confident enough to proclaim that 'the logic is compelling' (Saunders, 2010: 60), which, for anyone doing social scientific research, is about as certain as it is possible to be. The key point to remember for any student of education is that most social sciences, and that includes psychology, are speculative disciplines and they should be treated as such. Sociology and psychology sometimes offer seductively simple solutions to complex human problems and it is easy to be lulled into accepting an elegant, yet simple, theory about human nature for which the evidence is contested and the validity uncertain. Nikolas Rose (1999: 214) refers to this as the 'power of the single number' and it is not uncommon for policy makers, students and academics to take an idea or a theory that they have learnt and, because it seems so convincing, stake their entire careers and reputation on it, but this is generally ill advised. Hence the caution exercised by most sociologists when dealing with issues of intelligence. For example, how reasonable is it to base a theory of social mobility on the outcome of a few cognitive tests and thereby downplay the influence of other factors including socialisation, family context, environmental influences, uncontrolled occurrences and countless numbers of possible variables that have an impact on an individual's life-course? Most sociologists are not prepared to commit themselves to such a position, especially as much of the evidence upon which the heritability of intelligence is based is either highly contested or flawed (Gould, 1981; Kamin, 1977; Rose et al., 1984).

Thinking point 5.1

Is it all in the genes? The flaws in genetic determinism

James Fallon is an American neurophysiologist who specialises in the genetics of mass murderers. He claims to be able to identify such individuals from their brain scans. Moreover, these patterns, he claims, can be identified from childhood using some simple tests because he believes pathological killers are born not bred. The possible application for such a predictive tool is not lost on Fallon who sees in it a means of identifying potential killers and of preventing them from entering society and becoming a danger to the rest of us. A simple and elegant solution to a potentially serious threat.

And yet, it transpires that by some strange coincidence, Fallon himself has the brain patterns and presumably the genes of a 'psychopath'. But he is clearly not a mass murderer; he is a highly respected neuroscientist with a great deal of talent in his field of research, as well as a loving husband and father. If genes are so predictive, why is it that Fallon has not even got a criminal record? Indeed, Fallon concedes that there are many with such genes who never get into trouble and who live useful and crime-free lives. In effect individuals are not prisoners of their genes. This comes as an epiphany to Fallon who realises the folly of basing his theory of psychopathy on genetic testing alone.

> I'm a committed scientist ... and this fact has shaped the way I view behaviour, motivation, and morality for my entire adult life. In my mind we are machines, albeit machines we don't understand all that well, and I have believed for decades that we have very little control over what we do and who we are. To me nature (genetics) determines about 80 per cent of our personality and behaviour and nurture (how and in what environment we are raised) only 20 per cent.

> This is how I have always thought about the brain and behaviour. But this understanding took a stinging and rather embarrassing blow, starting

(Continued)

(Continued)

in 2005, and I continue to reconcile my past with my present reality. I have come to understand – even more than I did before – that humans are, by nature, complicated creatures. And to reduce our actions, motivations, desires and needs to absolutes is doing each of us a disservice. We are not simply good or evil, right or wrong, kind or vindictive, benign or dangerous. We are not simply the product of biology, either, and science can only tell us part of the story. (Fallon, 2014: 6–7)

1. How important do you think it is for us to know information about the 'pathological' characteristics of children as identified by Fallon?
2. To what use do you think it should be put?
3. How fair would it be to 'label' someone from the age of 5 as having 'psychopathic traits'?
4. What might be the implications of Fallon's findings for theories of intelligence?

Is inequality inevitable?

In his Margaret Thatcher Lecture in 2013, Boris Johnson (2013) suggests that Britain needs to nurture all of its talent in order to succeed in an increasingly 'impatient' and competitive global economy. He warns against a politics of envy in which the wealthy are targeted by those who resent their good fortune, pointing out that as a small minority blessed with God-given talents, the wealthy should be hailed as heroes not only for the wealth they create, but also for the fact that they pay a disproportionate amount of tax on which we rely to keep our public services functioning. In his speech Johnson conflates the wealthy with the highly intelligent; they are, in his mind, one and the same thing ignoring such factors as inherited wealth (Piketty, 2014) or, indeed, wealth illegally or unfairly acquired. He suggests that economic equality is undesirable because it discourages competition and because we are born with unequal and fixed amounts of intelligence. He goes on to state that only about 2 per cent of the population are born with an above average Intelligence Quotient (IQ) of over 130 and that about 16 per cent of the population are unfortunate enough to be endowed with an IQ of only 85 or below. The key message Johnson conveys in his lecture is similar to that propounded by Saunders: the wealthy are wealthy because they are more able and intelligent than the rest of us and that this ability is there at birth and remains fixed throughout our lives. Just as Young hypothesised in 1958, in a meritocracy we are able to separate children at an ever earlier age and allocate them to forms of education most suited to their ability levels thus making for a more efficient society, and one that is led by those believed to be the most able.

What is intelligence?

How have we reached a point of such certainty about the heritability of intelligence on the part of some biologists, psychologists, politicians and sociologists on one hand, and one of clear scepticism on the part of others? In 1904 the French psychologist Alfred Binet developed the first intelligence test to identify pupils who were struggling in their studies and in need of extra support. The tests involved the use of a number of cognitive questions that a child might be expected to understand by a certain age. The results enabled Binet to calculate the difference between the child's mental age and physical age and this would be used to identify any extra support the child might need. Binet had no intention of using his intelligence tests as anything other than as a diagnostic tool, but he was concerned they might be used as a means of labelling some children as congenitally, that is innately, 'feeble-minded' thereby ignoring their potential to learn and to improve their intelligence (Kamin, 1977). In 1912 Wilhelm Stern devised the IQ, which he defined as the ratio of a child's mental age, as measured by the intelligence test, and their chronological (actual) age. So, if their mental age is 10 but their chronological age is 8, then the ratio of this is $10/8 = 1.25 \times 100 =$ an IQ of 125. With adults the issue becomes more complicated because after a certain chronological age, mental age becomes meaningless when comparing adults of vastly differing ages. As a result, a deviance IQ is used by comparing a person's mental age with the mean level of intelligence in the population.

IQ, eugenics and immigration

Had IQ testing been limited to diagnostic assessment and a means of devising ways of helping children to improve their 'intelligence', then it might not have been such a controversial issue. However, Binet's worst fears were realised when psychologists in the USA began to employ it as a tool of the eugenics movement. In 1916 the American psychologist and eugenicist Lewis Terman created the Stanford-Binet Test, which, he hoped, could be used to identify the 'feeble-minded' with the aim of controlling their reproduction. This had the purpose of helping to eliminate what was thought to be the source of the criminal classes and thereby helping to preserve the genetic integrity of the American population. The work of the American Eugenics Research Association had already played a prominent role in the enactment of sterilisation laws in a number of states from 1907 onwards.

The USA at the turn of the twentieth century was a young nation that was growing rapidly as a result of its dynamic economy and the consequent demand for labour. However, there was a growing fear amongst the dominant white establishment that the influx of 'inferior races' threatened their preeminent position. In 1916 Madison Grant wrote a survey of the 'great races', which was written as a warning to America of the 'melting pot' approach to immigration (Grant, 1916). Placing the Anglo-Saxon and Nordic groups at the top of the racial hierarchy, Grant claimed that unrestricted immigration to the USA would bring an end to these superior races and result in the dying out of the qualities and characteristics that once made Europe great and which could also make America great. For Grant these characteristics are genetically transmitted and therefore are seen to be in need of management through eugenic policies.

Thinking point 5.2

Eugenics

Read this extract from Madison Grant's (1916: 48) *The Passing of the Great Race, or the Racial Basis of European History* and discuss the points that are raised at the end.

The value and efficiency of a population are not numbered by what the newspapers call souls, but by the proportion of men of physical and intellectual vigour. The small Colonial population of America was, on an average and man for man, far superior to the present inhabitants, although the latter are twenty-five times more numerous. The ideal in eugenics toward which statesmanship should be directed is, of course, improvement in quality rather than quantity. This, however, is at present a counsel of perfection and we must face conditions as they are. The small birth rate in the upper classes is to some extent offset by the care received by such children as are born and the better chance they have to become adult and breed in their turn. The large birth rate of the lower classes is under normal conditions offset by a heavy infant mortality, which eliminates the weaker children. Where altruism, philanthropy or

(Continued)

(Continued)

sentimentalism intervene with the noblest purpose and forbid nature to penalize the unfortunate victims of reckless breeding, the multiplication of inferior types is encouraged and fostered. Indiscriminate efforts to preserve babies among the lower classes often result in serious injury to the race. At the existing stage of civilization, the legalizing of birth control would probably be of benefit by reducing the number of offspring in the undesirable classes.

1. What are the main assumptions behind eugenics?
2. Why do those who propose eugenic theories urge governments to carry out eugenic policies?
3. Why does Grant criticise philanthropy?

Terman saw this as a clarion call to engage in the testing and control of immigration to America with the intention of restricting the entry of races that he believed to have lower intelligence, especially those from south eastern and eastern Europe. In fact, it was partly a result of the activities of the American Eugenics Research Association that the Johnson-Lodge Immigration Act of 1924 was passed, which imposed quotas on those 'races' designated as biologically inferior. This was a time of great turmoil in Europe during which Nazi persecution of Jews and other 'undesirable' groups led to huge numbers of refugees seeking entry to the USA. The quotas imposed on southern and eastern Europeans by the 1924 Act had clear consequences and, according to Kamin (1977), probably led to the deaths of hundreds of thousands of European refugees directly or indirectly at the hands of the Nazis.

IQ tests

Intelligence as a concept has become so much part of our discourse in education that we tend to accept it as an innate quality that can be measured accurately through intelligence tests. Those with IQs of 150 are deemed to be of exceptional mental ability and, according to Mensa, make up only 2 per cent of the population (Mensa, 2014). Those with IQs of less than 100 are deemed to be of below average intelligence. In effect, IQ is usually viewed as synonymous with intelligence, often referred to as g, which is the symbol for general intelligence, with the former providing a quantitative measure of g. The question is: what precisely is g? This is a real problem because it is believed by hereditarians such as Jensen (1969), Herrnstein and Murray (1994) and Saunders (2010, 2012) that g refers to the strength or power of an individual's linguistic, mathematical and spatial skills uncontaminated by any cultural or social factors. Moreover, they suggest that such individual differences are overwhelmingly inherited, with environment playing only a very small role. Furthermore, and in a clear rejection of Binet's claim that it is possible to improve one's intelligence, hereditarians emphasise the fixed nature of an individual's abilities.

These individual differences are said to be reflected in group characteristics because according to Saunders (2010) those with similar levels of intelligence tend to seek each other out and, because they tend to have jobs of similar status, are more likely to meet and have children together. This, for Saunders, explains the reason why children of middle class professional parents have a relatively better chance than children from working class backgrounds of becoming middle class professionals themselves.

Do IQ tests measure pure ability?

Despite the seemingly objective and value-free nature of intelligence, it is a concept that for some is socially constructed and is seen to measure qualities and skills identified and valued by particular groups at a particular time (Dorling, 2011). Furthermore, IQ tests are criticised by psychologists such as Otto Klineberg (1935b) for not being culture-free, but instead, of being biased towards white middle class children to the disadvantage of working class, Black and other ethnic children. This is clearly demonstrated by Klineberg in a study carried out in 1928 (Klineberg, 1928). The experiment involved administering intelligence tests to a sample of white American children, Black American children and Native American children from the Yakima tribe of Washington State. The results showed that under timed conditions the Black and Yakima children did less well on average than the white children. However, when the time element was removed and the children could do the tests at their own pace, the differences in the scores were no longer evident. Klineberg concludes that intelligence tests are more about measuring cultural differences between groups rather than pure ability. In his book *Race Difference* (1935b) Klineberg asserts that in every society those with power tend to provide ways of justifying their superiority and of the intellectual and cultural inferiority of those at the bottom of the hierarchy. These ideas, he suggests, are based on stereotypes rather than any scientific explanation. Klineberg's evidence and his views at the time, however, were not very popular with policy makers, who were more likely to be influenced by the ideas of eugenicists such as Nathaniel Hirsch (1930) and Madison Grant (1916).

A key point that is raised by many experts is the very narrow focus of intelligence tests on cognitive skills which are measured in a restricted time frame, usually decided by the test designer. For example, timed tests may suit those with more of an impulsive personality type rather than those who are of a more reflective disposition. Sternberg and Grigorenko (2001: 2) refer to performance in tests as related not just to ability but to *cognitive styles*, which point to how individuals process information. Cognitive styles may be *creative* as opposed to *analytic*, and intelligence tests, or indeed public examinations such as GCSEs, rarely test creativity.

A further point to make is that the genetic trait of intelligence is not fixed and unchanging within groups. Klineberg (1935a) produced evidence of an improvement in the IQ scores of Black pupils who moved from the southern states, such as Alabama and Mississippi, to the better resourced schools in the north of the USA such as Delaware. His conclusion was that the differences in intelligence were the result of social and economic differences, not fixed racial and genetic ones (Klineberg, 1935a). More recently, the Flynn effect (Flynn, 1998) shows that intelligence scores for populations all around the world are increasing and this has resulted in the regular revision of the standard deviation by 15 percentage points. This means that intelligence tests need to be recalibrated to ensure that the standard or average score remains at 100.

It is significant that as early as 1923 the American psychologist and pioneer of IQ testing, Carl Brigham, found evidence that there was a relationship between the measured intelligence of immigrants entering and the number of years they had been resident in America. However, he chose to ignore these data to pursue a line of argument, using statistical analysis, which satisfied his beliefs that increased immigration to the country of non-Nordic or non-Anglo-Saxon 'races' had actually led to an overall deterioration of intelligence of those entering the country (Kamin, 1977). This is a clear example of the way statistical manipulation can be used to make one's case, which in this instance was that of the innateness and fixed nature of intelligence. It is an approach used to alarming levels by Cyril Burt – the psychologist who probably had the most influence on twentieth-century English education policy.

How do we know that intelligence is mainly hereditary?

It would be unreasonable to claim that we are all born with the same cognitive, creative or analytic potential, but we do not know whether or not intelligence is mainly inherited, nor do we know how individual ability and environment interact to enable individuals to demonstrate their potential – cognitive, creative or otherwise. Despite Saunders' (2010: 57) claim that the evidence is 'compelling and incontrovertible', the original research upon which it is based is highly tainted and based on prejudice, and more recent research is not as conclusive as he claims (Rose et al., 1984).

Many of our beliefs about the heritability of intelligence come from the assumptions made by the American psychologist and eugenicist Nathaniel Hirsch (1930). In his study, *Twins*, Hirsch sets out to quantify the precise contribution of genes and environmental factors to an individual's 'intelligence' and comes up with the ratio of 80:20, the higher figure being attributed to innate biological factors. In the same book Hirsch echoes the views of other eugenicists such as Madison Grant and Lewis Terman by lamenting the decline of western civilisation and he suggests how the study of twins can provide the scientific knowledge with which politicians can halt this decline. Hirsch's claim triggered a number of studies of twins in order to test his hypothesis. The principle behind such studies is very simple and focuses on the degree to which monozygotic twins (MZ); that is, twins from the same egg and fertilised by the same sperm and therefore sharing identical genes, demonstrate the same levels of intelligence even when reared apart. This is usually measured as a level of correlation, or the degree of match between the scores of twins after separation, with 1.0 indicating a perfect match and 0 indicating no match. Should they demonstrate very similar or exactly the same measurable intelligence after such separation, ideally from birth, then it can be taken as strong evidence to support the hereditarian hypothesis of intelligence. If, on the other hand, such separated twins do not show a high degree of similarity in terms of intelligence then it can be assumed that environment plays a strong part in intelligence. In practice, however, it is much more difficult to test such a hypothesis given the lack of proper control over environmental factors and the problems of obtaining samples of such twins.

How reliable and valid is the evidence?

We know from a review of the evidence (Gillie, 1976; Kamin, 1977; Rose et al., 1984) that much of the early work on intelligence and IQ was flawed as a result of the preconceptions held by many of the researchers. This can certainly be seen in the work of Carl Brigham and his colleagues in the American Eugenics Research Association, who were driven more by the prejudice they held about other 'races' than by objective scientific findings. The work of Cyril Burt, however, is so flawed it is difficult to understand why he was not challenged more effectively at the time by other experts. Instead, the ideas of Burt were so accepted as representing the truth that they constituted an ideology which pervaded all levels of society, creating the rules and the parameters by which the issue of intelligence could be discussed and understood. We saw in Chapter 3 how Foucault argues that it is this relationship between power and discourse that creates knowledge and anyone attempting to speak outside this accepted framework is dismissed as having no credibility.

The reputation of Burt during much of the early to mid-twentieth century was so great and his ideas so influential that few psychologists or other experts dared to challenge his evidence, such as it was, or his methods of measuring the intelligence of MZ and dizygotic twins (twins born from separate eggs) reared both together and apart, as well as his measurement of the heritability of intelligence within populations. We now have a pretty good idea that Burt probably made up much of the evidence to support his theory of the heritability of intelligence (Kamin, 1977; Rose et al., 1984). This makes his alleged correlations in intelligence test scores for MZ twins reared together (0.944) and for MZ twins reared apart (0.771) highly suspicious, particularly as he claimed to have repeated these correlations to three decimal points even when the sample size increased. This is a result that is statistically highly unlikely to occur (Kamin, 1977).

Although Saunders (2010) accepts that Burt's evidence is unreliable and recognises the problems associated with the creation of valid experimental conditions that adequately test the heritability thesis, he suggests that subsequent twin studies are generally reliable and that they all demonstrate high levels of correlations in intelligence test scores between MZ twins raised in similar environments and MZ twins raised in different environments. He believes that this evidence confirms we are all born with fixed levels of intelligence which we inherit from our parents and that this intelligence remains stable over our lifetimes. However, the evidence is not quite so clear cut and is difficult to compare as studies tend to use different measures of intelligence, sampling methods and methodologies.

Thinking point 5.3

- What do you think intelligence is?
- From what you have read, do you think it is something that is fixed at birth?
- What might be the implications of discovering an 'intelligence gene'?

You might like to examine some of the alternative views of intelligence such as Howard Gardner's (1983) theory of *multiple intelligences* or Sternberg's (1977; Sternberg and Grigorenko, 2001) theory of *cognitive styles*. Hart and

(Continued)

(Continued)

Drummond (2014) take the view that there are no limits to children's potential except for the externally imposed factors of the education system and the fatalism of teachers who impose limits on what children can do. This approach sees the problem as being the result of determinist beliefs that locate limitations as lying within the individual who is believed to be born with a fixed ability. According to Hart and Drummond, teachers and educators tend to give priority to ability labelling rather than to seeing the child as an individual and to using their skills to create a learning environment. We can see how such labelling of children can lead to self-fulfilling prophecies (see Chapter 8).

The current state of the debate

The issue of genes and intelligence is still highly emotive and often causes extreme reactions in the media and amongst academics whenever new research is published. This is hardly surprising given the amount of harm and suffering that have been caused throughout the world in the name of eugenics and theories of human difference.

When in 1969 Arthur Jensen published his analysis of the evidence on intelligence testing available at the time and reported that on average Black Americans scored 15 IQ points below the average of the white American population, he understandably caused outrage by suggesting that this possibly had a genetic origin rather than being the result of such factors as poverty and inequality of opportunity. Jensen's interpretations of the evidence have been heavily criticised (Kamin, 1977) as has his claim that IQ tests measure pure cognitive ability *g* (Gould, 1981). Jensen's findings were particularly controversial at a time when America, supposedly the greatest democracy in the world, was locked in a civil rights dispute in which Black Americans in the Southern states were only beginning to win the right to vote under the 1965 Voting Rights Act and protection from discrimination through the Civil Rights Acts of 1964 and 1968. In suggesting that policies such as the Head Start program, which were set up to help Black Americans improve their levels of educational attainment, were destined to fail because of the differences in intelligence between Blacks and whites, Jensen had arguably given support to the white supremacist leaders and politicians in the South who were reluctant to succumb to the entirely legitimate demands of the Black population. Jensen claimed that his views were misinterpreted, but there was certainly no ambiguity when in 1998 he suggested that there was a biological basis for these differences between Blacks and whites (Jensen, 1998). There was a similar reaction in 1994 to the publication of *The Bell Curve* in which Herrnstein and Murray also claimed to have found evidence of the genetic basis of class and racial inequality in the USA.

In response to the generally negative reaction by the media to the *Bell Curve*, 52 academics signed a declaration that was published in *The Wall Street Journal* in December 1994 asserting that the media had misrepresented what was generally considered to be mainstream knowledge based on sound evidence regarding the heritability of intelligence (Gottfredson, 1994). However, it would seem that the claims by Gottfredson and her co-signatories that their conclusions represented mainstream views on intelligence were not well-founded. Only 51 of the 131 academics approached by Gottfredson agreed to sign the declaration, suggesting that the majority for one reason or another were not prepared to endorse the declaration and its 25 conclusions (Gottfredson, 1997).

Schools don't matter

One of the 52 signatories of the *Mainstream Science on Intelligence* declaration in 1994 was Robert Plomin, an American neuroscientist working in Britain who has been involved in one of the most recent controversies about intelligence and genetics. He is a convinced hereditarian who believes that inherited genes play by far the biggest role in children's performance in education and that schools, family environment and socialisation play only a minor part (Shakeshaft et al., 2013). Plomin argues that research evidence suggests that the conventional model of education as a place of instruction (*instruere*) that involves teachers putting knowledge into children, should be replaced by an active process in which teachers bring out (*educare*) children's innate abilities (Shakeshaft et al., 2013: 1). They conclude that children will tend to seek out experiences and activities that feed their natural level of intelligence and schools should be set up to facilitate this.

Plomin professes surprise and frustration at the response of the media and indeed other academics such as Leon Kamin who refuse to accept the evidence supporting the genetic basis of intelligence (Wakefield, 2013), and believes that it is only a matter of time before we isolate the gene responsible for *g*; that single and elusive piece of genetic material which is believed by some to determine each individual's future academic performance. However, as we have witnessed from the work of James Fallon, it is highly inadvisable to base a theory of human traits and future performance on a single factor. Moreover, other recognised experts in the field of genetics such as Steve Jones (Wilby, 2014) argue that it is very unlikely that intelligence can be narrowed down to one gene. Jones points to the fact that the variation in human height alone is associated with a combination of hundreds of genes, so something as complex as human intelligence is likely to be the result of the interplay of many more (Wilby, 2014). Nevertheless, Plomin has absolute faith that in the future genetic research will provide the means to create a genetic profile, or what he calls a 'Learning Chip', for every child and thereby enable us to create the appropriate educational environment to suit their talents (Wilby, 2014).

The growth of IQism

Testing of all kinds has become an increasing part of children's lives in England. English primary pupils are tested earlier and more often than almost anywhere else (Alexander, 2009). Ever since 2000 (except 2003) Britain has taken part in the Programme for International Student Attainment (PISA) tests, which monitor the performance of national samples of 15-year-olds around the world in maths, language and science every 3 years. The tests are seen as a measure of the effectiveness of individual governments in developing the human capital of their respective nations. There is also an increasing tendency of schools in England to divide children up into 'ability groups', ostensibly on the basis of aptitude, which results in labels that follow children throughout their school careers. Evidence gathered since the 1960s, however, shows that teachers are more likely to underestimate the ability of children from working class backgrounds and to place them in lower ability groups, thereby limiting their chances of academic success (Ball, 1981; Gillborn and Youdell, 2001; Jackson, 1964).

Equality of opportunity

So where does this leave the debate about meritocracy and equality of opportunity in England? Well, if we assume that the children of middle class parents are up to three times more likely to end up in the middle class themselves (Saunders, 2010), and if we also assume that there is such a thing as g, and that g is evenly distributed throughout the population, then it could be assumed that we do not have equality of opportunity in England, as the relative chances of social mobility are better for those children born to middle class parents. In Britain there have been a number of reports and policy papers produced by the New Labour government (CASE, 2010; Her Majesty's Government, 2009,) and the coalition government (Her Majesty's Government, 2011) suggesting that social mobility in Britain has ground to a halt and that Britain has become a closed society in which class privilege still dominates young people's progress in life. Former Secretary of State for Education, Michael Gove believes that social mobility in England has not just halted but gone into reverse (Gove, 2012).

Saunders (2010, 2012) however, rejects any such claims. Moreover, he rejects the assumption that g is spread evenly throughout the population. Instead, he claims that children from more affluent backgrounds have inherited their intelligence from their parents and are therefore likely to be of above average intelligence themselves. This, for Saunders, is the main reason for the different levels of relative mobility upwards between middle class and working class children. What Saunders is rejecting is the notion that a privileged and more stimulating infancy and early childhood make any appreciable difference to a child's cognitive and intellectual development because he believes that it is what they are born with that matters most.

It could be suggested that children from more affluent backgrounds do better because of their advantaged backgrounds. The work of Jefferis et al. (2002) (see Chapter 10) shows how children born in 1958, who experienced poverty in childhood, fell behind children from more affluent backgrounds in school tests at age 7 and that the gap widens with age. In a more recent study that compared the cognitive development of a sample of children from low socio-economic backgrounds with children from high socioeconomic backgrounds born in 1970, Feinstein (2003) administered a variety of age-appropriate tests to monitor and compare their progress at 22, 40, 60 and 120 months. He identified what can been described as a crossover in intelligence scores between initially low-scoring middle class children and high-scoring working class children. The latter group of children who had started with high scores in their cognitive tests at 22 months were passed on their way down by the initially lower-scoring middle class children on their way up. Feinstein suggests that the family climate and early educational experiences of the middle class children have a positive effect on the more 'average' middle class children, whereas what is likely to be a poorer and less stimulating early childhood experience of the working class children tends to hold them back.

A statistical artefact?

Saunders (2012) admits that the evidence produced by Feinstein appears at first sight to be quite compelling, but then rejects the results as merely a statistical artefact rather than the real effects of social and environmental differences. He claims that cognitive tests of young children are notoriously unreliable, revealing extreme results in which some children score much higher or much lower than they 'should' (Saunders, 2012: 21), which in later tests are evened out when genetic factors become more pronounced. The apparent crossover of bright working class children and 'dull' middle class children is put down to a regression to the mean. In other words, they are not accurate measures of their ability later on in life because the effects of genes increase gradually and strengthen as the child gets older. This is a statistical artefact, which is believed to be common in such tests. Saunders' use of the word 'should' is significant in that he seems to have already decided what the children from the different socioeconomic backgrounds should be achieving and his approach to the evidence suggests this.

Environmental influences on children's linguistic and other cognitive abilities have even been detected before birth (Molfese, 1987; Molfese and Molfese, 1985, 2002) and, rather than seeing this growing gap in intelligence between middle class and working class children as the cumulative effect over time of social and environmental factors, Saunders claims it is a statistical phenomenon caused by the gradual and ever increasing influence of genes.

Individual problem or public issue

For Gove though this is evidence of less able rich children overtaking able poor children due to their socioeconomic advantages (Paton, 2010); however, the solution, he believes, lies not in the reduction of this gap between the rich and the poor but in increasing the effectiveness of schools through curriculum reform, increasing school discipline, the imposition of 'higher standards' and the removal of schools from local authority control through the free schools programme (Gove, 2010, 2012). Gove refuses to accept that poverty and disadvantage should be used as reasons why poorer children don't do as well as children from more affluent backgrounds, although much of the evidence shows that structural factors and growing inequalities play a significant role in this process (Wilkinson and Pickett, 2009).

In this context, the ideas of C. Wright Mills (1959) are highly relevant. A key aspect of the *sociological imagination* according to Mills is the interconnectedness between *individual problems* and *public issues*. The low educational attainment of working class children is a public issue; however, politicians refuse to acknowledge this by insisting it is an individual problem that lies with the inadequacies of the individuals concerned and their specific *milieu* rather than the structures within which these individuals exist and act. Politicians such as Gove and Cameron believe that the poor need to take responsibility for their actions and make more appropriate lifestyle choices for themselves and their children (Jones, 2011; Smyth and Wrigley, 2013).

There is an assumption by Gove and other politicians that parents and children from poor backgrounds are fatalistic in their attitudes and display poverty of aspiration (Gove, 2012), a view that has been perpetuated by sociologists (Sugarman, 1970) and anthropologists (Lewis, 1961), who describe a world of the poor characterised by fatalistic attitudes and an obsession with immediate gratification. More recently the work of Charles Murray (1996) has conjured up images of a dissolute 'underclass', which has become so dependent on benefits that there is no incentive for them to gain qualifications for a job.

What we have then, is a continuation of the use of deficit models by politicians who are determined to reject the evidence which shows that wider structural and social factors affect educational achievement. It is a common strategy for politicians to blame their predecessors, local authorities, a lack of discipline, failing schools, poor teaching and irresponsible parents for the failings of the system (Smyth and Wrigley, 2013). Summing up the work of three studies by the Joseph Rowntree Foundation, Carter-Wall and Whitfield (2012) claim they reveal no shortage of aspiration amongst young people living in deprived areas. They suggest that what at first sight might appear to be a sense of fatalism and a negative attitude to education and school by parents and children may actually be the consequences of negative experiences, poor parent and school relations as well as limited knowledge of how to access systems of support.

In his analysis of the underachievement of working class children and what he calls the 'waste of talent', and 'the grotesque failure to give all our fellow citizens an equal chance', Michael Gove identifies what he sees as the causes of this situation by pointing to 'vested interests', the 'tragic inequality we inherited', the breakdown of discipline in schools, 'ideologues' and 'bureaucrats' (Gove, 2010). His pronouncements and policies echo the beliefs of Sir Keith Joseph (Ball, 2013) and Cox and Dyson (1969, 1975) in his distrust of state education (see Chapter 10).

Schools matter most

At the forefront of the debate about inequalities in educational attainment and the assertion that social mobility has stagnated is the issue of school effectiveness. In any common-sense approach it seems logical to see schools as part of 'the problem' and to suggest that many of them are not teaching effectively, are poorly led, that they lack discipline and do not push their children sufficiently. They are, in the words of Nick Gibb the former Schools Minister, 'letting children down' (Department for Education, 2012). He points to the fact that only 33.9 per cent of pupils from deprived backgrounds achieve five A*–C grade GCSEs including English language and maths, compared to the national average of 58.2 per cent in state-maintained schools. Gibb asks if 21 state schools with more than 10 pupils from disadvantaged backgrounds can ensure that 80 per cent of these pupils achieve five A*–C grades including English language and maths, then why can't the 329 schools with 10 or more deprived children where only 20 per cent achieve five A*–C grades at GCSE do the same?

You do not have to be a statistician to be aware of the problem with Gibb's question. The 21 schools, which make up only 0.6 per cent of a total of 3,268 state-funded mainstream secondary schools (January 2012) in England (Department for Education, 2014), are clearly outliers which are likely to occur. Moreover, what Gibb does not reveal is the location of these outliers, their size or what proportions of these schools are made up of deprived pupils. Stating that they had 10 or more tells us very little. According to Smyth and Wrigley (2013) it transpires that half of these 21 schools are grammar schools that select the brightest pupils in the area and a quarter of them are high-achieving comprehensive schools in affluent areas with very small numbers of deprived pupils.

In making such accusations on the basis of such weak data the government is placing high expectations on schools in terms of reducing levels of inequality in society, of increasing social mobility and of providing a highly skilled workforce able to compete with the best in the world. The question is how realistic is it to expect schools to compensate for the current effects of inequalities in England (Mortimore and Whitty, 1997; Wilkinson and Pickett, 2009)? In a summary of the hundreds of studies on school effectiveness Bangs et al. (2010) claim that the school effect, in terms of educational achievement, accounts for only between 8–15 per cent of the total. Other factors such as family, income levels, social class, peer influences and neighbourhood, together play a much bigger role.

In general, politicians do not want to hear about problems and obstacles to their policies, they want solutions to problems they have identified and expect quick solutions. As Gove (2010) stated in a speech in 2010:

> People sometimes ask me why I'm in such a hurry to change our education system. Slow down, they say. Opt for a gentler pace. You've got five years. Your reforms can be introduced all in good time. But children only have one chance. Five years for them is their entire life at secondary school. And I don't want to see another generation of poor children travel through school only to leave at the end without qualifications, without a place at college, without hope.

> I couldn't live with myself, if, having been given the chance to serve I put the enjoyment of office before the power to do good – so that is why every moment I have in this job – every day I do it, I won't stop pressing, pushing, fighting to give every child the chance to succeed. (Gove, 2010)

This is possibly one reason why they do not have much time for the views of sociologists who suggest that there are wider social and structural barriers to children from less advantaged backgrounds. For politicians such as Gove and Cameron poverty is not something that has cumulative effects which, when deeply embedded in communities, cause wider social problems in terms of community breakdown. Poverty is instead treated as a state of mind rather than something that affects people's lives, and the actions and behaviour of the poor are seen as 'lifestyle choices' (Jones, 2011). This is clearly evident in school improvement policies, which are usually devoid of the social context of those on the receiving end (Smyth and Wrigley, 2013). In some places there are clearly exceptional groups of individuals working together, headteachers, teachers, pupils and parents, who sometimes succeed despite all the odds. The question is whether it is reasonable or realistic for the government to expect all schools in poorer areas to do so.

Going private

A further dimension to the debate about equality of opportunity is the advantage conferred upon those who receive a private education. Any attempt to point to this is often greeted with accusations of envy as well as emphasis on the right of parents to choose how their children are educated. However, in any analysis of inequalities in educational attainment and social mobility the advantage of a private education is palpable. Even Gove comments with astonishment that so 'many of the positions of wealth, influence, celebrity and power in our society are held by individuals who were privately educated' (Gove, 2012). However, rather than accepting that the privilege of such pupils will inevitably confer upon them an unfair advantage over the rest of the school population, Gove instead berates state schools for not being more like private schools, insisting 'that a difficult start in life can be overcome, with hard work and good teaching' (Gove, 2012).

In his interviews with young people attending private and state schools, Riddell (2010) examines their aspirations and ambitions. He suggests that these are influenced by their social circumstances and the culture of school and family. Interviews with pupils from less privileged backgrounds revealed a general lack of support in their schools and the need to make great sacrifices by effectively reinventing themselves in order to achieve their aspirations. Interviews with pupils attending private schools reveal school and family working seamlessly together to create a climate of expectation, if not entitlement, to a place at a prestigious university and ultimately to a top profession. This is also evident in Stephen Ball's (2003) ethnographic study of pupils from a variety of state and private school backgrounds. The research focuses on the 'privilege' of the middle class and how this enables it to mobilise different kinds of *capital* to maintain and improve its social position in relation to the working class. He carried out interviews with 120 students and 35 families from both the state and the private school sectors and uses Bourdieu's (1984, 1986) notions of *social capital* and *cultural capital* to illustrate how the middle class is able to access the sources of influence and power in the education system. This provides them with greater choice in terms of schools and higher education institutions.

Social capital relates to social (class) groups and their networks in the form of exchange, social obligations and other connections that create a sense of belonging to a class or a class fraction (section). It helps to act as a barrier excluding those, such as the working class, who do not fit in, and as a means of creating class solidarity and cohesion. Cultural capital consists of the cultural values and objects of the dominant class that are recognisable through language, interests and style, and which indicate status. Such cultural capital is usually recognised as superior or official in its status in comparison to popular culture in its various forms. This is seen by Bourdieu (Bourdieu and Passeron, 1977) as part of the symbolic violence committed by the middle class against the working class (see Chapter 3).

Middle class parents who buy into the private sector are able to develop networks and relationships beyond their relatives, friends and acquaintances thereby maximising their options in the education system. This process of bridging (Putnam, 2000) is essential for 'getting ahead'. Private schools provide access to such bridging opportunities through the links they have with the elite universities. So when Gove muses on why 'more Etonians make it to Oxbridge than boys and girls on benefits' (Gove, 2012), or why social mobility seems to have stagnated, Ball's (2003) research findings provide some relevant insights. His interviews with middle class pupils, particularly those who went to private schools, are replete with references to social networks and support systems beyond their immediate families, whereas those with working class pupils rarely include references to adults beyond their family. In terms of the development of these networks, elite private schools enable their pupils to invest in and develop their cultural capital, which is displayed at relevant points such as at interviews and in accessing support.

Chapter summary

This chapter has covered the wide-ranging debate relating to inequalities in educational attainment between children from affluent backgrounds compared to those from less affluent backgrounds, as well as the related issues of meritocracy and social mobility in England. It is a debate that encompasses theories of intelligence, cultural differences and the effects of wider social and economic inequalities. From the theories and the evidence presented it could be suggested that no single approach or explanation can on its own explain these inequalities in educational attainment.

Sociologists are likely to be cautious about genetic and biological theories of difference and their contribution to educational differences. They are particularly mindful of hereditarian theories and their origins in eugenics, which has been the intellectual and ideological basis of so many oppressive regimes such as Nazi Germany, the Apartheid system in South Africa and even the racial segregation in the South of the United States until the late twentieth century. In addition, the evidence upon which hereditarian theories are based is highly contentious. In general, sociologists focus on socioeconomic and cultural factors in attempting to explain inequalities in educational attainment. Politicians, on the other hand, are more likely to point to the inadequacies and deficits of the poor rather than the advantages experienced by privileged groups in society and the wider socioeconomic divisions in English society. They prefer to focus on the personal troubles of the poor rather than the wider public issues as the causes of educational underachievement.

References

Alexander, R. (ed.) (2009) *Children, their World, their Education: Final Report and Recommendations of the Cambridge Primary Review*. London: Routledge.

Ball, S. (1981) *Beachside Comprehensive: A Case Study of Secondary Schooling*. Cambridge: Cambridge University Press.

Ball, S. (2003) 'Social capital, social class and choice', in S. Ball (ed.), *Class Strategies and the Education Market*. Abingdon: Routledge Falmer.

Ball, S. (2013) *The Education Debate* (second edition). Bristol: Policy Press.

Bangs, J., MacBeath, J. and Galton, M. (2010) *Reinventing Schools, reforming teaching: From political vision to classroom reality*. London: Routledge.

Banks, O. (1955) *Parity and Prestige in English Secondary Education*. London: Routledge and Kegan Paul.

Bourdieu, P. (1984) *Distinction: A Social Critique of the Judgement of Taste*. London: Routledge and Kegan Paul.

Bourdieu, P. (1986) 'The forms of capital', in J. Richardson (ed.), *Handbook of Theory and Research for the Sociology of Education*. New York: Greenwood.

Bourdieu, P. and Passeron, J. (1977) *Reproduction in Education, Society and Culture*. London: Sage.

Carter-Wall, C. and Whitfield, G. (2012) *The role of aspirations, attitudes and behaviour in closing the educational attainment gap*. York: Joseph Rowntree Foundation.

Centre for Analysis of Social Exclusion (CASE) (2010) 'An anatomy of economic inequality in the UK, Summary Report of the National Equality Panel'. London: Government Equalities Office.

Cox, C.B. and Dyson, A.E. (eds) (1969) *Black Paper One*. London: Critical Quarterly Society.

Cox, C.B. and Boyson, R. (1975) *Black Papers on Education*. London: Critical Review Quarterly.

Department for Education (2012) Press release: 'New data reveals the truth about school performance'. London: Department for Education. Available at: www.gov.uk/gov ernment/news/new-data-reveals-the-truth-about-school-performance (accessed 14 January 2015).

Department for Education (2014) FOI Release: 'Number of secondary schools and their size in number,' 9 January 2014. London: Department for Education. Available at: www.gov.uk/government/publications/number-of-secondary-schools-and-their-size-in-student-numbers (accessed 14 January 2015).

Dorling, D. (2011) *Injustice: Why Social Inequalities Persist*. Bristol: The Policy Press.

Fallon, J. (2014) *The Psychopath Inside: A Neuroscientist's Personal Journey Into the Dark Side of the Brain*. New York: Penguin Group.

Feinstein, L. (2003) 'Very early evidence', Centre for Economic Performance Paper No. 146, June. London: London School of Economics.

Floud, J., Hallsey, A.H. and Marton, F.M. (1956) *Social Class and Educational Opportunity*. London: Heinemann.

Flynn, J.R. (1998) 'IQ gains over time: Toward finding the causes', in U. Neisser (ed.), *The Rising Curve*. Washington, DC: American Psychological Association.

Gardner, H. (1983) *Frames of Mind: The Theory of Multiple Intelligences*. London: Fontana.

Gillborn, D. and Youdell, D. (2001) 'The New IQism: Intelligence and, "ability" and the rationing of Education', in J. Demaine (ed.), *Sociology of Education Today*. Basingstoke: Palgrave.

Gillie, O. (1976) 'Crucial data was faked by eminent psychologist', 24 October, *Sunday Times* (London).

Gottfredson, L. (1994) 'Mainstream science on intelligence', 13 December, *Wall Street Journal*.

Gottfredson, L. (1997) 'Mainstream science on intelligence: An editorial with 52 signatories, history and bibliography', *Intelligence*, 24(1): 13–23. Available at: www.udel.edu/educ/gottfredson/reprints/1997mainstream.pdf (accessed 14 January 2015).

Gould, S.J. (1981) *The Mismeasure of Man*. New York: W.W. Norton and Company.

Gove, M. (2010) 'Michael Gove: All pupils will learn our island story', speech given on 5 October 2010. Available at: http://toryspeeches.files.wordpress.com/2013/11/michael-gove-all-pupils-will-learn-our-island-story.pdf (accessed 14 January 2015).

Gove, M. (2012) 'Education Secretary Michael Gove's speech to Brighton College'. Available at: www.gov.uk/government/speeches/education-secretary-michael-goves-speech-to-brighton-college (accessed 14 January 2015).

Grant, M. (1916) *The Passing of the Great Race, or the Racial Basis of European History*. New York: Charles Scribner's Sons.

Green, A. (1991) 'The peculiarities of English education', in CCCS Education Group (ed.), *Education Limited: Schooling and Training and the New Right since 1979*. London: Unwin.

Hart, S., and Drummond, M.J. (2014) 'Learning without limits: Constructing a pedagogy free from determinist beliefs about ability', in L. Florian (ed.), *The Sage Handbook of Special Education*. London: Sage.

Her Majesty's Government (2009) 'Unleashing aspiration: The final report of the panel on fair access to the professions (the Milburn Report)'. London: Cabinet Office.

Her Majesty's Government (2011) 'Opening doors, breaking barriers: A strategy for social mobility'. London: Cabinet Office.

Herrnstein, R. and Murray, C. (1994) *The Bell Curve: Intelligence and Class Structure in American Life*. New York: Free Press.

Hirsch, N. (1930) *Twins: Heredity and Environment*. Cambridge, MA: Harvard University Press.

Jackson, B. (1964) *Streaming: An Education System in Miniature*. London: Routledge and Kegan Paul.

Jefferis, B.J., Power, C. and Hertzman, C. (2002) 'Birth weight, childhood socioeconomic environment, and cognitive development in the 1958 British birth cohort study', *British Medical Journal*, 10 August, 325: 305–88.

Jensen, A. (1969) 'How much can we boost IQ and academic achievement?' *Harvard Educational Review*, 39(1): 1–123.

Jensen, A. (1998) *The g Factor: The Science of Mental Ability*. Westport, CT: Praeger.

Johnson, B. (2013) 'Boris Johnson: 3rd Margaret Thatcher Lecture (FULL)'. Available at: www.youtube.com/watch?v=Dzlgrnr1ZB0 (accessed 14 January 2015).

Jones, O. (2011) *Chavs: The Demonization of the Working Class*. London: Verso.

Kamin, L.J. (1977) *The Science and Politics of IQ*. Harmondsworth: Penguin.

Klineberg, O. (1928) 'An experimental study of speed and other factors in "racial" differences', *Archives of Psychology*, 15(93): 1–111.

Klineberg, O. (1935a) *Negro Intelligence and Selective Migration*. New York: Columbia University Press.

Klineberg, O. (1935b) *Race Differences*. New York: Harper and Brothers.

Lewis, O. (1961) *The Children of Sanchez: Autobiography of a Mexican Family*. New York: Random House.

Mensa (2014) 'What is Mensa?' Available at: www.mensa.org (accessed 14 January 2015).

Ministry of Education (1954) 'Early Leaving Report: Report of the Central Advisory Council for Education (England)'. London: HMSO.

Ministry of Education (1959) 'Fifteen to Eighteen. Report of the Central Advisory Council for Education (England) (The Crowther Report)'. London: HMSO.

Molfese, D.L. (1987) 'Electrophysiological indices of categorical perception', in S. Hanard (ed.), *Categorical Perception*. New York: Cambridge University Press.

Molfese, D.L. and Molfese, V.J. (1985) 'Electrophysiological indices of auditory discrimination in newborn infants: The bases for predicting later language development?' *Infant Behavior and Development*, 8: 197–211.

Molfese, V. and Molfese, D. (2002) 'Environmental and social influences on reading skills as indexed by brain and behavioral responses', *Annals of Dyslexia*, 52: 121–37.

Mortimore, P. and Whitty, G. (1997) *Can School Improvement Overcome the Effects of Disadvantage?* London: Institute of Education.

Murray, C. (1996) 'The Emerging British Underclass', in R. Lister (ed.), *Charles Murray and the Underclass: The Developing Debate*. London: IEA.

Paton, G. (2010) '"Rich thick kids do better at school" says Gove', 28 July, *Daily Telegraph*.

Piketty, T. (2014) *Capital in the Twenty-First Century*. Tr. A. Goldhammer. Cambridge, MA: The Belnap Press.

Putnam, D. (2000) *Bowling Alone: The Collapse and Revival of American Community*. Touchstone: New York.

Riddell, R. (2010) *Aspiration, Identity And Self-Belief: Snapshots of Social Structure at Work*. Stoke-on-Trent: Trentham.

Rose, N. (1999) *Powers of Freedom: Reframing Political Thought*. Cambridge: Cambridge University Press.

Rose, S., Lewontin, R. and Kamin, L. (1984) *Not in Our Genes: Biology, Ideology and Human Nature*. London: Penguin.

Saunders, P. (1996) *Unequal but Fair: A Study of Class Barriers in Britain*. London: Civitas, Choices in Welfare No. 28.

Saunders, P. (2010) *Social Mobility Myths*. London: Civitas.

Saunders, P. (2012) *Social Mobility Delusions: Why So Much of What Politicians Say about Social Mobility in Britain is Wrong, Misleading or Unreliable*. London: Civitas.

Shakeshaft, N.G., Trzaskowski, M., McMillan, A., Rimfeld, K., Krapohl, E., Haworth, C.M.A., Dale, P.S. and Plomin, R. (2013) 'Strong genetic influence on a UK nationwide test of educational achievement at the end of compulsory education at age 16', *PLOS ONE*, 8(12): 1–10.

Smyth, J. and Wrigley, T. (2013) *Living on the Edge: Rethinking Poverty, Class and Schooling*. New York: Peter Lang.

Sternberg, R. (1977) *Intelligence, Information Processing and Analogical Reasoning: The Componential Analysis of Human Abilities*. Hillsdale, NJ: Erlbaum.

Sternberg, R. and Grigorenko, E.L. (2001) 'a capsule history of theory and research on styles', in R. Sternberg and L. Zhang (eds), *Perspectives on Thinking and Cognitive Styles*. Mahwah, NJ: Lawrence Erlbaum Associates.

Sugarman, B. (1970) 'Social class, values and behaviour in schools', in M. Craft (ed.), *Family, Class and Education*. London: Longman.

Terman, L.M. (1916) *The Measurement of Intelligence*. Boston, MA: Houghton Mifflin.

Tomlinson, S. (2005) *Education in a Post Welfare Society*. London: Routledge.

Wakefield, M. (2013) 'Revealed: How exam results owe more to genes than teaching', 27 July, *The Spectator*.

Wilby, P. (2014) 'Psychologist on a mission to give every child a Learning Chip', 18 February, *The Guardian*.

Wilkinson, R. and Pickett, K. (2009) *The Spirit Level: Why More Equal Societies Almost Always Do Better*. London: Penguin.

Wright Mills, C. (1959) *The Sociological Imagination*. New York: Oxford University Press.

Young, M. (1958) *The Rise of the Meritocracy 1870–2033: An Essay in Education and Equality*. London: Thames and Hudson.

CHAPTER 6

MULTICULTURALISM, 'RACE' AND POWER

Chapter Aims

This chapter will explore the historical development of multiculturalism in education and will reflect on the contested notion of Britishness as a political dimension of multiculturalism. In addition, this chapter will introduce an international perspective in the exploration of multiculturalism in America and biculturalism in Australia as contrasting examples. To conclude, this chapter will consider Critical Race Theory (CRT) and will unpack discourses around *whiteness* and *white privilege* that will draw on ideas of 'race', education and power. You will notice that we have chosen to capitalise the term 'Black', we have done so in order to acknowledge the powerful political dimensions of this term, in particular in relation to CRT.

Key words: Britishness, segregation, Islamophobia, acculturation, domination, identity, hybridity, white privilege, power structures, intersectionality, convergence.

Multiculturalism in Britain

In order to consider the impact of multiculturalism on education it is important to briefly consider the historical and political context of this discussion. The transformation of Britain into the current multicultural society it is and the associated challenges of racism and discrimination that this transformation has encountered have taken place over many centuries; however, from a political perspective a focus on mass migration of Asian and Black people in the latter part of the twentieth century paints a different picture. This period of modern history is often referred to as the era of immigration suggesting a heightened peak of activity; however, migration and pathologising of external groups is by no means a new phenomenon to this island. Celts, Romans, Saxons, Danes and Normans have established roots in historic Britain, with Jews and Huguenots arriving later and a new wave of Celts in the Irish. Modern history includes migrants from the British Empire and Commonwealth including whites from Australia, Canada and South Africa and Blacks and Asians from Africa, the Caribbean, India, Pakistan, Bangladesh and Hong Kong. Historically, discrimination against the perceived or created 'other' has a troubled history in the British Isles as illustrated by the ongoing tensions between England and Ireland embedded in a long-standing tradition of colonialism that presented the Irish as a primitive, uneducated, unclean nationality, originating from the observations of medieval commentators in the twelfth century and stretching through the massacre of the Irish in Ulster in the sixteenth century (Gibbons, 2005).

A turning point towards a framework of 'Blackness' in relation to 'others' in Britain was the 1948 Empire Windrush era, the start of the Black immigration in the 1950s and 1960s, and the consequent race riots of 1958. A powerful irony is noted by academics and commentators reflecting on this period in that the immigrants travelling to the UK were invited Commonwealth citizens who arrived to help the 'mother country' after the end of the Second World War (Panayi, 2010). Instead, they were met with acute experiences of racism and discrimination, prompting the government to respond with so-called equalities legislation such as the first Race Relations Act (1965, under Labour), which outlawed racism in public places, and made it unlawful to refuse access to anyone on racial grounds to public places such as accommodation and social spaces. The subsequent impact of mass Black and Asian immigration on housing, education, the health service and how British society is perceived is the context within which this discussion of multiculturalism in education is framed.

Contested notion of Britishness

Rabbi Jonathan Sacks addressed the question of what it takes to make a society a 'home we build together' rather than a 'hotel', in his consideration of the contested notion of Britishness and in particular the idea of shared values (Sacks, 2007). He argues that neither individualist liberalism (with its focus on rights) nor multiculturalism (with its focus on identity) can offer anything beyond a 'hotel'. Both lead to a position that rests on an agreement only on minimal and fragile rules of co-existence and excludes any substantive notion of shared human values. In capturing a sense of shared values, as a multicultural nation, we are able to celebrate our Britishness as supported by politician and community leaders such as Munira Mirza, cultural advisor to Boris Johnson and advocate of tolerance as a core British value. Sacks' proposal is a revival of the idea of a social covenant in which the hyperdiverse citizens of multi-cultural Britain are able to retain their particular identities but yet commit themselves wholeheartedly to the common project of society-building founded on shared (British) values. Academics such as Tariq Ramadan also support this emerging grand narrative illustrating that faith communities are tasked with being proactive in finding the common ground that unites us. Ramadan (2009) is now taking up the challenge of delving deeply into his own tradition to ask himself what Islam has to contribute to the moral sustenance of a western democracy like the UK, and coming up with hopeful answers to contribute to a cohesive and unified sense of Britishness. These are bold and proactive, positive steps dependent on wider ideological support and ultimately need to be translated into pragmatic notions that can shape a postmodern conceptu-alisation of what it is to be British today. This chapter started by framing the discussion in a historical context in order to clarify and demonstrate how we have arrived at the current state of play. This historical perspective and its impact are acutely relevant to an exploration of Britishness. This is a contested idea perhaps because traditional and historically framed notions of what con-stitutes Britishness are both exclusive and outdated, though still highly influential. This is typified by the word picture painted in 1993 in a speech by Conservative Prime Minister John Major who stated that 'fifty years from now Britain will still be the country of long shadows on county grounds, warm beer, invincible green suburbs, dog lovers and pools fillers and – as George Orwell said – "old maids cycling to holy communion through the morning mist"' (Kumar, 2003). Further evidence of the enduring nature of historical views of what it means to be British is captured in Norman Tebbit's infamous 'cricket test' and convincingly in a series of lectures given to Cambridge under-graduates in 1882 by Sir John Seeley at the height of his enthusiasm for empire and in a carefully manipulated strategy to shape Victorian values: 'We seem, as it were, to have conquered and peopled half the world in a fit of absence of mind. While we were doing it ... we did not allow it to affect our imagina-tion or in any degree to change our ways of thinking' (Seeley, [1883] 1971: 15). Finally, there is the undeniable influence of Enoch Powell on contemporary UK independence Party (UKIP) policy as illustrated in the classic notion that 'the West Indian or Indian does not, by being born in England, become [ever?] an Englishman' (Paul, 1997: 178).

A more current reflection of how blurred the lines are in defining Britishness would be to take account of the impact of glocal (local and global) factors such as the impact of globalisation on how we live, work and enjoy leisure time. Britain's entry into the European Union, an impetus for more rigid definitions for what it means to be Scottish (illustrated by the Commonwealth Games, 2012 and the 'yes' campaign for the Referendum, 2014) or Welsh. As Parekh reports, we cannot unpack Britishness without encountering 'race':

> Britishness, as much as Englishness, has systematic, largely unspoken, racial connotations. Whiteness nowhere features as an explicit condition of being British, but it is widely understood that Englishness, and therefore by extension Britishness, is racially coded. 'There ain't no black in the Union Jack', it has been said. Race is deeply entwined with political culture and with the idea of nation. (The Runnymede Trust, 2000: 38)

Perhaps it is a movement of popular consciousness; this nation made up of hybrid identities and founded on intellectual and political discourses that should now reinvent our national identity, reflecting who we are now and what we share as unifying values.

Multiculturalism in America

Multiculturalism has had a complex and complicated past in American history, the legacy of which, some would argue, continues into the present and the future. Wilbur Zelinsky the American cultural geographer defended the position that American had always been 'a stratified caste-ridden society, practicing a rather primitive form of multiculturalism … now due to quantitative growth, increasing complexities, the activism of minority populations and the globalisation of cultural and social processes, multiculturalism has come out of the closet, so to speak' (Zelinsky, 2001: 192). Cultural theorists have presented the argument that as a philosophical ideal, multiculturalism began as part of the pragmatism movement at the end of the nineteenth century in the USA, then as political and cultural pluralism at the turn of the twentieth. This timeline is reflected in postmodern manifestations of multiculturalism in the USA, where dissatisfaction with the traditional ideology of the 'melting pot' (diverse cultures assimilating into a single cultural identity) placed a spotlight on the acute and jarring inequalities embedded constitutionally. In order to contextualise the current political position, it is important to reflect on this 'complex' history of multiculturalism in the USA, as, it can be argued, the past is increasingly relevant to the present and the future.

America's role in the transatlantic slave trade during the Colonial era in the late seventeenth century secured national prosperity; however, it is also the bedrock of African-American discontent. This dehumanisation of Black people for economic gain has left a lasting legacy on the American psyche, a history that is revisited with frequency as illustrated in the Hollywood box office hit *Twelve Years a Slave* (2013), the film adaptation of Solomon Northup's book, one of the longest and most detailed slave narratives. The enslavement of Black people throughout American history is a common thread as noted in the American Revolutionary War (1775–83), where Americans won their freedom from British rule and the new nation the United States of America was created. However, this much sought after freedom was not extended to the Black slaves, as the notion of white supremacy and Black inferiority reinforced by popular culture and religious rhetoric demonstrate. During the American Civil War (1861–65) Black slaves occupied the lowest of Zelinsky's (2001) caste group. Though slavery was outlawed in 1865 new forms of racial discrimination and injustice were constituted by the 'Black Codes' and later 'Reconstruction' as laws restricting the rights of Blacks, which denied freed slaves the right to vote and to leave a job and move elsewhere. The perpetuation of racial segregation was the preoccupation of Southern states, which passed laws on racial segregation (separation of Black people from whites) known as Jim Crow laws in 1877. The term Jim Crow, noted in 1828 as a song performed by an actor with a 'blackened' face and stereotypical Black characteristics (poor, infirm and uneducated) later became associated with laws on segregation and then later still as a slur directed at Black people (Cockrell, 1997). By 1915, all Southern states had implemented some form of Jim Crow laws effectively sowing the seeds for the white supremacist group the Ku Klux Klan. In 1919 the National Association for the Advancement of Colored People (NAACP) published a record of this period in American history entitled *Thirty Years of Lynching in the United States: 1889–1918*, documenting sexual abuse, hanging, lynching and incidents of Black people being burned alive as examples of the extremes of hostility and violence directed towards Black people in the USA (NAACP, 1969). Protests against Jim Crow laws gathered momentum leading to the Civil Rights Movement led by Dr Martin Luther King Jr, a Montgomery Baptist minister. The 1950s and 1960s were a period of acute and sustained unrest in American social and political history with widespread state-sponsored violence and escalation of hostilities leading to the emergence of Black Power groups, such as the Black Panthers, and finally culminating in the passage of the landmark Civil Rights Act in July 1964. The enduring legacy of Jim Crow laws ensure that Black people are over-represented in the penal system and in inner city ghettos, and many fail to reach the lowest rung of the social mobility ladder, a result of poor educational and life chances (Chafe, 2001). Landmark cases such as the video recording of the assault on Rodney King in 1991 by four law enforcement officers (Stacey Koon, Laurence Powell, Timothy Wind and Theodore Briseno) leading to the 1992 Los Angeles riots, illustrate the fact that racial fault lines are both fragile and triggered intermittently with terrifying consequences in modern-day America.

Multiculturalism in America maintains the dominance of an 'American Culture' (white, Anglo, Christian), which embodies the motto of acculturation 'e pluribus anum' (one out of many). Captured within this ideology is the inferiority of subcultures that may offer a counter narrative, based on globalisation, as exemplified by President Barack Obama, who spoke of his new conceptualisation of multiculturalism as a national strength (Obama, 2009). In this new era, multiculturalism and biculturalism extend beyond an individual's sense of self-identity and also refer to nationhood (Nguyen and Benet-Martínez, 2010), valuing diversity and acknowledging the distinct contribution immigrant cultures make, thereby facilitating psychological well-being and self-worth amongst Americas diverse citizens.

Thinking point 6.1

Coca Cola's commercial at the Super Bowl (2014) entitled 'America the Beautiful' (www.youtube.com/watch?v=443Vy3I0gJs) provoked both support and outrage on Twitter as an unpatriotic public statement. The commercial echoed Harvard sociologist Nathan Glazer's declaration that 'we are all multi-culturalists now'; however, a prominent Tea Party member posted the following statement on his blog:

> I am quite sure there may be some who appreciated the commercial, but Coca Cola missed the mark in my opinion. If we cannot be proud enough as a country to sing 'America the Beautiful' in English in a commercial during the Super Bowl, by a company as American as they come – doggone we are on the road to perdition. This was a truly disturbing commercial for me, what say you?

Consider the impact of the commercial, delivered at an iconic event in popular culture, as a means to deliver a political agenda.

Biculturalism in Australia

An exploration of biculturalism from the Australian context offers an opportunity to introduce an international perspective in the process of developing the discourse on multiculturalism as a global phenomenon. A *bi*cultural identity, as opposed to a *mono*cultural identity (Lawrence et al., 2012) is a person's sense of self in relation to more than one culture, in an environment where multiple cultures co-exist. Australia is an interesting case study to explore as the increase in population mobilisation has made a significant impact on mainstream and adult educational provision predominantly caused by the rising numbers of immigrant and refugee communities. Researchers have noted the dual educational and cultural challenges these communities face incorporating educational challenges when entering a system that operates on a sound understanding of the English language and western learning styles, and that focuses on the sense of self, personal identity and maintaining a heritage culture. The process of negotiating a place within both cultures allows newcomers to adapt to their new surroundings, while maintaining their previous cultural values and resources as part of their acculturation process (Schwartz et al., 2010). Studies with learners in adult education settings have concluded that students who were more biculturally committed appeared to experience some advantages in tackling specific challenges. These studies argue that the ways in which newly arrived immigrants develop their bicultural identities can have implications for how they address educational challenges, and the subtle negotiations of how they find a place for themselves within the new culture and their heritage culture. A strong bicultural identity is therefore understood as the means by which an individual can achieve a strong identity in one's heritage culture, which in turn can help to develop greater inter-cultural awareness. This latter aspect of biculturalism is particularly proactive in managing discrimination, and contributes to a heightened psychological sense of well-being (Syed, 2010). Psychologists have applied Erikson's (1968) concept of ego-identity to assess how cultural identities are sustained, concluding that biculturalism is a complex process and cannot be simplified to excluding one or other cultural identity from one's consciousness. This discussion focuses on the experiences of young adults; however, an interesting dimension of biculturalism is the process of identity construction in schools, an area of increasing research (Hird, 1996) with bicultural communities and, in particular, with bicultural boys in the school setting.

A creative example is noted in the work of Anita Jetnikoff and her research conducted with bicultural boys in a mainstream setting with a specific focus on literacy. In her application of personal narratives as a research tool, Jetnikoff (1997) allows the bicultural male pupils to disclose how their experiences of biculturalism are played out in the classroom. This method captures the aim of making space for marginalised voices that may otherwise remain unreported (Singh, 1995). In other words, the bicultural boys and their lived experiences are made visible, present and relevant in the research project in the sharing of their personal narratives; in contrast to the mainstream classroom structures that render them silent. Jetnikoff draws attention to dominant discourses on anti-intellectualism, masculinity and exclusion as key themes in the narratives shared in her research, concluding that:

> At school, bicultural boys have to constantly construct and reconstruct themselves in order to fit in. They must be 'one of the boys' on the football field, and sociable and 'not too smart' in class. Some bicultural boys, therefore, have to become tricksters, slaving at home to make up for what they pretend not to do at school. Even though they work hard at school, they do not do so loudly. They try to keep their intelligence inconspicuous, so that peers do not construct them as 'skids', and to maintain a sense of fitting into school life.' (Jetnikoff, 1997: 36)

Navin, a 14-year-old Pakistani participant explained that in order to fit in at school it was important that he did not appear engaged in his studies, despite the hours of supervised homework that took place privately under the watchful gaze of both parents and older siblings, illustrating how the entire family invested in Navin's education. Navin also allowed academic competitors, in the form of fellow classmates to beat him in tests, in order to facilitate this all-important process of belonging. What seemed a priority to Navin in the school setting appeared at odds with his home life, resulting in a binary existence. At school the priority was to 'joke around', 'fit in' and 'be Australian'. At home, a strong faith (Muslim), cultural (Pakistani) identity and close-knit family dynamic influenced Navin to 'be himself'. This distinction between school and home had to be carefully managed and is the process of construction and reconstruction Jetnikoff speaks of in the extract above. It was important that Navin did not feel different at school, or was not exposed to scenarios that shone a spotlight on his differences, as he explains:

> Like, sometimes in history or something the teacher might ask me to get up and talk about Islam, and that makes you feel really different. Then of course you feel different, but when you're doing maths, or playing football, you're just one of the crowd I suppose. When you're openly telling everyone else that you're different, of course you feel different.

To conclude this discussion on biculturalism Navin demonstrates how the notion of an inclusive curriculum (while addressing the range of religious heritages in the school community) also serves to define Navin as 'other', thereby heightening his experience of exclusion at that moment. His careful negotiations of a strong bicultural heritage must be managed within the context of school structures and may perhaps be impeded by the best intentions of the teachers delivering an inclusive curriculum.

Critical Race Theory (CRT)

CRT finds its origins in an American intellectual movement in the late 1970s and early 1980s and is born out of legal theory. It was formulated in an era during which some academics and political thinkers, worried by what they perceived as a loss of momentum in the sustained campaign for racial equality, began to question whether the constitutional and legal system itself had the capacity for change. They felt that the Civil Rights movement, which had set out to achieve so much, had in effect, been halted in its tracks. This awareness was made acute when, as legal professionals, they were confronted by what the Constitution and other policy statements promised and what they actually delivered: the perpetuation of an acutely unequal society (Bell, 1992). This movement was embedded in a Marxist conceptualisation where the ordinary (Black) citizen suffered multiple layers of exclusion caused by a Constitution that was incapable of allowing for the redistributionist change necessary to create a more equal world. In other words, it existed to sustain an inequality. To create a more equal world, the Constitution and the legal system would have to be challenged and dismantled from within. The Marxist criticism of the system was called critical theory; the legal criticism of the system was known as Critical Legal Studies (CLS) and the most radical aspect was the racial criticism of the system, which is known as Critical Race Theory (CRT) and is the focus of this discussion. CRT is therefore a radical intellectual movement committed to challenging power structures and racial inequality in society (Ladson-Billings, 1998). Despite the original foundation in legal scholarship where it provides a critical analysis of race and racism from a legal standpoint, CRT has evolved into a flexible, interdisciplinary framework that can be applied to a myriad of disciplines including sociology, history, literature, culture and science (Bell, 2009). In addition, spin-off minority groups have formulated their own principles to champion their own change-making movements including Latino-critical (LatCrit), which addresses issues of immigration and integration, and Asian American (made of Indian scholarship) who focus on indigenous people's rights. Both these splinter groups illustrate the diversity of potential under the CRT banner.

Reading suggestion

The forefathers of CRT are Derrick Bell and Alan Freeman, who are credited with starting the movement. Key scholars of influence within the movement include Richard Delgado, Kimberlé Crenshaw, Cheryl Harris, Gloria Ladson-Billings,

Patricia Williams, Tara Yosso and William Tate. CRT is also of significance in British academia and includes the work of John Preston, Nicola Rollock, David Gillborn, Mike Cole and Ann Phoenix. The following references support wider reading on CRT:

Hylton, K. et al. (eds) *Atlantic Crossings: International Dialogues on Critical Race Theory*. Birmingham: CSAP/Higher Education Academy CRT.

This book explores 'race', racism, racialisation, gender, class, sexuality, age and disability in the UK and in other European countries.

Warmington, P. (2014) *Black British Intellectuals: Multiculturalism's Hidden History.* London: Routledge.

This book presents the counter-narrative Delgado speaks of in this chapter by exploring histories of race, education and social justice through the work of Black British public intellectuals: academics and campaigners. The book provides a critical history of diverse currents in Black British intellectual production, from the eighteenth century, through post-war migration and into the 'post-multicultural' present, focusing on the sometimes hidden impacts of Black thinkers on education and social justice. The book defends the position that Black British thinkers have helped fundamentally to shape educational policy, practice and philosophy, particularly in the post-war period. Additionally, it argues, that education has been one of the key spaces in which the mass consciousness of being Black and British has emerged, and a key site in which Black British intellectual positions have been defined and differentiated.

Due to its origins in a legal movement, the ways in which CRT is applied as a theoretical framework in understanding 'race' and racism is complex and orientated towards policy reconstruction. However, at the heart of the movement are some very basic principles: first, CRT explains that racism is endemic in the fabric and system of American society. Second, CRT recognises that power structures in society are based on white privilege and white supremacy. Third, CRT defends the position of convergence, where white elites will support the advancement of Blacks only if this also supports white self-interest. Fourth, CRT challenges legal 'truths' of a colour-blind, liberal and meritocratic system of governance in America replacing it with rule by a white minority of extreme wealth and power. Finally, CRT recognises the role of intersectionality, the complex ways in which inequality and subordination can combine to exclude minority groups in a socio-cultural, economic and political context.

The forefathers of CRT, Derrick Bell, Alan Freeman and Richard Delgado, positioned these principles at the heart of their initial campaigns to motivate support for CRT, often using personal narratives and the foundational experience of slavery and the enduring impact on the African-American as a starting point. As Simmons (2012) clarified 'Derrick Bell and other CRT scholars have challenged us to do more than talk about it – but *be* about it' (2012: 3). This rallying call is epitomised in Simmons' own account of how encountering CRT guided his work as a doctoral candidate in education, powerfully recounting how the realisation of his Blackness during the era of the 'Obama effect' (Emdin and Lee, 2012) was reminiscent of the rise in consciousness as expressed through Negro spirituals such as 'Swing Low, Sweet Chariot' when African slaves passed on words of hope, faith and resistance from plantation to plantation via musical narrative. Simmons shares his frustration and anxiety as an African-American teacher in an urban setting, as a role model and an activist undermined by a dominant narrative sold by Hollywood in films such as *Dangerous Minds, Half Nelson, Freedom Writers,* and *The Ron Clark Story,* which projected a notion that privileged the stories of white teachers who appeared to be over-represented in urban schools, rescuing the receptive and grateful African-American and Latino students who (inevitably) were involved in life stories of extreme dysfunction, abuse, crime and neglect. This is an example of convergence (Stovall, 2005) and also intersectionality (Bhopal and Preston, 2012) and illustrates the many layers of complexity associated with CRT. None the less, the challenge presented by CRT is to give voice to the marginalised (Simmons accomplishes this as a researcher) and to be active at grassroots level, which Simmons achieves by dismantling the dominant narratives of convergence and re-presenting the critical significance of the Black male teacher in urban settings as a catalyst for self-recognition and as a change maker. As Richard Delgado clarifies:

> Critical Race Theory's challenge to racial oppression and the status quo sometimes takes the form of storytelling in which writers analyse the myths, presuppositions and received wisdoms that make up the common culture about race and that invariably renders Black and other minorities one-down. Starting from the premise that a culture constructs its own social reality in ways that promote its own self interest, these scholars set out to construct a different reality. Our social world with its rule, practices, and assignments of prestige and power, is not fixed, rather we construct it with words, stories and silence. But we need not acquiesce in arrangements that are unfair and one sided. By writing and speaking against them, we may contribute to a better, fairer world. (Delgado, 2000: xvii)

In a British context David Gillborn has applied CRT to the education system in the course of his research over many years. He argues that a traditional conceptualisation of racism in education would suggest that it is in fact an exceptional occurrence, notable due to high profile media cases such as the

1986 murder of Ahmed Ullah (MacDonald et al., 1989) in the playground of Burnage School or the 1993 murder of Stephen Lawrence and driven by race hatred. It is important to momentarily reflect on the timeline of Stephen's murder not only as a watershed exemplar of institutional racism, but also as an indicator of how CRT emerges in the course of this particular case study.

The murder of 18-year-old Stephen Lawrence in April 1993 by a group of white youths as he waited for a bus in Eltham, south-east London, has dominated the political and social psyche for decades for many differing reasons. The original police inquiry generated no arrests and instead Stephen's parents, Doreen and Neville, and his brother Stuart were viewed as troublemakers rather than grieving parents and family members. Their first-hand experience of the Metropolitan Police and media hype in the aftermath of the murder led to the conclusion that Stephen's death was not a pressing matter because of his colour. After years of campaigning, the Lawrences' demands for a public inquiry were finally met by Home Secretary Jack Straw as part of the New Labour administration in 1997. Gillborn likens the Stephen Lawrence Inquiry and the reporting of subsequent campaigns regarding private legal action by the Lawrence family as the closest British parallel yet to the kinds of national furore over high profile cases of institutional racism in America, such as the beating of Rodney King in 1992 and the shooting of Trayvon Martin in 2012, thus making the Stephen Lawrence Inquiry a watershed moment in British cultural and political history. The Inquiry Report concluded that institutional racism was confirmed as a factor in the key agencies of society, including the police, education and the health service, leading to a position where the New Labour government, the Conservative opposition and, in particular, the Metropolitan Police were forced to accept the inquiry's findings of institutional racism. As Ambalavaner Sivanandan, Director of the Institute for Race Relations observed 'the unrelenting struggle of the Lawrences has put institutional racism back on the agenda … they changed the whole discourse on race relations and made the government and the media and the people of this country acknowledge that there is a deep, ingrained, systematic racism in the institutions and structures of this society' (Sivanandan, 2000: 7). It was not until 2012, some 20 years after Stephen's murder, that Gary Dobson and David Norris were found guilty of his murder and sentenced to minimum terms of 15 years and 2 months and 14 years and 3 months, respectively. To bring this timeline up to date, in May 2014, an independent inquiry (Ellison Report) into corruption and the role of undercover policing revealed that the Metropolitan Police tried to smear the Lawrence family in the aftermath of Stephen's murder. In response to this *confirmation* Doreen Lawrence, now Baroness Lawrence of Clarendon stated 'I'm not shocked. It's something I suspected all along' (BBC News, 2014).

A more critical conceptualisation of racism in education would support the position that racism is endemic throughout the education system (Graham and Robinson, 2004) and enacted through 'colour blind' policy and rhetoric and sustained by actions that are assumed to apply fairly to all. To illustrate, the discourses on the underachievement of Black students (Christian, 2005; Crozier, 2005) pathologise young Black students (in particular, male students), viewing the Black family structure as disrupted and therefore unsupportive of both the learner and the education system; drawing attention to the heightened need to discipline Black students more severely and disproportionately placing them in lower ranked teaching groups, often as a response to issues of disaffection and behaviour rather than academic ability (Gillborn, 2008). Research conducted by Chadderton (2013) applying CRT in the British educational context gives weight and authority to the work of Leonardo (2009) and Lynn and Parker (2006) from the American context, and identifies many parallels, including the prevalence of institutional racism and evidence of intersectionality. Therefore, research suggests that the basic principles of CRT, as explained earlier in this chapter, are also applicable in the British educational context. This evidence is presented in a discussion on 'Masculinities' in Chapter 7, where recommendations for teacher education are considered in light of evidence on the educational experiences of African-Caribbean boys. Finally, Chadderton argues that there is no new critique of schools as spaces reproducing wider social inequalities and she draws attention to the increasingly consumer-orientated language of the market place linked to schools in Britain, the increase in competition-orientated measures of school success and the impact of intersectionality on pupil attainment overall. To further develop the focus on intersectionality, this chapter will now move onto a consideration of whiteness and white privilege as an increasingly pressing sociological aspect of identity construction.

Whiteness and white privilege

As this chapter explores the importance of 'race' in the context of identity and the impact on multiculturalism, it is important also to reflect on the development of whiteness as deconstruction of 'race' and white privilege. Johnson (1999) suggests that in discussions about issues of race, be they in the law, literature, sport, music, fashion or religion, in fact in all aspects of society, it is evident that whiteness is privileged, raceless and normalised, and therefore, cannot be understood in the same way as Blackness. To expand on this point applying Edward Said's orientalist position, the Black is the 'other' that will always occupy the peripheral, while the white is the dominant, the majority, the powerhouse and as a consequence, commands the centre. The concept of normalisation is derived from the notion that white people are not subject to racialisation, they are neither perceived nor do they self-identify in the context of their 'race'. In comparison, it is very common and indeed a feature of institutional racism to refer to 'black crime'. Similarly, in professional football one would not hear about 'the white footballer Steven Gerrard'; however, it is an integral part of the commentary and possibly footballing culture that one would be made aware of the Ivorian (or African) Yaya Toure. This simple everyday example is 'the fact of Blackness' of which Fanon (1992) writes – an ideological position that is rooted securely in CRT, from a historical sociological position whiteness has been taken to signify a 'raceless', normalised identity belonging to the majority. Consequently, whiteness as a means of understanding how society functions signals the production and reproduction of dominance rather than subordination and the presence of privilege. Whiteness theory treats whiteness not as a biological category but as a social construction. CRT theorists would argue that whiteness is best thought of as a form of property, both legal and cultural and symbolic, and can therefore be defined as an ideology that provides material and symbolic privilege to whites. This material privilege can take the form of access to better schools and established institutions, such as the Inner Temple where a student may qualify as a barrister, or to an elitist, Oxbridge or 'red brick' university and senior positions in key institutions, such as top-ranking positions in the army and navy. From the examples cited here, it is clear to see that whiteness engages in power structures that are both discrete and hidden, a form of embedded dominance that allows people to use their white status, which is allegedly normative, to exploit other non-whites.

The French sociologist Pierre Bourdieu's work on class inequalities and cultural capital is of relevance in understanding how whiteness operates; however, it is his influential work on 'habitus' that can be applied directly to this discussion. The concept of 'habitus' is at the heart of Bourdieu's theoretical framework, and reflects many shades in terms of application and complexity. It has been effectively applied in the British educational context by academics such as Reay (2004) and is important in establishing links between 'race', class and educational attainment. The word habitus is commonplace in the classical Greek reflections of Aristotle, who applied it to mean those acquired virtues that were the prerequisites for a virtuous life. In contemporary American psychology habitus is taken to mean being conscious of one's upbringing, which shapes the person one becomes; it also combines primary and secondary socialisation with situations and events that are of notable influence while growing up. Despite his focus on Algerian and French society, Bourdieu's approach is insightful in analysing power in terms of social change, and his work is considered in the context both of the debate

on class inequalities and educational attainment in advanced capitalist societies. Bourdieu defends the position that the theory of cultural reproduction is
concerned with the link between original class membership and ultimate class
membership, and explains how this link is mediated by the education system.
Accordingly, the education systems of advanced and industrialised societies
operate in such a way as to reinforce class inequalities so that achievement
in the education system is facilitated by the possession of cultural capital and
of higher class habitus. Pupils occupying a different original class position, by
this Bourdieu means a lower class, do not possess these traits, so the failure of
the majority of these pupils is an inevitable consequence that explains class
inequalities in educational attainment. Providing this background context
is of relevance in understanding 'white habitus' as it facilitates the conceptualisation of theory in the bigger picture – that ability to stand back and see
how theory can become apparent in practical contexts. To demonstrate how
'white habitus' operates in an everyday context, the social segregation of
housing often results in white people living in areas with a white majority. As
a consequence, if whites mainly interact with only each other, then this can
result in the sharing of similar cultural and racial experiences. This can influence the formulation of shared attitudes, thereby reinforcing their habitus and
developing 'white habitus'. For the CRT advocate this allows for further white
supremacy ideologies to prevail because in a setting where shared values
and attitudes about non-whites dominate, white privilege becomes invisible
(Akintunde, 1999). In other words, whiteness becomes transparent, neutral
the norm, while other non-white races or ethnic groups are 'othered', thereby
subjecting them to prejudice and potent negative assumptions.

Atkinson (2010) offers a powerful self-reflection on her personal narrative
of encountering and understanding white habitus and white privilege in her
encounters during her college years. In the extract captured below she recounts
experiences of travelling with the basketball team and how this provided concrete evidence of both 'white habitus' and white privilege:

> I remember visiting different schools in our district. The schools east and
> south of mine were predominantly black or Hispanic and the schools
> north and west were mainly white. More memorable were the trips into
> inner-city Austin, where our coach would tell us to keep all of our valu-
> ables with us and to take a buddy when going to the restroom. These
> statements were only made when we travelled in certain areas. They were
> obviously based on assumptions about the people at certain schools
> because of the location and type of school it was. At the time, I do not
> recall thinking it was out of the ordinary that we would need to be care-
> ful in these 'types' of areas. I did not see these reactions as having
> anything to do with race because race was not discussed; the idea was
> just there, and it just made sense. (Atkinson, 2010: 5)

White privilege is the historical, conscious and unconscious privileging of white people over Black people and can be understood in a comparison to Eurocentrism, which is a more commonly placed ideology in relation to 'race' and multiculturalism. Eurocentrism refers to standards and values that are embedded in the notion that European-based culture and experience are superior to other (non-European) cultural values and experience. The Eurocentric stand-point is a historical legacy of colonialism and imperialism and the version of history that places western discovery and achievements at the centre of the grand narrative. To illustrate, in the history of mathematics, as taught in the west, there is a notable failure to formally include and celebrate the discoveries of ancient civilisations such as those of Indian (theory of trigonometry), Chinese (development of negative numbers) and Islamic (algebra) mathematicians, opt-ing instead for a world view which suggests that the great mathematical discoveries are European (Said, 1994). Similarly, in sociology Ibn Khaldun is neither a familiar name linked to the academic development of sociological ideas, nor is his culture a celebrated tradition of academic endeavour and excel-lence. To conclude this discussion a further exemplar from the world of sport is noted by McIntosh (1997), who identified 46 outcomes of privilege associated with her whiteness, which her Black fellow sportsmen and women were unable to experience. Her research is interesting as it marries the binary challenges of 'race' and gender in the sporting context; however, based on her personal expe-riences she is able to locate and describe her white privilege as an 'invisible package of unearned assets that indicate a subtle but ultimately destructive process of power relations' (Long and Hylton, 2002: 97). The assets to which she refers are captured in an extensive list, thereby demonstrating the all-encompassing nature of white privilege, and include the fact that she is not represented as role model for her 'race'; that she is never placed in a position where she is expected to know about other sportsmen and women of her 'race'; that she is not aware of or concerned by racist chanting; and finally that her sporting ability is not attributed to her 'race'. This snapshot into the 'assets' McIntosh speaks of incor-porates the role of the media, spectators and also governing bodies in sport further demonstrating the endemic nature of white privilege.

Chapter summary

This chapter has explored the historical development of multiculturalism in education and reflected on the contested notion of Britishness as a political dimension of multiculturalism. From an international perspective, multicultural-ism in America and biculturalism in Australia are noted as exemplars of contrast in the debate on how diverse peoples are viewed. By way of conclusion, this chapter has explored Critical Race Theory (CRT) and discourses around *white-ness* and *white privilege* that have drawn on ideas of 'race', education and power.

References

Akintunde, O. (1999) 'White racism, white supremacy, white privilege, and the social construction of race: Moving from modernist to postmodernist multiculturalism', *Multicultural Education*, 7: 2–8.

Atkinson, A. (2010) 'Understanding white habitus and white privilege', in *Race, Ethnicity, and Me*. Philadelphia, PA: Trinity University Press.

BBC News (2014) 'Reaction to undercover police inquiry', 7 March. Available at: www.bbc.co.uk/news/uk-26468327 (accessed 14 January 2015).

Bell, D. (1992) *Faces at the Bottom of the Well: The Permanence of Racism*. New York: Basic Books.

Bell, D. (2009) 'Who's afraid of critical race theory?' in E. Taylor, D. Gillborn and G. Ladson-Billings (eds), *Foundations of Critical Race Theory in Education*. New York: Routledge, pp. 37–50.

Bhopal, K. and Preston, J. (2012) *Intersectionality and Race in Education*. London: Routledge.

Chadderton, C. (2013) 'Towards a research framework for race in education: Critical Race Theory and Judith Butler', *International Journal of Qualitative Studies in Education*, 26: 8.

Chafe, W.H. (2001) *Remembering Jim Crow: African Americans Tell About Life in the Segregated South*. New York: W.W. Norton.

Christian, M. (2005) 'The politics of black presence in Britain and black male exclusion in the British education system', *Journal of Black Studies*, 35(3): 327–46.

Cockrell, D. (1997) *Demons of Disorder: Early Blackface Minstrels and their World*. Cambridge: Cambridge University Press.

Crozier, G. (2005) 'There's war against our children: Black educational underachievement revisited', *British Journal of Sociology of Education*, 26(5): 585–98.

Delgado, R. (2000) *Critical Race Theory: The Cutting Edge*. Philadelphia, PA: Temple University Press.

Emdin, C. and Lee, O. (2012) 'Hip-Hop, the Obama effect, and urban science education', *Teachers College Record*, 114(2). Available at: www.tcrecord.org/Content.asp?contentid=16245 (accessed 14 January 2015).

Erikson, E.H. (1968) *Identity: Youth and Crisis*. New York: W.W. Norton.

Fanon, F. (1992) 'The fact of blackness', J. Donald and A. Ratansani (eds), *Race, Culture and Difference*. Milton Keynes: Open University Press.

Gibbons, L. (2005) '"Into the Cyclops Eye": James Barry, historical portraiture, and colonial Ireland', in F. Cullen and J. Morrison (eds), *A Shared Legacy: Essays on Irish and Scottish Art and Visual Culture*. London: Ashgate.

Gillborn, D. (2008) *Racism and Education: Coincidence or Conspiracy?* London: Routledge.

Graham, M. and Robinson, G. (2004) 'The silent catastrophe: Institutional racism in the British educational system and the underachievement of black boys', *Journal of Black Studies*, 34(5): 653–71.

Hird, B. (1996) 'EAP: Teaching Chinese learners to be impolite', *English in Australia, ESL Policies and Practice*, no. 115, March: 11–18.

Jetnikoff, A. (1997) 'Concealing and revealing: Boys – literacy and biculturalism', in N. Alloway and P. Gilbert (eds), *Boys and Literacy: Professional Development Units*. London: Curriculum Corporation, pp. 34–43.

Johnson, P. (1999) 'Reflections on critical white(ness) studies', in T. Nakayama and N. Martin (eds) *Whiteness: The Communication of Social Identity*. Thousand Oaks, CA: Sage, pp. 1–9.

Kumar, K. (2003) *The Making of English National Identity*. Cambridge: Cambridge University Press.

Ladson-Billings, G. (1998) 'Just what is Critical Race Theory and what's it doing in a nice field like Education?' *International Journal of Qualitative Studies in Education*, 11(1): 7–24.

Lawrence, J.A., Brooker, A. and Goodnow, J. (2012) 'Finding a cultural home in Australia', in J. Bowes and R. Grace (eds), *Children, Families, and Communities: Contexts and Consequences*, 4th Edition. Melbourne: Oxford University Press.

Leonardo, Z. (2009) *Race, Whiteness, and Education*. New York and Abingdon: Routledge.

Long, J. and Hylton, K. (2002) 'Shades of white: An examination of whiteness in sport', *Leisure Studies*, 21: 87–103.

Lynn, M. and Parker, L. (2006) 'Critical race studies in education: Examining a decade of research on U.S. Schools', *The Urban Review*, 38(4): 257–334.

Macdonald, I., Bhavnani, R., Khan, L. and John, G. (1989) *Murder in the Playground: The report of the Macdonald Inquiry into Racism and Racial Violence in Manchester Schools*. London: Longsight Press.

McIntosh, P. (1997) 'White privilege and male privilege: A personal account of coming to see correspondence through work in women's studies', in R. Delgado and J. Stefancic (eds), *Critical White Studies: Looking Behind the Mirror*. Philadelphia, PA: Temple University Press.

National Association for the Advancement of Colored People (NAACP) (1969) *Thirty Years of Lynching in the United States: 1889–1918*. New York: Negro Universities Press.

Nguyen, A.-M.D. and Benet-Martínez, V. (2010) 'Multicultural identity: What it is and why it matters', in R. Crisp (ed.), *The Psychology of Social and Cultural Diversity*. Hoboken, NJ: Wiley-Blackwell.

Obama, B.H. (2009) 'Inaugural address', 21 January. Available at: www.whitehouse.gov/blog/inaugural-address/ (accessed 14 January 2015).

Panayi, P. (2010) *An Immigration History of Britain: Multicultural Racism since 1800*. Harlow: Longman.

Paul, K. (1997) *Whitewashing Britain: Race and Citizenship in the Postwar Era*. Ithaca, NY and London: Cornell University Press.

Ramadan, T. (2009) *Western Muslims and the Future of Islam; Radical Reform: Islamic Ethics and Liberation*. Oxford: Oxford University Press.

Reay, D. (2004) '"It's all becoming a habitus": beyond the habitual use of habitus in educational research', *British Journal of Sociology of Education*, 25(4): 431–44.

The Runnymede Trust (2000) *The Future of Multiethnic Britain: The Parekh Report*. London: Profile Books.

Sacks, J. (2007) *The Home We Build Together: Recreating Society*. London: Continuum Press.

Said, E. (1994) *Culture and Imperialism*. London: Vintage Books.

Schwartz, S.J., Unger, J.B., Zamboanga, B.L. and Szapocznik, J. (2010) 'Rethinking the concept of acculturation: Implications for theory and research', *American Psychologist*, 65(4): 237–51.

Seeley, J.R. [1883] (1971) *The Expansion of England*. Chicago, IL: University of Chicago Press.

Simmons, R. III (2012) *Don't Just Talk About It – Be About It: The Role of Narrative and Activism in the Life of a Critical Race Theorist*. Baltimore, MD: Loyolla University, Maryland, University Press.

Singh, P. (1995) 'The politics of identity and speaking positions in the conditions of postmodernity', paper presented at the Fourth International Literacy and Education Research Network Conference on Learning 1995, Sheraton Breakwater, Townsville, Australia.

Sivanandan, A. (2000) 'Reclaiming the struggle – One year on', *Multicultural Teaching*, 18(2): 6–8 and 20.

Stovall, D. (2005) 'Critical race theory as educational protest: Power and praxis', in W. Watkins (ed.), *Black Protest Thought and Education*. New York: Peter Lang Publishing, pp. 197–211.

Syed, M. (2010) 'Developing an integrated self: Academic and ethnic identities among ethnically diverse college students', *Developmental Psychology*, 46(6): 1590–604.

Zelinsky, W. (2001) *The Enigma of Ethnicity: Another American Dream*. Iowa City, IO: University of Iowa Press.

CHAPTER 7

RE-IMAGINING GENDER ROLES

Chapter Aims

This chapter will examine the sociology of gender roles by reflecting on key theoretical perspectives including feminist sociological theory and feminist peace and conflict theory as an alternative lens through which to re-imagine gender. This examination will also explore the radical feminist standpoint on historic educational developments in the UK focusing in particular on how girls and young women have experienced the education system. In addition, this chapter will consider the feminist perspective on research as an emancipatory process for both the researcher and the researched. The chapter also aims to re-imagine gender by exploring masculinity as a socio-cultural phenomenon and finally by considering the role women played in the Arab Spring as an example of radical transformation.

Key words: masculinity, education feminism, genderquake, empowerment, transformative change.

Sociological theories of gender

Feminist sociological theory is a political as well as an academic approach to the study of how society operates in terms of gender. Embedded within a global tradition of change making, this approach is both challenging and critical, and aims to ensure a secure place for gender in classical sociology. This theoretical position argues that classical sociology (from within a European context) has failed to explore a gendered basis of how social institutions function, opting instead to represent women's roles and identities in relation to men and painting a picture of oppression, domination and inferiority. Working closely with other academic disciplines such as political theory, literature, history, geography and philosophy, feminist sociological theory sets out to destabilise this narrow vision by shifting the focus from the margins to the centre of the discourse and applying the knowledge and understanding of the experiences and insights of women into a sociological imagination with a focus on gender and education in particular. Comte, Marx, Durkheim and Weber are generally regarded as being the 'fathers' of classical sociology in the western conceptualisation, thereby revealing a clear gender imbalance in sociological knowledge production. Furthermore, the interpretation of women's roles captured in the work of the 'fathers' reinforces the marginalisation of women including ideas of (male) intellectual superiority and of women being powerless as a consequence of patriarchy. The balance is somewhat redressed in the latter part of the nineteenth century and the early twentieth century in the work of key theorists such as Beatrice Potter Webb, who wrote about the basis of a Welfare State following the First World War; Marianne Weber, who addressed the influence of modernity on the legal position of women; and Ida B. Wells-Barnett from the African-American perspective, who documented evidence of events such as lynching and applied a sociological lens to societal conflict and the treatment of Black people in America.

The origin of the term 'feminism' is a disputed historical story that provides a fitting backdrop for the many varied and complex definitions of the terms. This process of definition is compounded by the variety of types of feminism such as familial feminism, Christian radical feminism, socialist feminism, queer feminism and male feminism to name just a few subcategories. A traditionalist focus on feminism would acknowledge the strand of feminism that sought to champion women's economic independence alongside campaigns which addressed issues such as birth control, the role and status of women in marriage and equality in the workplace. Historical global periods including the First World War, the Great Depression, the baby boom years (1940s and 1950s) and the three waves of feminism, from the early part of the twentieth century to the present day, are notable for their impact in reducing the progression of the feminist march. However, in the aftermath of the Second World War an ideological shift towards feminist matters is identifiable in relation to women's potential in building a productive economy, in higher education and as equal to men in society. A key influential text reflecting themes of this era is Simone de Beauvoir's *The Second Sex* (1952), which identified two clear goals for women in the post-war era: first women should shape and embrace their own history as authentic subjects; and second, it was incumbent upon society to change in order for women to achieve the first goal.

An alternative historically rooted, yet postmodern lens through which to re-examine gender is feminist peace and conflict theory (FPCT), which focuses on the visibility of women in conflicts and in relation to violence, both domestic and state-based. FPCT is a transformative movement grounded in a historical context highlighting women's reality during war and conflict, thus presenting 'her-story' as opposed to 'his-tory', which is the traditional historiography (Reardon, 1985). The participation of women in warfare globally (Bennett et al., 1995) and the depiction of the iconic warrior queen (Mernissi, 1993) contribute to a representation of women as powerful; however, this is in the wider context of war in which public domination of women is linked to domination of women in the private sphere. As Benhabib (1992) reflects from a philosophical perspective, women are situated in a 'timeless universe', thus rendering them as disempowered and ultimately invisible. This aspect is evident in the classical work of Virginia Woolf in her 1938 essay 'Three Guineas', which explores the enforced invisibility of women (Woolf, 1938). Woolf's work is similar to that of Mary Wollstonecraft (1975), who wrote about the French Revolution and the notion that private and public violence is interrelated and that domination of man over women is legitimised from domestic relations to warfare. This ideological standpoint, the motivation behind FPCT, aims to destabilise women's lack of political power and how this has silenced women's experiences of violence in the home. In FPCT, a role for women is carved out to challenge how society perceives women as equal citizens and agents of political change. To summarise, feminist sociological theory and feminist peace and conflict theory are therefore best understood as parts of an intellectual movement with a vast array of subcategories representing feminist thought.

Education through the lens of radical feminism

In this section education policy and practice is explored through the lens of radical feminism, a movement of transformative change by women, for women that rose during the 'second wave' of feminism circa 1960 (in the UK, USA and Australia) and was heavily influenced by the civil rights movement in America, which was itself a catalyst for a global women's liberation movement. The main concern of the radical feminist is to campaign for and establish equality for women and thereby bring about transformation in society, an aim that has drawn parallels with Marxism and its ideological battle with patriarchy and class analysis. A radical feminist would argue that women's oppression is the result of patriarchy, a system of domination through which men as a group has power over women as a group – as a consequence of this manifesto they would seek freedom from being placed under the power of men and would celebrate systems of self-empowerment. To illustrate, the radical feminist would campaign for a woman's right to be in control of her own body, particularly in relation to reproductive capabilities, but also including freedom from the oppressive control of men, medical professionals, religious authorities, and would also support, the right to state support for childcare so that women can play an active role in society. As the name suggests, radical feminists espouse a more extreme set of solutions to the problems faced by women in society in comparison to liberal feminists. In relation to education the radical feminist would argue that from a historical perspective, economic and political structures embedded in patriarchy and implemented by male dominated institutions (the government, funding authorities, local authorities) have compounded gender inequalities resulting in a movement within education to close the 'gender gap' (Cruddas and Haddock, 2003). Historically, the education of girls has been at the margins of policy and curriculum design as evident in the focus in the 1960s on providing a range of vocational options for boys in the tripartite system and higher education for an elite minority of young men. In the 1970s through to the 1980s the demand for women's equality on social policy, see for example the Equal Pay Act in 1970 and the Sex Discrimination Act in 1975, gave rise to 'education feminism' (Forbes, 2002) advocated by female teachers and academics who championed a radical movement that challenged systems of oppression including patriarchy, social class and 'race'-based discrimination. It was in this period that female underachievement both in school and higher education was attributed to the socialisation processes to which girls were subjected, including gender blindness and gender stereotyping in curriculum subjects (e.g. girls being guided to the arts and away from maths and science) as well as low teacher expectations (Arnot and Mac an Ghaill, 2006). Radical feminists sought alternatives to male-centric schooling, such as single sex schools that supported the creation of a gendered identity based on an autonomous female-learning culture; a safe space where girls were included in the curriculum and challenged academically. In this period a heightened focus by academics on the triple exclusion of Black girls in the education system at this time (Mirza, 2009) noted the construction of the marginalised 'other' as a result of institutional racism and sexism. Further research by Dillabough et al. (2009) explores the notion of multiple femininities, a fluid social construction which supported the radical feminist position that the education system both produced and reproduced identities, and therefore by altering the structures of the system (such as how schools are managed, ethos, feminine culture of teaching and learning) strong radical feminist identities could be nurtured, in effect creating a 'genderquake' (Wilkinson, 1997). This period reflects a time of adjustment in terms of gender reforms based on inequalities in the education system; however, a girl-friendly ideology was never established to any real degree and the ensuing period, from 1980 to the era of New Labour in 1997 noted rapid and significant developments that demanded a prompt response from radical feminists (Osler and Vincent, 2004). The review of the national curriculum (Education Reform Act, 1988) under Prime Minister Margaret Thatcher marked an era of assumed equality of opportunity both in education and in work. This new politically motivated era in education embraced a highly technology-centred, global and competitive vision in which girls could and would achieve alongside boys in order to build a flexible and highly educated workforce. Interestingly, Thatcher's administration also supported traditional family values and the roles and identities captured therein; leading the radical feminist to question and challenge education policy such as the Education Reform Act and the establishment of regulatory organisations such as Ofsted and the Qualification and Curriculum Authority (QCA) in the late 1980s. A significant shift from 'education feminism' to 'managerialism' occurred, which is reflected in the consolidation of a male-orientated performance culture of testing and competition, with a marked change in language around gender matters from social justice to performance. To some extent, the notion that not only can women compete on an equal basis with men but outperform them appealed to a sector of the radical feminist ideology. This was reflected in media scrutiny of Black male underachievement (Sewell, 1998) linked to ideas about a crisis in masculinity and a 'lost' generation of young men alongside growing academic interest in the performance levels of girls and young women in higher education. It can be argued that the previous period of education feminism provided a solid foundation for such successes to become a reality; however, the cost of such successes was apparent to radical feminists and others in the persistence of the 'glass ceiling' in senior management positions across most sectors resulting in high achieving women, like Margaret Thatcher, representing an acute minority unable to destabilise the status quo. Under New Labour a refocusing on the performative culture of schools projected an inclusive, neoliberal agenda that focused on addressing the underachievement of different ethnic groups (Gillborn and Mirza, 2000) and closing the gender gap by careful monitoring of girls and boys in school in comparison to high-performing education systems around the world. The preoccupation with data-driven policy change meant that children's performance was measured from age 7 and this emerging picture (embedded in data generated through a culture of testing) of the continued underachievement of boys led to the conclusion that the previous era of reform has produced (not reproduced) this culture of disaffection and failure. The post-1997 New Labour era is notable for placing the educational needs of boys at the centre of reform, including challenging controlling teacher pedagogies that perpetuated disaffected masculinities (Arnot, 2006), setting out to recruit male primary teachers in order to provide much needed positive role models and developing 'boy-friendly' schooling practices such as using more information technology and physical activities in teaching all curriculum subjects but especially English and maths. Despite the momentum of change, radical feminists continued to question entrenched notions of gender stereotyping that remained constant in the education system, such as fewer women recruited in science, engineering and technology in higher education and the fact that on vocational courses women were in the overwhelming majority in childcare, hairdressing and beauty courses, while men dominated courses linked to the motor industry, construction and information technology. This new era set out to address the gender gap and in doing so cement gender equality, however, the social, cultural and economic divisions women were subject to, compounding their social exclusion, were also apparent, as reflected in the following commentary on New Labour's economic policy at the time:

> In the repositioning of family and state responsibilities what is of real significance is the placing of gender at the heart of state actions: the 'out of control' and uneducable boy is in need of reigning in; the parent at home, oftentimes the single parent/mother, is made responsible for and penalised for his actions; at the same time, she is culpable in the production and sustenance of family poverty by not having a real job, and will be further penalised by changes to tax and benefit support. (Raphael Reed, 1998: 64–5).

To conclude, the radical feminist perspective on education in the UK acknowledges that significant economic restructuring, the dismantling of traditional male preserves (in terms of curriculum areas and employment options) alongside the closing of the gender gap, the transformation of family life and the changing role and status of women in society have all contributed to a genderquake effect. Genderquake as a sociological concept celebrates positive generational change for women and refers to the radical change in perceptions and attitudes (in education, society and work) as experienced by younger women compared with women of previous generations. It can be argued that the reverberations from the genderquake effect are ongoing as illustrated by the appointment of Nicky Morgan, who was appointed Education Secretary *and* Minister for Women and Equalities on 15 July 2014, with a vast remit including early years, adoption and child protection, teachers' pay, the school curriculum, school improvement and the establishment of academies and free schools. Educated at the University of Oxford and formerly a solicitor specialising in corporate law, Nicky Morgan's new dual responsibility has been challenged by radical feminists (and other branches of feminism) as an act of reducing women's issues into a 'non-role' as it can be accomplished alongside major global and national educational developments.

It is important to credit the role of the radical feminist movement as a catalyst for change, despite the initial reservations and concerns expressed by more liberal or conservative feminists. Academics such as Germaine Greer and Ann Oakley (often referred to as 'feminist foremothers') argue that it was this version of feminism that has helped to bring about radical changes in the ways girls perceived themselves; consequently, they no longer constructed their identity in relation to the domestic domain. Instead, women's identities embraced the notion of intersectionality with dominant intersections of 'race', class, ethnicity and even religions, resulting in an ideological shift whereby women saw themselves as career professionals first and as homemakers at a later stage. This range of progressive developments has established and maintained a sense of ownership and self-realisation that achieves the ultimate aim of radical feminism – to escape patriarchy. As such, the tireless campaign of the radical feminist claims that the postmodern era is the best time to be a woman. This is because a critical foundation to knowledge production has been established, facilitating the process by which we come to learn about women's lives through their experiences.

Reading suggestion

The further reading sources below capture the ideological basis of the radical feminist standpoint as a position that nurtures women's knowledge production (through women's experiences) and challenges theoretical ideas and truth claims which may limit or oppress the advancement of women. The selection of sources includes contemporary debates in women's studies including sexual politics, identity construction and women as change makers.

Brah, A. and Phoenix, A. (2004) 'Ain't I a woman? Revisiting intersectionality', *Journal of International Women's Studies*, 5(3): 75–86. Available at: http://vc.bridgew.edu/jiws/vol5/iss3/8 (accessed 14 January 2015).

Gunew, S. (2013) *Feminist Knowledge, Critique and Construct*. Routledge Library Editions: Feminist Theory. New York: Routledge.

Ringrose, J. (2013) *Postfeminist Education? Girls and the Sexual Politics of Schooling*. New York: Routledge.

Walby, S. (2011) 'The impact of feminism on sociology', *Sociological Research Online*, 16(3): 21. Available at: www.socresonline.org.uk/16/3/21.html (accessed 15 January 2015).

Masculinity

In exploring the socio-cultural phenomenon of masculinity it is important, first and foremost, to secure a definition of masculinity; however, this is challenging. Academics in a wide range of disciplines including anthropology, cultural theory, psychology and politics would argue that 'masculinity' is composed of many masculinities (Kilmartin, 2010). In other words, there are many creative forms and expressions of this gender identity, including 'being masculine', which refers to the process of adopting a gender identity that is securely manly or masculine in orientation. To illustrate, Black masculinity and gay masculinity are two contemporary exemplars of the diverse forms of masculinity that exist in society. It is important to mark, at the outset of this discussion, the distinction between masculinity and gender in that masculinity is the degree or extent of being masculine or man-like, while (as a verb) gender is preoccupied in being assigned, meaning to assign a gender, or to engender.

The term masculinity is embedded in social, political, cultural, historical and geographical locations and time periods adding further complexity to the process of finding a definition. Masculinities are also plural and dynamic in that they are shaped by structural factors and the individual. From a psychological perspective, researchers have argued that boys are socialised in a variety of cultural ideals of masculinity from the world of sport, media, popular culture and schooling. As a consequence, this complex range of influences can have a limiting impact on their emotional expression and capacity to respond to, or acknowledge feelings. From the sociological perspective, masculinities can be understood in terms of qualities or attributes ascribed to men; for example, a muscular physique (Grogan and Richards, 2002). Research suggests that even from as young as 4, boys are aware of and interested in their muscles. By the age of 8 this awareness has intensified and is evident in discussion about muscle-gaining behaviours such as diet, interest in icons in popular culture who are very muscular (Superman, Wolverine) and role-playing in sport or play that requires physical strength (McCabe and Ricciardelli, 2003). This research suggests that socialisation, gender cultures and social interaction are all key factors in the construction of masculinities. The powerful role of the media cannot be underestimated in terms of projecting and maintaining ideas of masculinity that are internalised and become the norm overnight. An exemplar of the sociologically driven characterisation of what it means to be masculine can be found in the cult American series *Breaking Bad* and *Sons of Anarchy*. *Breaking Bad* tells the story of Walter White, a high school chemistry teacher with a PhD, played by Bryan Cranston, who 'breaks bad', deciding to make a dramatic U-turn in his life by leaving his profession to produce and eventually traffic crystal methamphetamine across New Mexico. A key facet in the storyline is that Walt is a loyal family man, devoted to his pregnant wife, Skyler, and teenage son, Walt Jr, who suffers from cerebral palsy. This cult series has won critical acclaim as demonstrated by its global popularity and the way archive episodes are tagged in online sociology discussion forums in an exploration of masculinity, deviance, crime, family and class. *Sons of Anarchy* is loosely based on Shakespeare's *Hamlet* and tells the story of a motorcycle gang called 'Sons of Anarchy Motorcycle Club, Redwood Original' or SAMCRO, referred to as Sam Crow. The gangs operate as a vigilante organisation, trafficking powerful weapons and engaging in violent gang culture. The series finale in 2013 was described as a bloodbath where the main characters die a violent death because of the poor choices they make. The main character is Jax Teller (played by Charlie Hunnam) who is divorced from his drug addict partner and has a young son who was born with premature cardiac problems. There are many overlapping themes in both examples of media-manipulated notions of masculinity, which also dominate academic discourses, including crime, violence, disrupted family life (Williams, 2009) and contested ideas about fatherhood (Lamb, 2004). Research commissioned by the Joseph Rowntree Foundation on masculinity and associated themes based in the UK (Hauari and Hollingworth, 2009; Lewis, 2000; Lewis and Lamb, 2007) also expands on themes of disruption, isolation, being an outsider, striving to be a role model and anger. Moreover, this research emphasises the impact of economic social exclusion and 'race', arguing that attitudes to fathering are influenced by a complex web of factors, including the fathers' personal experiences of being parented, culture, faith, housing, (un)employment and mental health; concluding that the fathering role in modern Britain is a fragile balancing act of many competing elements set within a framework of social and economic challenges.

In terms of a global perspective, a further illustration of re-imaging gender is captured from American research and the empowering conceptualisation of masculinity, which is aligned with 'race' and how Black masculinity draws on psychological attributes and life chances as opposed to physicality. hooks (2004), who writes about 'plantation patriarchy', offers a sobering insight into the enduring notion of Black masculinity:

Negative stereotypes about the nature of black masculinity continue to over determine the identities black males are allowed to fashion for themselves. The radical subculture of black maleness that begins to emerge as a natural outcome of militant anti-racist activism terrified racist white America. As long as black males were deemed savages unable to rise above their animal nature, they could be seen as a threat easily contained. It was the black male seeking liberation from the chains of imperialist white-supremacist capitalist patriarchy that had to be wiped out. This black man potential rebel, revolutionary, leader of the people could not be allowed to thrive. (hooks, 2004; xi)

In a highly emotive and compelling account, hooks argues that the male African-American experience is framed within a myriad of entrenched stereotypes but starting within the context of slavery, which denied men their manhood, and moving through associations with violence (towards other men as well as women), disaffection in schooling, absent father syndrome and a preoccupation with being 'cool'. Academic literature on Black masculinity addresses the recurring notion of 'cool' in relation to rap music (Baker-Kimmons and McFarland, 2011), sport (Abdel-Shehid, 2005) and violence (Collins, 2004), concentrating in particular on hip hop as a movement where Black masculinity can exist in its own world as demonstrated by the motto FUBU: 'for us, by us' (Alim, 2006: 39). While historical Black masculinity may have attempted to seek acceptance in the mainstream, hip hop (which is rooted in the civil rights movement) embraced 'gangsta' culture, having a good time and existing within a separate world unconcerned with integration into the mainstream and founded in the rhetoric of the dominator. Boyd (2003), a leading voice in the reign of hip hop as a radical pedagogy, suggested that this popular subculture offered a radical alternative, explaining 'Hip hop is concerned with being "real," honouring the truth of one's own convictions, while refusing to bend over to accommodate the dictates of the masses. Unlike the previous generation of people who often compromised or made do, in search of something bigger, hip-hop sees compromise as false, fake, and bogus.' It is important to emphasise that Boyd's insight is just one of many voices about hip hop as a way for Black masculinity to be reformulated and re-fashioned for the postmodern world. hooks (2004) is a vehement critic of Boyd's vision, arguing that a lack of spiritual fulfilment and the denial of a true self was more fake and bogus than any allegiance to this particular ideology. For hooks, the dominator mindset was not a rearticulation of Black masculinity but a denial of true potential and an indication of wounded souls. To conclude this discussion on Black masculinity hooks therefore advocates the need for Black men to embrace their unique masculinity by seeking wholeness through first and foremost resilience as exemplified by an alternative hip hop pedagogy by music icons such as Kanye West, Jay-Z and 50 Cent (Young, 2007), who embody and celebrate the socio-cultural attributes of Black masculinity as life-enhancing, rooted in positive self-esteem, liberatory and self-healing. Moreover, economic well-being and a grounded sense of self-worth complete the rearticulation of Black masculinity as captured in the work of the acclaimed poet of the Black male revolution, Haki R. Madhubuti: 'Gender equality, like human rights, is not modern paper talk, is not a reward given to smart women or good "girls", but enlightened men. Gender quality is a hard fought right, earned by women and men who are not afraid of their own shadows, mistakes and histories' (Madhubuti, 1990: 18).

Thinking point 7.1

Gosai, N. (2009) 'Perspectives on the educational experiences of African/Caribbean Boys. PhD Thesis, University of Birmingham.

The doctoral research cited above made the following recommendations to support a positive rearticulation of Black masculinity in schooling. Consider how these recommendations may act as a catalyst for change in the British schooling context.

- Teachers need to learn to view cultural language, for example, Creole/ Patois, in a positive manner as part of a wider school policy on language.
- As suggested by Black parents, teachers need to learn to give positive encouragement to Black boys in all curriculum subjects and not to direct them to take 'non-academic' subjects.
- Black boys and their parents need to receive a very thorough explanation of current exclusion policies within the context of a whole-school policy on discipline.
- The secondary school environment needs to engage more systematically with Black history and culture.
- Teachers need to perceive Black student peer groups more positively and as a potential cultural resource within the classroom.
- The Teacher Development Agency is well placed to address the above recommendations and to translate them into practice through teacher-training courses.
- Currently employed teachers could be offered workshops and senior management training that emphasise the need to establish an inclusive curriculum, pedagogy and assessment for all pupils, thus ensuring that they act as change agents in their schools. In keeping with the requirements of Race Relations (Amendment) Act 2000, training on race equality issues should be part of continuing professional development and should constitute a keystone in initial teacher training and training for management positions.
- The National College for School Leadership could prioritise as a central curriculum issue the question of academic achievement and Black boys' accounts of schooling as a racialised space of learning

Women's voices: A feminist perspective on research

In this discussion a consideration of the many complex and varied interpretations of the feminist perspective on research is framed within a context of how knowledge about women's lives and experiences is shaped. We start with a quote from Maeve Landman articulating what sets feminist research apart from other types of research:

> It is argued that feminist research is exclusively feminist because it is the feminist beliefs, motives, concerns and knowledge that act as the guiding framework to the whole research process. The methodology of feminist research differs from that of traditional social science researches on the basis of three reasons. First, feminist research explores and challenges the power imbalance between the researcher and the researched. Second, the feminist research is politically driven and has a sense of purpose and has an important role in removing the social inequalities. And finally, it asks for the experiences of women to guide the whole research process. (Landman, 2006: 38)

Feminist scholars such as Sandra Harding, Kathryn Norberg, Elizabeth Potter, Linda Alcoff, Margaret Fonow and Judith Cook all promote the idea that traditional approaches to research are undesirable as they do not reflect the diverse nature of the feminist perspective. They argue that a feminist perspective (captured in research approach, design and methodology) is significant as it creates a framework that is more receptive and sensitive to gender issues, whereas traditional approaches to research adopt an unbiased male-centred focus (Ramazanoglu with Holland, 2006). This feminist perspective suggests, first and foremost, that the researcher must be personally involved with the subject and that they must experience the subject of research for it to be a meaningful research exercise. In addition, it is argued that the research must be emancipatory in nature and must take the individual's perspective, making it both an empowering and a unique approach to research. To illustrate, Sarah Harding, Professor of Education at the University of California – Los Angeles (UCLA) and feminist philosopher of science, makes reference to this position as a standpoint, suggesting that any emancipatory social movement will include a group of people who argue 'from my standpoint, this is how I see things'.

It is critical to engage with the various feminist perspectives on research as this field of enquiry is fluid, ever-changing and representative of a multiplicity of voices. There are many dimensions to the feminist perspective on research including liberal feminist theory, Marxist–socialist feminist theory, radical feminist, psychoanalytical feminist, African feminist, ecofeminist and global feminist theory. The many shades of feminist theory suggest a powerful political influence in formulating ideas about how we can learn about women's lives and their experiences; it is integral to speak of and to the experiences of women as means of knowledge production. Therefore, the feminist perspective on research is a movement that aims to place women at the centre of the discourse and establish knowledge production from this point. To expand further, there are many integral aspects of feminist research, as clarified by Reinharz (1992), including the notion that a multiplicity of research methods can be creatively applied, it is multi-disciplinary and it aims to create social change. Moreover, feminist research strives to represent and celebrate human diversity; to include the researcher as a research subject; and also to nurture strong relations with the people studied (Reinharz, 1992: 240).

Women and the Arab Spring

In this chapter the notion of re-imagining gender and gender roles aims to capture the progressive nature of how women have delivered a counter narrative to more traditional ways of being presented and represented. With this in mind, it is timely to focus on the Arab Spring as a groundbreaking period of gender reshaping potential with its capacity to transform socio-political notions of gender. The Arab Spring is a grassroots movement of social, cultural and political reform engineered via social media and through people power where women were catalysts in bringing about revolutionary change. As such, it is a time of immense significance, with a domino effect still being felt to this day. Additionally, the Arab Spring can be regarded as a geo-political space where ideologies are made and re-made and with this potential in mind we will now consider the role women played in its overall impact.

The Arab Spring began in 2011. Global media report that it was triggered by the actions of 26-year-old Mohamed Bouazizi in the rural town of Sidi Bouzid, Tunisia, who was allegedly slapped by Fedia Hamdi (a policewoman) when he refused to hand over his wooden cart of fruit and vegetables. It is reported that Bouazizi did not have a permit to sell the goods and that this action of the policewoman, the violence of the act, the public humiliation and the desperation in his attempt to work to feed his family, led Bouazizi to set himself on fire in front of a government building as an extreme act of protest.

News reports of the incident portrayed a scenario where an ordinary man, struggling to make a living, was met by an unjust and authoritarian symbol of a corrupt regime, which had widespread impact throughout Tunisia. Local residents identified with Mohamed Bouazizi's suicide, sharing his frustration and despair and took to the streets gathering outside the governor's offices. Social media was instrumental in making wider local and global communities aware of the protests gathering momentum and it was immediately clear that the target of their rage was the dictatorial state rule, led by President Ben Ali, which had remained unchallenged for too long. At the same time, in Cairo, Asmaa Mahfouz, a 26-year-old blogger, posted a video on Facebook calling for a demonstration in Tahrir Square to protest against the Mubarak regime, marking the start of the Egyptian Arab Spring. In Tunisia, videos were uploaded onto Facebook depicting the graffiti sprayed onto the white walls of government buildings and the students gathering in nearby towns and in Kasbah Square, the political centre of Tunis. The protesters attracted even more media attention in their chants against a lack of freedom of speech, poverty and unemployment and of corruption. The speed at which events took place and the interest generated triggered mass gatherings across the country in a matter of hours. President Ben Ali was likened to a mafia don with stories of greed, abuse and violence now widespread. Within a matter of days the world was watching live footage as the people of Tunisia made a stand to reclaim their country. On 14 January, 4 weeks after Bouazizi's self-immolation, the President fled to Saudi Arabia. Tunisia was free and the Arab Spring was born.

As the Arab Spring spread across North Africa and the Arabian Gulf, the role of women as campaigners for change, alongside men, was a notable phenomenon, challenging orientalist (Said, 1978) notions of how women are perceived in Arab states. As protest organisers, bloggers, hunger strikers and medics on the ground, women in Tunisia, Egypt, Libya, Yemen and Bahrain were visible as leading the march to change. Mona Eltahawey, an Egyptian-American activist presented a two-part documentary for the BBC World Service entitled *The Women of the Arab Spring* exploring the notion of a gendered Arab Spring. A paradigm shift was evident from national issues of unemployment, exclusion and corruption as experienced by all citizens to issues of women's rights, sexual violence and exploitation, unequal representation of women and women's security, which dominated women's lived experiences. Iranian-American scholar Farzaneh Milani, captured the dynamic shift in focus, engineered by women, for women.

> The year 2011 will probably be remembered for its perennial spring: the Arab Spring, a time of transformative change and rejuvenation. A non-violent, desegregated, transgressive, youth-generated, and technologically savvy movement has swept across many countries in the Middle East and North Africa. The massive participation of throngs of women, walking shoulder to shoulder and side by side with men, is a turning point in the contemporary history of the region. It is indeed a revolution within revolutions. Although there will be many challenges ahead, particularly for those women who have transgressed all conventional boundaries and traditional spaces, the genie is out of the bottle. (Youssef and Heideman, 2012)

Reading suggestion

Cherif, K., Bernard, A. and Bessis, S. (2012) *Women of the Arab Spring: Taking their Place?* Paris: FIDH – Fédération internationale des ligues des droits de l'Homme.

This publication was produced and distributed with support from the Democratic Governance Mission of the French Ministry of Foreign and European Affairs, the British Foreign and Commonwealth Office, the Norwegian Ministry of Foreign Affairs, the Takreem Foundation and the Mairie de Paris. The publication addresses women's engagement in revolutions in Tunisia, Egypt and Libya. In addition, a consideration of the differing demands of women in Yemen, Bahrain, Algeria and Morocco culminates in recommendations entitled '20 measures for equality'.

Chapter summary

In this chapter an examination of the sociology of gender roles reflected on key theoretical perspectives including feminist sociological theory and feminist peace and conflict theory as an alternative lens through which to re-imagine gender. Additionally, a consideration of the radical feminist standpoint on historic educational developments in the UK focused on how girls and young women have experienced the education system. A feminist perspective on research as an emancipatory process for both the researcher and the researched offered an alternative lens on how research is viewed. Finally, the chapter re-imagined gender by exploring masculinity as a socio-cultural phenomenon and by exploring the role women played in the Arab Spring as an example of radical transformation.

References

Abdel-Shehid, G. (2005) *Who Da Man? Black Masculinities and Sporting Cultures.* Toronto: Canadian Scholars' Press.

Alim, H.S. (2006) *Roc the Mic Right: The Language of Hip Hop Culture.* New York: Routledge.

Arnot, M. (2006) 'Gender equality and difference in education: Affirmative and transformative pedagogic approaches', *Theory and Research in Education*, 4(2): 131–50.

Arnot, M. and Mac an Ghaill, M. (eds) (2006) '(Re) contextualising gender studies in education: Schooling in late modernity', in M. Arnot and M. Mac an Ghaill (eds), *Gender and Education Reader*. London: Routledge.

Baker-Kimmons, L. and McFarland, P. (2011) 'The rap on Chicano and black masculinity: A content analysis of gender images in rap lyrics', *Race, Gender and Class*, 18(1/2): 331–44.

Benhabib, S. (1992) *Situating the Self: Gender Community and Postmodernism in Contemporary Ethics*. Cambridge: Polity Press.

Bennett, O., Bexley, J. and Warnock, K. (eds) (1995) *Arms to Fight – Arms to Protect*. London: Panos.

Boyd, T. (2003) *The New H.N.I.C.: The Death of the Civil Rights Movement and the Reign of Hip Hop*. New York, NY: New York University Press.

Cherif, K., Bernard, A. and Bessis, S. (2012) *Women of the Arab Spring: Taking their place?* Paris: FIDH – Fédération internationale des ligues des droits de l'Homme.

Collins, P.H. (2004) 'Booty call: Sex, violence, and images of black masculinity', in P.H. Collins, *Black Sexual Politics: African Americans, Gender, and the New Racism*. New York: Routledge.

Cruddas, L. and Haddock, L. (2003) *Girls' Voices: Supporting Girls' Learning and Emotional Development*. London: Trentham Books.

de Beauvoir, S., (1989) [1952] *The Second Sex*. H.M. Parshley (Trans.). London: Vintage Books.

Dillabough, J., McLeod, J. and Mills, M. (eds) (2009) *Troubling Gender in Education*. London: Routledge.

Forbes, I. (2002) 'The political meanings of the Equal Opportunities Project', in E. Breitenbach, A. Brown, F. Mackay and J. Webb (eds), *The Changing Politics of Gender Equality in Britain*. London: Palgrave.

Gillborn, D. and Miza, H.S. (2000) *Educational Inequality: Mapping Race, Class and Gender*. London: Ofsted.

Grogan, S. and Richards, H. (2002) 'Body image: Focus groups with boys and men', *Men and Masculinities*, 4: 219–233.

Hauari, H. and Hollingworth, K. (2009) *Understanding Fathering: Masculinity, Diversity and Change*. York: Joseph Rowntree Foundation.

hooks, b. (2004) *We Real Cool: Black Men and Masculinity*. New York, Routledge.

Kilmartin, C.T. (2010) *The Masculine Self* (fourth edition). Cornwall-on-Hudson, NY: Sloan.

Lamb, M.E. (ed.) (2004) *The Role of the Father in Child Development*. New York: John Wiley.

Landman, M. (2006) 'Getting quality in qualitative research: A short introduction to feminist methodology and methods', *Proceedings of the Nutrition Society*, 65: 429–33.

Lewis, C. (2000) *A Man's Place in the Home: Fathers and Families in the UK*. York: Joseph Rowntree Foundation.

Lewis, C. and Lamb, M.E. (2007) *Understanding Fatherhood*. York: Joseph Rowntree Foundation.

McCabe, M.P. and Ricciardelli, L.A. (2003) 'Sociocultural influences on body image and body changes among adolescent boys and girls', *Journal of Social Psychology*, 143: 5–26.

Madhubuti, H. (1990) *Black Men: Obsolete, Single, Dangerous?* Chicago, IL: Third World Press.

Mernissi, F. (1993) *The Forgotten Queens of Islam.* London: Polity Press.

Mirza, H. (2009) *Race, Gender and Educational Desire: Why Black Women Succeed and Fail.* London: Routledge.

Osler, A. and Vincent, K. (2004) *Girls and Exclusion: Rethinking the Agenda.* London: Routledge Falmer.

Ramazanoglu, C. with Holland, J. (2006) *Feminist Methodology Challenges and Choices.* Thousand Oaks, CA: Sage.

Raphael Reed, L. (1998) 'Zero tolerance: Gender performance and school failure', in D. Epstein, J. Elwood, V. Hey and J. Maw (eds), *Failing Boys: Issues in Gender and Achievement.* Milton Keynes: Open University Press.

Reardon, B. (1985) *Sexism and the War System.* London: Teachers College; Columbia University.

Reinharz, S. (1992) *Feminist Methods in Social Research.* New York: Oxford University Press.

Said, E. (1978) *Orientalism.* New York: Random House.

Sewell, T. (1998) 'Loose cannons: Exploding the myth of the "black macho" lad', in D. Epstein, J. Elwood, V. Hey and J. Maw (eds), *Failing Boys: Issues in Gender and Achievement.* Milton Keynes: Open University Press.

Wilkinson, H. (1997) *No Turning Back: Generations and the Genderquake.* London: Demos.

Williams, R.A. (2009) 'Masculinities and fathering', *Community Work and Family*, 12(1): 57–73.

Wollstonecraft, M. (1975) *A Vindication of the Rights of Woman.* Harmondsworth: Penguin Classic, 1792. Reprint, 1975, Pelican Books.

Woolf, V. (1938) *The Three Guineas.* New York, NY: Harcourt Incorporated.

Young, V.A. (2007) *Your Average Nigga: Performing Race, Literacy, and Masculinity.* Detroit, MI: Wayne State University Press.

Youssef, M. and Heideman, K. (eds) (2012) 'Reflections on women in the Arab Spring: Women's voices from around the world', Middle East Program, Woodrow Wilson International Center for Scholars.

CHAPTER 8

INCLUSION, DISABILITY AND SPECIAL EDUCATIONAL NEEDS

Chapter Aims

This chapter will examine the issues of disability and special educational needs (SEN), and the policy of inclusion against a background of increasing political activism by disability rights groups and new ways of thinking about disability in the context of an increasingly performance-driven education system.

Key words: special needs, social model, medical model, affirmative and rights based models of disability, social construction of disability, impairment, disability, deficit approaches, labelling, integration, inclusion.

Introduction

In 1982 Sally Tomlinson wrote a seminal work on special needs education from a sociological perspective (Tomlinson, 1982). It was written at a time when, as Tomlinson admits, there was a distinct 'hostility to sociology as an academic activity' (Tomlinson, 1982: 1). In addition, sociology's contribution to the academic debate, policy making and practice in the field of special education had been negligible up to that point. For example, there were no sociologists on the groundbreaking Warnock Committee, which was set up in 1974 to examine existing special education provision at the time in order to recommend changes based on the findings and opinions of experts in the field. These experts came primarily from the disciplines of psychology and medicine, which dominated thinking on special education and who had for decades set the agenda on policy and practice relating to special education. What Tomlinson did was to apply the sociological imagination to the issue of special education, which adds another dimension to the area of special needs and challenges the individualised approach to disability dominant at the time. Special education now draws on a wide variety of academic fields and sociology is recognised as one of its many foundational disciplines (Farrell, 2010).

The emergence of disability studies

What may be seen as the diverse and often limiting experiences of children and adults with specific impairments that represent many seemingly unconnected personal problems, can in fact be connected to the wider social and cultural context. Since the 1980s there has been an increasing number of sociologically inspired works relating to disability and special needs that have identified the structural and social origins of the disabilities experienced by those with impairments. Crucially, many of the most influential of these have been written by academics and activists within the disabled people's movement (Finkelstein, 1980; Oliver, 1990; Shakespeare et al., 1996). These writers were attempting to establish a new discipline, disability studies, as distinct from psychology, medicine or sociology, which would be multidisciplinary and have a focus on 'disabled people's lifestyles and aspirations' (Finkelstein, 1998: 33). So, it was in fact academics and activists in the disability rights movement who started to claim that individuals with impairments are unable to make progress in education and society generally, not primarily because of their impairments, but because society disables them through the way it is organised, the way it defines them, as well as what it defines as educational success and failure. Writers in the disabilities studies field wish to create a new way of thinking about impairment that is not dominated by other professionals and experts who claim to know what is best for those with disabilities.

Using C. Wright Mills' (1959) notion of private troubles and public issues (see Chapter 1), Oliver (1990) suggests that professionals and those in power such as politicians and policy makers play a key role in this process as they have the power to define the problem and tend to locate it within the individuals concerned rather than in society and how it functions. By focusing on the so-called pathological traits and deficits of those who underachieve in the education system, professionals and policy makers are able to deflect blame away from such things as how education is funded, the way schooling is organised to fit the so-called 'normal' pupil and the existing curriculum.

A further dimension of this approach relates to the interests of those involved in defining and treating people with impairments. As Tomlinson (1982) points out, social life is based on struggles for influence and power between status groups, each trying to assert their rights to control relationships. If there is anything sociologists have shown us in the study of the professions, it is that professionals do not always function in the interest of their patients or clients (Illich, 1976; Turner, 1995). This is as much the case in special education as in any other field of social life. In this struggle, the primary definers tend to be those higher up the hierarchy of credibility, in particular doctors and psychologists (Becker, 1967).

The individual problem of disability

Disability has historically been viewed as a personal and individual problem. Tomlinson's (1982) account of the social origins of special education examines the emergence of special needs education during the nineteenth century in England ostensibly as a humanitarian mission to help those seen as unfortunate enough to have acquired or to have been born with impairments become useful and productive members of society. The impairment, physical or mental, was seen as a personal tragedy, which was defined as the problem. With the increasing role of the state in education and welfare of children generally and of children with impairments in particular, the role of professionals such as doctors and psychologists became more prominent in entrenching this view. Indeed, the discourse of disability has been dominated by notions of deficit relating to children with special needs. Negative labels and pathological terms still tend to dominate academic and professional practice and this has a strong influence on common-sense assumptions held by policy makers and the public.

The role of the professions

With the growing involvement of the state in mass public education in England through the introduction of the 1870 Elementary Education Act, there was a clear growth in the role of experts and professionals, including teachers, employed by the state to administer and run the education system. There was a perceived need to classify and sort people with impairments into groups relating to their degree of educability (Finkelstein, 1980; Tomlinson, 1982). Finkelstein argues that in the preceding feudal period there had been no segregation of people with impairments, who tended to form part of the poor and marginalised labouring peasantry who made a living selling their labour or begging. However, with the growth of factory based production those with impairments were deemed to be incapable of operating machinery designed for the 'average' worker. The disciplines of medicine and psychology were enlisted in the process of identifying, classifying and allocating those with impairments to appropriate roles and institutions. Segregation of those with impairments from the rest of the community became the norm. Those who were deemed educable and capable of being productive were provided with training and offered work. Henry Dannett, for example, set up the first school for the blind in 1791 that was primarily commercial in nature. Those pupils who were incapable of working productively were expelled (Tomlinson, 1982). Doctors were enlisted to identify and categorise those with impairments as it was believed that they possessed new knowledge of the human mind and body based on rational science and they were thought to be able to create order out of the diverse characteristics and seemingly confusing behaviour of those with impairments.

It was from the late nineteenth century and early twentieth century that, according to Foucault (1973), this new approach to sickness emerged, based on the rational principles of observation and classification. This *clinical gaze* as Foucault called it created a new language, or *discourse*, which has come to define and dominate thinking about the human mind and body. The medical knowledge created through this clinical gaze has gained the status of 'truth' that acts as a form of power over us all. In any discussion of special educational needs (SEN) there is a focus on the individual and their particular deficits. As such the disabled came to be seen not only as a burden but also as a threat to the well-being of society. Segregation from the community in large Victorian asylums became the norm and this continued well into the twentieth century. The fear stemmed from the belief that the mental or physical defects of the disabled could be passed on from one generation to the next and this brought about the establishment of the eugenics movement. Eugenics is the philosophy concerned with promoting the improvement of the human race through the encouragement of individuals with socially desirable physical and intellectual traits to reproduce, and the discouragement of those considered by society to have socially undesirable physical and intellectual traits from reproducing.

The science of segregation: the role of psychology

Along with the growing role of medicine in the control of people with impairments there was the rise of the psychologist who used the new method of mental testing to identify those requiring separation from the rest of the 'normal' population. Foremost amongst psychologists at the time was Cyril Burt, who made it his duty to assess children using the new intelligence test that had become the preferred way of identifying the 'innately dull' and 'backward child' (Burt, 1937). Burt was the first official psychologist to be appointed by the

London County Council in 1913 and, by all accounts, his ideas and methods were generally accepted without question (Tomlinson, 1982). As we saw in Chapter 5, psychologists were at the forefront of the eugenics movement and Burt's ideas were based on somewhat dubious scientific assumptions as well as rather sinister political intentions.

The scientific bases of Burt's theories are highly contested: he claimed to have developed a way of measuring a child's potential using a standardised test that could be administered to any child from any background. He assumed that a child's ability is fixed by the age of 11 and that this was the best way of allocating children to different types of school. Burt's ideas were so highly respected that they formed the basis for the 11-plus exam and grammar school entrance, which still exists in some local authorities, as well as the legislation that led to the official categorisation and segregation of children with special needs in special schools.

It is easy in hindsight to accept that some ideas developed by scientists in the past were simply mistaken or not well developed. Burt was certainly a man of his time in which eugenics had a popular following. However, Burt was not the average misinformed or mistaken scientist. He was a highly skilled researcher and statistician, and there is strong evidence (Gillie, 1976; Kamin, 1977) to suggest that Burt forged much of his data on the heritability of intelligence in order to artificially promote his idea that those at the bottom of the social ladder were there because they had inherited their low intelligence from their parents and those at the top of society were there also because they had inherited their abilities from their parents. The corollary of this was a belief that it was a waste of time providing an expensive extended education for the masses as they would not benefit from it and nor would society.

During the 1920s and 1930s Burt was an influential member of the Eugenics Society, which advocated the segregation and even the forced sterilisation of those with low intelligence. It is not too strong to suggest that Burt was committed to the social control of the 'problem classes' (Burt, 1937) of which those with impairments were considered to be a part. For pupils deemed to be subnormal, Burt recommended they be educated in special schools with a much less demanding curriculum to accommodate their impaired cognitive abilities. This is pretty much what happened: by 1913 the Mental Deficiency Act was passed, ensuring the removal of so-called defective children from local elementary schools and their placement in special schools, and by the end of the Second World War there was an Education Act (1944) that required local education authorities to test children with a view to identifying whether they were in need of special education in a separate educational institution. The stigma of segregation and negative labelling of children with impairments now had official state sanction and the medical model of disability became the official discourse of educationalists.

Special education and identity formation

As Tomlinson (1982) points out, there has been, until relatively recently, a lack of interest by sociologists in the field of SEN. However, there is no shortage of potential insights that can be provided by sociological theories and perspectives. As we saw in Chapter 1, sociology is a discipline that challenges many of our taken-for-granted assumptions and subjects them to a sociological imagination through the application of sociological analysis, research and perspectives. Such analyses do not provide the whole picture or, indeed, the truth, which would be too much to expect, but they provide insights that may enable us to better understand many aspects of social life. If we take the notions of special needs and the idea of disability we can immediately see the association of such terms with ideas of deviance, sickness and deficit. Indeed, the work of labelling theorists such as Becker (1963) and Goffman (1964, 1968) provide an excellent starting point in an attempt to understand the effects of the segregation of children with special needs from the rest of society.

In *Stigma*, Goffman (1964) draws on a variety of sources of data including his own experiences to explain the effects of stigmatising labels on those who come to be seen as somehow different. The discourse surrounding special needs is located within the fields of medicine and deviance as well as education and it is generally the first two that attract the negative labels, which eventually affect the third field, education and ultimately such things as job prospects and other social and personal relationships. What Goffman suggests is that the stigmatising labels spoil the relationships individuals seek to create with others because such labels tend to dominate and override others' perceptions of them. In effect the stigma of deviance such as ex-con, epileptic, ex-mental patient or disabled becomes the *master status* of the person concerned: it becomes the individual's prime source of identity.

Thinking point 8.1

Identify some labels that can be seen as master statuses. The labels could be positive ones as well as negative ones. How might these labels affect social interaction, for example, in applying for a job or forming personal relationships?

As with other forms of deviance, those with impairments may present *discrediting stigmas*; that is, those that are immediately evident when there is a social encounter such as where someone has missing limbs. This disrupts 'normal' interaction in that the so-called normal person often does not know how to react and the person with the impairment does not know how the other will respond. However, it may be the case that a person has a *discreditable stigma* that is not immediately evident but, should it be revealed, it could potentially disrupt social interactions. For example, a person with epilepsy will generally appear 'normal' but they will usually try to manage such information about themselves in an attempt to continue to appear normal. However, should such information become manifest, it could seriously affect such things as personal relationships and job prospects. Research on epileptics by Scambler and Hopkins (1986) (cited in Marsh and Keating, 2006) reveals that only 1 in 20 revealed their epilepsy to their employers and 1 in 2 of those studied had not informed their spouse of their condition before they got married. Those with such stigmata clearly fear the effect a general disclosure of this information may have on those with whom they interact, particularly those who may have a significant influence on their lives.

Labels of handicap

As we have seen, the treatment of children diagnosed as having special needs in the immediate post-war period involved incarceration in some form or other. Under the 1944 Education Act those children diagnosed as having one or more of the 10 official designations were defined as 'handicapped'.

Table 8.1

Categories of handicap under the 1944 Education Act
Severely subnormal (SSN)
Blind/partially sighted
Deaf/partially deaf
Epileptic
Educationally subnormal
Maladjusted
Physically handicapped
Speech defect
Delicate
Diabetic

Under the 1944 Act it was only medical officers who had the statutory right to certify a child as having a handicap relating to the mind or body. A positive diagnosis was then followed up by a series of tests by an educational psychologist, who determined what kind of educational support was needed. This usually involved the child being allocated to an appropriate special school. Often it was a special day school if it was located near the child's home or a special residential school if there was no suitable institution nearby. In some circumstances a child diagnosed with special needs was sent to a special class perhaps at their local school. In cases involving severe chronic handicap there was the prospect of long-term confinement in a hospital.

Very little sociological research or evidence exists relating to the experiences of children attending special schools. Indeed there is very little information generally and this is in part due to the fact that pupils in such institutions had little or no voice, and access to them by outsiders such as researchers and even parents was highly restricted (Brignell, 2010). Brignell describes how children's letters to their parents were usually censored and staff tended to accompany the child when parents visited. As a result what testimonies we do have do not provide a representative picture of life in special schools at the time. However, what evidence there is seems to confirm much of what Goffman (1968) found in his examination of the supposedly therapeutic and caring role of such institutions. In a review of the literature on the experiences of the disabled in special institutions, Brignell (2010) reveals the many humiliating experiences, degrading rituals and mortifications experienced by disabled children in the immediate post-Second World War period. Goffman's own ethnographic evidence and experience reveal a similar picture leading him to conclude that such 'total institutions' tend to serve the interests and routines of the staff rather than the inmates. In addition, he found that rather than providing places of asylum, they were in reality environments where the self-concept of the inmate is constantly undermined and any sense of individuality they may display is removed, destroyed or ignored. This usually involves the confiscation of personal possessions including clothes, the shaving of hair and the subjection to a regime of petty rules and regulations. Attempts on the part of patients to be taken seriously such as by giving an opinion or to try to be involved in decisions about their treatment are usually greeted with condescension. Goffman refers to these as *spurious interactions* which form part of the process of taking away any autonomy an inmate may have because, by virtue of their defect, they are seen as incapable of making decisions for themselves. In line with Foucault's ideas of medical control and surveillance, inmates' behaviour and movements are constantly monitored and recorded as a means of exercising total control.

Such treatment also seems to be confirmed by Jenny Morris (1991) from her interviews with individuals such as Ruth Moore, who is more aptly described as a victim rather than a patient and who spent time in a variety of institutions for the handicapped as a child in England during the 1940s and 1950s. It makes very disturbing reading. One of Moore's friends from those times managed eventually to get a job in the county council where an institution they had attended as children was located. Having gained access to the hospital records relating to the children who had been inmates there, Moore's friend established that two-thirds of those children had died. More recently, allegations about the celebrity Jimmy Savile, who had been an active worker for disability charities, suggest that he had abused as many as 500 children, many of them handicapped, over a 40-year period (Laville and Halliday, 2013). Such revelations reveal not only the hidden levels of abuse that are only now coming to light, but also the inability of the victims to be heard and protected due to the alleged complicity of many of those in authority.

Reading suggestion

It is certainly worth reading the accounts of those born with disabilities in the past. They provide a personal and important first-hand account of their experiences that sociologists generally can't provide. A good place to start is *Pride Against Prejudice* by Jenny Morris (1991), Chapter 5.

If asylum means a place of safety or refuge, then the testimonies of former inmates who experienced life in such institutions indicate that many were far from being safe and secure havens, but were instead places of humiliation and degradation. What the existing evidence suggests is a system that displayed, certainly in a number of places, institutional abuse and neglect, which is a terrible stain on the record of the education system in England and the work of policy makers, politicians, professionals and even celebrities who dealt with a highly vulnerable group of children and young people. In their analysis of a variety of studies on long-term institutional care, Jones and Fowles (1984, cited in Morris, 1991) conclude that there are five features that are common to life in such institutions: 'loss of liberty; social stigma; loss of autonomy; depersonalisation and low material standards' (Jones and Fowles, 1984, cited in Morris, 1991: 119).

A lack of prospects

Furthermore, if special schools were supposed to be places of education and training in order to enable young people with disabilities to live independent lives, then the prospects for those with severe chronic handicap were limited. However, those with mild handicaps such as the mildly educationally subnormal (ESN-M) were provided with training designed to prepare them for routine manual work. The development of 'good' work habits such as conformity and obedience to authority were all part of a regime of creating compliant but self-sufficient workers (Tomlinson, 1982). In general, those with some training in basic skills did find work after leaving their special schools in the early post-war period; however, with the downturn in the national and global economy during the mid-1970s this group was particularly 'affected by the recession and those requiring routine or semi-skilled work found the most difficulty' (City of Birmingham, 1977, cited in Tomlinson, 1982: 143). For most pupils with special needs then, the lack of an autonomy and choice in their education, and the inability to progress any further than the kinds of basic training recommended by experts such as Burt and general prejudice against the disabled meant that the life chances of those who were defined as handicapped meant a future of poor job prospects and higher than average levels of poverty. This has been confirmed in studies of poverty at the time. In his highly regarded and comprehensive research on poverty in the UK during the late 1960s, for example, Peter Townsend (1979) found that 'More than half those with appreciable or severe incapacity were in households in or on the margins of poverty, compared with only a fifth of those with no incapacity' (Townsend, 1979: 711).

The USA

A similar picture seems to emerge from evidence collected in the USA during this period. In his excellent account of the history of special needs education in the USA, Osgood (2007) examines the growth in the role and size of special schools there during the 1940s and 1950s. He states that this was partly due to a growing belief amongst experts and policy makers that there was a link between maladjusted youth and delinquency, and also a belief that those with mild learning difficulties required an education that would enable them to become independent. However, he found evidence of officials putting pressure on families to rid themselves of a burdensome family member with a serious disability by placing them in long-term institutions from which there was little prospect of release. Osgood (2007) found that although public (state) schools were increasing their intake of children with officially defined special needs, these institutions were seen by many experts as inadequate and unable to provide an effective education for 'slow learners'. As a result, special schools, particularly residential ones, grew in number. However, just as we saw from the case of English special schools and long-term care institutions, the evidence collected by Osgood suggests that they were not, in general, very caring, educational or therapeutic places either. From a series of personal accounts of inmates and employees as well as photographic portrayals of life in American special schools he concludes that 'many if not most such places offered nothing but hellish, brutal worlds for those entrusted to their care' (Osgood, 2007: 89–90). Overcrowding, poor staffing and little in the way of care for these children seems to have been a common feature of residential special schools in the USA at the time and, on leaving, there were poor job prospects due to widespread prejudice and discrimination.

A self-fulfilling prophecy?

As we have seen, labelling theory can help us to understand the way the medical model creates negative labels that affect the way those with impairments are seen and treated by professionals as well as other 'normal' people. It also provides an insight into the way labels can affect those who are labelled. Labels relating to special needs are rarely positive and as a consequence those labelled as slow learners may come to see themselves as such and conform to people's expectations of them. This is sometimes called a self-fulfilling prophecy and it has been claimed by writers such as Coard (1971) that African-Caribbean children in the UK are more likely to be labelled as disruptive and also as having special needs. He suggests that this results in their lower than average levels of academic achievement and higher than average levels of exclusion. He sees this as being due to prejudice and a self-fulfilling prophecy. Coard provides no hard evidence of such a phenomenon but a study by Rosenthal and Jacobson (1968) seems to suggest there is some evidence for a self-fulfilling prophecy. Their experiment involved selecting at random a sample of pupils from a number of classes in an elementary school in California and dividing them into two groups in terms of their measured ability. The teachers were advised that one group was expected to make rapid progress, but that they should not expect too much progress from the other group. As predicted, the former group performed as expected and the latter made less progress as indicated by IQ tests administered the following year. Just as one would expect, you might say. However, what the teachers were not aware of is that the pupils had not actually been divided by ability but instead they had been allocated to each group at random, making the outcome of the subsequent test results difficult to explain on the basis of ability alone. Rosenthal and Jacobson suggest that it has to do with the way the children were treated by the teachers and the differing expectations the teachers had of them. As with most research in the social sciences, the evidence is rarely conclusive because no single study will tend to settle a debate. Subsequent studies have shown both supporting and opposing results, which seem to depend on such variables as the age, ethnicity and socio-economic class of the children and the quality and nature of the data a teacher has on pupils as well as how teachers respond to such data in relation to the pupils' performance (Woolfolk, 2013).

As we have seen, labelling theory can help us to understand the way the medical model creates negative labels that affect the way individuals with impairments are seen and treated by those in authority as well as by other 'normal' people. Such labelling can also be exacerbated by racism and sexism (Morris, 1991). It also provides an insight into the way labels can affect those who are labelled. However, labelling theory has been accused of being too deterministic – that those who have been labelled as deviants are portrayed as passive victims. It is clear that not everyone who is labelled as deviant accepts the limitations imposed on them by the label; the label may be rejected, however, given that challenging professionals such as doctors or psychologists would be difficult for most patients, what match is a child against the weight of such institutional authority? Indeed, it could be argued that children with impairments have had very little option but to conform to the medical labels attached to them and tend to become dependent on others who 'know better'. As the disability rights activist Simon Brisenden (1998: 23) writes of the label 'disabled':

> It teaches us a conditioned uselessness, which is not based upon our actual physical or intellectual capacities, but upon the desire to make us believe that we are a drain upon society's resources. It teaches us to be passive, to live up to the image of ourselves as objects of charity that we should be grateful to receive, and to ignore the possibility that we may be active people who have something to contribute to society.

Tomlinson (1982) suggests that there is little sociology can offer special education in terms of tools and procedures; however, if we take into account the potentially negative self-concepts that might result from the frequent labelling of children with special needs, then a policy of more positive labelling in terms of the classification of children with disabilities might be a starting point. This is indeed happening and what we have been witnessing over the past 30 years is a series of reports, policy developments and a growth in the activities and successes of civil rights movements both in England and world-wide, which have had a significant influence on how disability is defined and treated. The perception of handicap clearly does not occur in a political and social vacuum: it is subject to change and redefinition. Perhaps one of the most significant events of the past decade, which has challenged many people's assumptions about those with impairments, was the London Paralympics of 2012. Research suggests that the impact of the games has generally been positive in terms of public attitudes towards those with disabilities (EFDS, 2012; Ferrara, 2012).

However, as Ferrara (2012) suggests, although there is evidence of significant changes in attitude in a positive way, certainly in the short term, the likely long-term impact is unclear. It is probable that a more sustained positive and informed coverage of people with impairments is necessary for such a long-term change to occur.

The politicisation of disability

The political organisation of those with disabilities is not new. As early as 1890 the British Deaf and Dumb Association was set up by Francis Maginn to promote the right of deaf people to be taught via the medium of sign language, which had been banned in 1889. In 1894 the National League for the Blind was formed by Benjamin Purse who had himself been born with a visual impairment. One of Purse's first policies was to affiliate the new organisation to the Trades Union Congress (TUC) and to campaign vigorously for the right of blind workers to a minimum wage. This campaign highlighted the link between impairment and poverty, for the new piece rate system of production placed an emphasis on speed and output rather than quality and this worked to the disadvantage of blind workers who, though just as skilled as sighted workers, tended to be slower. The issue of poverty and disability has been a prominent issue in terms of the campaigns and activities of such groups ever since.

However, what became clear from these early organisations is that they tended to be dominated by non-disabled 'experts' who often took it upon themselves to speak on behalf of the disabled. What many disabled activists wanted was to be able to speak for themselves. As the disabled writer and activist Simon Brisenden puts it:

> Our experiences must be expressed in our words and integrated in the consciousness of mainstream society, and this goes against the accumulated sediment of a social world that is steeped in the medical model of disability.

> It is vital that we insist on the right to describe our lives, our disabilities and that we appropriate the space and proper occasions to do so. (Brisenden, 1998: 21)

It could be argued that disability as an issue was entering a new and increasingly politicised phase. Despite the sporadic campaigns and demands by groups representing the disabled up until the 1960s the disabled were not generally self-organised or able to speak with their own voice. They were expected to accept definitions of their situation imposed on them by experts (Brisenden, 1998).

As such, they did not challenge the existing hierarchy of credibility as the non-disabled expert members of these groups had been able to impose their ideas of what is reasonable for the disabled to decide for themselves. This compliance, however, was starting to be challenged. A good example of this is provided by Barnes (1998), who gives an account of the campaign in the 1960s by physically impaired residents of Cheshire Homes to take more control over the running of their residential accommodation. The residents were frustrated by the very restrictive regime and wanted to decide for themselves such things as when they went to bed or watched television. In order to provide an evidence-based assessment of their abilities they enlisted the services of two psychologists from the Tavistock Institute in London, Eric Miller and Geraldine Gwynne, to evaluate their demands. However, though the researchers claimed to have sympathy for the residents' position, they concluded that the residents were being unrealistic and recommended the employment of the 'enlightened guardian model of care' (Miller and Gwynne, 1972, cited in Barnes, 1998: 68), which essentially means that the nursing staff and management should take account of the residents' wishes but that the responsibility for decisions should still lie with nurses and management.

The residents felt that they had been betrayed by the researchers who, in assessing the residents' needs, had effectively resorted to a deficit-based medical model approach rather than one based on a serious consideration of their views and natural desire for autonomy. This, and other similar events as well as the growth of the academic field of disability studies, led to the challenge of conventional approaches to disability and the existing hierarchy of credibility (Goffman, 1968). In 1972 the Union of the Physically Impaired Against Segregation (UPIAS) was founded, which claimed to:

> reject the whole idea of 'experts' and professionals holding forth on how we should accept our disabilities, or giving learned lectures about the psychology of impairment. We already know what it feels like to be poor, isolated, segregated, done to, stared at and talked down to – far better than any able bodied expert. (UPIAS, 1976, cited in Barnes, 1998: 68)

UPIAS together with a number of academics such as Oliver (1990, 1993, 1996) and Finkelstein (1980) developed a social model of disability. Oliver (1990), for example, makes a pioneering attempt to provide a critique of the individualistic approach to disability characterised by the medical model using Mills' ideas relating to individual troubles and public issues. By making the distinction between the impairment an individual may have been born with or have acquired, such as a missing limb or in terms of the functioning of an organ or part of the body, and the way that impairment is defined, labelled and treated, we have the basis of a social model of disability. So for Oliver it is not the specific impairment that causes disability, but instead it is the effects of negative labelling and the processes of exclusion caused by a lack of consideration of the needs or wishes of those with impairments by policy makers and professionals, or a positive act of exclusion of people with impairments from mainstream society and its institutions be they schools or places of employment. In terms of the neglect in considering the needs of individuals with impairments in the built environment and modes of transport, an impaired person may become excluded and thereby disabled because of issues of access. With regard to positive acts of exclusion, many children with impairments are still denied full rights of access to their local schools.

Challenging essentialist views of disability

Oliver (1993) suggests that the focus of attention should be on society and not on the disabled person for, as the quote from UPIAS above suggests, we already have a wealth of information about the experiences of the disabled. Moreover, Finkelstein (1981) argues that disability is the result of a process in which those with impairments have become defined by their biological condition rather than in terms of their other qualities as human beings. This is known as an essentialist view of disability and implies that because those with impairments are different biologically they are somehow deficient. Essentialist assumptions justify and provide a so-called rational basis for exclusionary practices. If it is assumed that those with impairments are fundamentally different from 'normal' people and are unable to live normal lives, then there is the clear implication that those with impairments cannot function within the world of the non-disabled. As Jenny Morris (1991) writes:

> This exclusion is associated with the way that our physical or intellectual differences make us less than human in the eyes of non-disabled people; we can be excluded from normal human activity because we are not normally human. A physically different body, or a body which behaves in a different way, means an incomplete body and this means that our very selves are similarly incomplete. (Morris, 1991: 27)

An excellent example of such essentialist ideas and their consequences with regard to a particular disabled group such as the blind is the claim by some psychologists that the condition of blindness causes a 'blind personality', which is characterised by displays of helplessness, docility and depression. For these psychologists the blindness is responsible for creating such a personality and the inability of the blind person to come to terms with the condition. However, in a pioneering sociological study in the USA in the 1960s that focuses on the adventitiously blinded; that is, those who are not born blind but become blinded, Scott (1969) argues that the blind learn such helplessness and therefore become disabled in the course of their (re)socialisation; that is, in their interactions with family members, agencies for the blind, medical and welfare professionals and peers. Scott suggests that what is needed is a fundamental change in attitudes and treatment of the blind so as to challenge the generally negative discourse surrounding the condition of blindness. In countries where blindness is treated primarily as a technical problem, rather than one of loss, blind personalities are much less in evidence (Taylor, 1994).

Divisions within the movement

The work of the pioneers of disability studies theory such as Oliver and Finkelstein has been highly influential in challenging the personal tragedy approach of the medical model and in showing how disability is a socially created problem rather than one that stems primarily from an impairment. As such it has encouraged us to rethink and challenge conventional ideas of disability, which have tended to dominate our understanding of the issue and which locate the problem of disability squarely on the shoulders of individuals with impairments. However, Light (2003) refers to the 'unsocial muddle' that has erupted amongst those involved in disability studies and the disability rights movement. What writers such as Morris (1991) argue is that by focusing on the ideology of 'disablism' and the common experiences of disability, the social model effectively excludes the diverse experiences of disabled people. As a result, issues such as gender, race and sexuality are ignored. In addition, for disabled feminists such as Morris, to ignore the differences of impairment is to fall victim to the normalising pressure of society. Morris suggests that by denying or downplaying their impairments disabled people are rejecting who they are: a politics of disability is about celebrating this difference and affirming it in order to develop a pride in one's identity. Moreover, she points to the myth of the personal tragedy approach to disability, which assumes that all people with impairments want to be 'cured' or to be 'normal'. It is this myth that Morris believes prevents the non-disabled from thinking of the disabled as anything other than deviants or tragic victims incapable of living valued and fulfilling lives.

Celebrating difference

Swain and French (2000) develop what they describe as an 'affirmative model of disability' that challenges disablist ideology whilst at the same time creating a positive image of impairment through a disability culture and also by rejecting the normalising pressure on those with disabilities. The affirmative model, however, though celebrating these differences, does not imply that those with disabilities do not have the same ambitions and aspirations as non-disabled people. Like anyone else, disabled people seek independence through gainful employment, which can only be achieved through education. For disabled activists, current policy and legislation still operate in terms of a medical and exclusionary model despite the rhetoric of inclusion used by politicians. This has a clear effect on the life chances of the disabled and their quality of life. Just as in the immediate post-war period the handicapped were reported to have higher than average levels of poverty, there seems to have been little change in recent years.

Disability and life chances today

The consequences of exclusion are evident in the terms of the life chances of disabled people today. Evidence from the Office for Disability Issues (ODI, 2013) reveals the continuing gap between the disabled and non-disabled in terms of educational attainment, levels of employment and living standards. Although there was an increase in the proportion of children with SEN statements achieving five or more GCSEs at grades A*–C from 8.7 per cent to 24.9 per cent between 2005/6 to 2010/11, there was an even more impressive increase during the same period for children without special needs from 66.3 per cent to 88.9 per cent, revealing an increasing gap between the two groups (ODI, 2013). Although there has been a reduction in the gap between the two groups in terms of the percentage in work there was still a 30 per cent gap in 2012, with 76.4 per cent of non-disabled people of working age in employment compared to 46.3 per cent of disabled people. This clearly has an effect on the proportion of disabled people living in poverty. In 2012, 21 per cent of children in families with at least one disabled member were living in poverty compared to 16 per cent of children in families without any disabled members (ODI, 2013).

The right to be included

Summing up a report by the Institute for Public Policy Research (IPPR) called 'Education: A different vision: An alternative White Paper' published in 1993, Thomas and Vaughan (2004) state that employers are generally not well disposed to children who have had a 'special education': the label 'special' itself creates disadvantage for the disabled with regard to employment so, for the IPPR, schools and colleges should become inclusive of all children regardless of their disabilities or differences, and the education they provide should cater for their individual needs. The IPPR asserts that the failure of any child is more the result of the poor management of schools, unnecessary and inappropriate testing, an inflexible curriculum, poor teaching and bad teacher–pupil relations, rather than the fault of the child. As such, for the IPPR, the onus is on schools to change and not their pupils.

There has, however, been a slow but clearly discernible change in attitudes to, as well as amongst, those with disabilities since the 1960s, which ultimately has had a clear influence on policy regarding special education. This process picked up a pace during the 1970s and 1980s, when the Warnock Report (Department for Education and Science, 1978) was published. This was a landmark in special education as it recommended the integration of disabled children into mainstream schools and, furthermore, shifted the focus on disabled children away from their impairments and towards their educational needs. By using the term special educational needs (SEN) and proposing the abolition of the term handicap, there was a clear shift in thinking away from the medical model of disability to a more social one. More recently in England in the 1990s and early 2000s New Labour (1997–2010) introduced a number of policies and legislation promoting the inclusion of disabled children in mainstream education. Much of this change can be attributed to the politicisation of disability issues and the demands for civil rights by disabled people who had started to organise themselves just as those campaigning for sexual equality and racial equality were beginning to organise in the 1960s. In addition, experts and professionals were starting to reassess their procedures and the evidence relating to the effectiveness of the segregation of those with impairments generally, as well as that of special education in special schools in particular (Christopolos and Renz, 1969; Dunn, 1968; Leyden, 1978). A further factor was the international impetus for the furthering of the rights of oppressed and minority groups by organisations such as the United Nations Convention on the Rights of the Child (UNICEF, 1989) and the United Nations Educational, Scientific and Cultural Organization (UNESCO) in the form of such pronouncements as the Salamanca Statement of 1994 and Inclusive Education for All on the Agenda (1998), which stated that it was the right of all children, regardless of their disability or learning difficulties, to be educated together.

Integration and Inclusion

The debate about the education of children with special needs has, over the past four decades, revolved around the concepts of integration and inclusion. As we have seen above, the Warnock Report (Department for Education and Science, 1978), and the subsequent legislation that enacted much of its recommendations in the 1981 Education Act, focus on a policy of integration. This refers to the requirement, under Section 2 of the Act, that Local Education Authorities (LEAs) are required to educate children with SEN alongside other children in mainstream schools. Considering the attitude to and treatment of children with disabilities up to the 1970s, the recommendations of the Warnock Report and the legislation that followed seem quite radical. However, if we examine the ideas of the Warnock Report and the legislative guidelines regarding integration in more detail we can see a lack of real commitment to integration. For a start, integration, as envisioned by Warnock and the 1981 Act took three forms. The first, *locational* integration refers to the placement of children with SEN in the same schools as other children, but in special units rather than the same classes. *Social* integration is where children with SEN mix with other children in the school generally such as during break times, social events and meal times, but are still educated in separate classes, and *functional* integration relates to the inclusion of children with SEN in all aspects of school life with other children, including being taught in the same classes.

Warnock did not make a strong commitment to any particular form of integration, suggesting that there will always be a need for separate facilities and special schools given the needs of some children, which ordinary schools cannot reasonably be expected to provide. This equivocal position was reflected in the 1981 Act in that the duty placed on LEAs to integrate was seriously undermined by the conditions set on the level and nature of integration that children with SEN and their parents could expect from their local school. Although integration was a duty of LEAs, and parents' views had to be taken into account, this could be overridden if three requirements could not be met: first, that the education of the other children would not be adversely affected by the such placements; second, the requirement to use resources efficiently; and third, if the child would not be able to receive the special educational support deemed necessary for them. This effectively gave LEAs a get-out clause if they did not agree with their duty to integrate. Indeed, they were under no legal obligation to make any changes as part of a general policy of increasing integration.

In a national survey by the Centre for Studies on Inclusive Education (CSIE, 1985, cited in Thomas and Vaughan, 2004), 'Caught in the act', conducted soon after the introduction of the 1981 Education Act, it was revealed that of the LEAs surveyed about the implementation of the legislation, only a small minority (11%) provided information in their literature for parents about their duty to integrate children with SEN into mainstream schools. This lack of communication and openness about their obligations, together with the ease with which LEAs and their professional staff were able to avoid their responsibilities, made the 1981 Education Act largely ineffectual as a means of promoting integration and, in addition, managed to infuriate many thousands of parents whose wishes to have their children integrated into mainstream schools were rejected. As Evans (1995, cited in Hodkinson and Vickerman, 2009) states, between 1985 and 1991, there was only a 12.5 per cent drop in the proportion of children in special schools and in some LEAs there was actually a rise.

From integration to inclusion

The key weakness of the legislation was the concept of integration, which puts the onus on parents of children with SEN to fight for a place in a mainstream school, and imposes no obligation on LEAs to make any changes to facilitate greater integration. This highlights a key difference between inclusion and integration: while the latter is permissive in terms of allowing LEAs to integrate if they so wished and could satisfy the provisos contained in Section 2, inclusion is based on an assumption of the right of all children to be educated with their peers. Once this right is established the obligation is reversed: the education providers are required to make the changes necessary to enable all children to

Table 8.2

CSIE Inclusion Charter

---

1   We fully support an end to all segregated education on the grounds of disability or learning difficulty, as a policy commitment and goal for this country.

2   We see the ending of segregation in education as a human rights issue which belongs within equal opportunities policies.

3   We believe that all students share equal value and status. We therefore believe that the exclusion of students from the mainstream because of disability or learning difficulty is devaluation and is discriminating.

4   We envisage the gradual transfer of resources, expertise, staff and students from segregated special schools to an appropriately supported, diverse and inclusive mainstream.

5   We believe that segregated education is a major cause of society's widespread prejudice against adults with disabilities or difficulties and that efforts to increase their participation in community life will be seriously jeopardised unless segregated education is reduced and ultimately ended. De-segregating special education is therefore a crucial first step in helping to change discriminatory attitudes, in creating greater understanding and in developing a fairer society.

6   For these reasons we call on Central and Local Governments to do all in their power to work as quickly as possible towards the goal of a de-segregated education system.

(CSIE, 2002: 1)

be educated together. Inclusion relates more closely to the views of disability rights groups such as CSIE, which were reflecting the changes in attitude towards SEN during the 1990s. Taking their lead from such documents as UNESCO's Salamanca Statement as well as the United Nations Convention on the Rights of the Child, which Britain ratified in 1991 and which states that all children including those with disabilities have the right to 'the fullest possible social integration and individual development' (United Nations, 1989: 3), CSIE produced an Inclusion Charter in 2002 containing six statements relating to the ending of segregation in education.

In its campaign to promote inclusive education in Britain CSIE has sought support for the charter from organisations representing the disabled. However, despite sending the Charter out for endorsement to potentially interested parties on several occasions over the past decade, CSIE has not met with universal support from all the relevant groups. The list is notable for the absence of such names as Scope, which represents disabled people and their families, the Royal National Institute for the Blind (RNIB), the Royal National Institute for the Deaf (RNID), as well as the Royal Society for Mentally Handicapped Children and Adults (MENCAP), all of which are arguably some of the most high profile and respected organisations in their respective fields.

A lack of consensus

The arguments in support of full inclusion can be summed up under the categories of the ethical and philosophical, the social and the educational. In terms of the ethical and philosophical justifications, there is a straightforward assertion that all children have the right to be educated together and not segregated on the grounds of difference (CSIE, 2002; IPPR, 1993; UN, 1989; UNESCO, 1994). Socially, the policy of integration is seen as an essential part of the process of challenging discriminatory attitudes and practices (CSIE, 2002; Wertheimer, 1997). For groups such as CSIE bringing children up and educating them separately sends all the wrong messages to young people who, it claims, need to be part of a fairer and more just society. Inclusion is justified on educational grounds on the basis that there is no convincing evidence supporting the claim that segregation benefits students (CSIE, 2003). In a clear reversal of traditional psychological approaches to the education of those with disabilities, the British Psychological Society published a position paper in 2002 that presented a very strong case for inclusion by endorsing the CSIE Charter and also suggests how psychologists might contribute to this policy (BPS, 2002).

In addition to these arguments, it is claimed that inclusion is more cost effective than segregated provision. The Organisation for Economic Co-operation and Development (OECD, 1999, cited in Thomas and Vaughan, 2004), a highly respected international development agency, suggests that it is more expensive to run a twin system of special schools and mainstream schools than a single inclusive one. However, these points are not sufficient to convince those who do not support the closure of special schools and wholesale inclusion. The debate was particularly polarised in the 1990s and early 2000s during which time those who did not support wholesale inclusion were labelled as somehow morally suspect by those who did (Garner, 2009). The debate was presented very much in black and white terms.

New Labour

In 1997 when New Labour came to power on a programme of social justice and inclusion, it seemed that real change was afoot in favour of inclusive education. It published a Green (discussion) Paper 'Excellence for all children: Meeting special educational needs' (1997), which started with what seemed like a manifesto for full inclusion. Quoting the Salamanca Statement's proposal for progressive steps towards greater inclusion there seemed to be a clear commitment to increasing inclusion. Indeed subsequent policy documents and legislation such as 'Meeting special educational needs: A programme of action' (1998) and the Special Educational Needs and Disability Act (SENDA) 2001, went a long way towards promoting inclusion as a right rather than just a desirable thing. The former set out five aims that identified a strategy involving parents, local authorities, schools, teachers and other relevant agencies in working together to bring about greater inclusion. The latter made it illegal for local authorities and schools to discriminate against those with disabilities in their admissions policies and the provision of services. Moreover, the get-out clause relating to the efficient use of resources, which was such a blatant feature of the 1981 Education Act and which allowed LEAs to escape their duty to integrate, was rescinded.

However, despite these developments, those who support full and unconditional inclusion such as CSIE are critical of what they describe as New Labour's contradictory position (Thomas and Vaughan, 2004), for whilst endorsing and promoting the idea of greater integration, New Labour also stated its belief in the continuing need for special schools and the rights of parents to have their child educated in a special school. Indeed, the Green Paper (1997) went on to suggest that such separate institutions would still have a place in the education system for the foreseeable future. For those who propose a rights based case for inclusion this is a real cause for concern (Thomas and Vaughan, 2004).

However, this rights based position has been subject to a greater challenge in recent years. For Garner (2009) there is now a growing acceptance that inclusion is much more complex than merely winning the right for children with SEN to be educated in mainstream schools alongside their peers. As Armstrong et al. (2010) point out, there is very little clarity or agreement not only about what inclusion is, but also about how it can be implemented as well as what the desired outcomes of inclusion might be. In addition, there is some scepticism about what inclusion might involve for some disabled groups. As we have seen above, a significant number of groups have declined to endorse CSIE's Disability Charter. The Royal National Institute for the Deaf (RNID), for example, represents a community with its own language and culture (Deaf culture) as well as identity. Deaf people generally have a strong allegiance to their community, which would be at odds with a mainstream education dominated by hearing pupils and teachers.

Thinking point 8.2

What would constitute an inclusive education?

As Armstrong et al. (2010) point out, there is little agreement as to what inclusive education is or should be. This creates a good deal of confusion in academic debate as well as policy development. You might like to read Ainscow et al. (2006), which examines this issue in some depth.

A further but related issue is that of children with SEN being included in mainstream classrooms where they are judged by the standards of what is expected from a 'normal' child. Under the existing system all children are expected to follow the same National Curriculum and to be judged by common criteria of success. Bateman (1995) suggests that the National Curriculum and its assessment criteria disadvantage those who fall at the extreme ends of the statistical norm. So what we have is an inclusive philosophy that works according to a system which measures all children against a notional norm outside of which children with SEN are more likely to fall.

It is true that under National Curriculum arrangements those performing outside the standardised performance indicators are now assessed according to alternative criteria known as P-Scales. However, being assessed separately in this way is in itself stigmatising because these scales are applied to those children who fall below Level 1, which is the lowest attainment level. This is unlikely to change because in the prevailing economic and political climate both nationally and globally, the measurement of performance and the adding of value are becoming the main ways in which schools are judged.

The purpose of education

The current priorities of the education system are based on a *neoliberal* approach. This refers to the notion that market principles should dictate the way education is delivered and assessed. Schools are required to compete with each other for pupils through funding systems based on performance criteria. In addition, the education system is now expected to be much more focused on providing for the needs of the economy through the creation of *human capital* in the form of skilled workers. As the Green Paper 'Higher ambitions' (Department for Business Skills and Innovations, 2009: 2) states with regard to the role of universities:

> In a knowledge economy, universities are the most important mechanism we have for generating and preserving, disseminating, and transforming knowledge into wider social and economic benefits.

Although the Green Paper goes on to discuss the importance of enabling each individual to reach their full potential as part of an agenda to promote social justice, the main thrust of the document, and many like it published under New Labour and the coalition government, is the need to increase Britain's economic competitiveness in the global economy.

It could be argued that this is incompatible with the right to inclusion of children with SEN into mainstream schools in that the main priority of the education system is to create employable citizens at the lowest possible cost to the state. Children with SEN are generally more expensive to educate and this has meant that schools have engaged in processes of excluding 'problem' pupils (Tomlinson, 2005) or have been reluctant to spend the extra resources needed for pupils with special needs (Ball et al., 1994). The government's own figures show that 'Pupils with SEN with statements are around eight times more likely to be permanently excluded than those pupils with no SEN' (Department for Education, 2011). With the expansion of the academies and free schools programme under the coalition it is feared by some that such practices will increase, particularly in light of the fact that free schools have much more autonomy as to how they spend their budgets and admissions policies. Evidence collected so far by Stewart (2004) (cited in Tomlinson, 2005) suggests that many of the new academies set up under New Labour were able to improve their examination performances by excluding pupils with behavioural problems or refusing to take certain children with special needs. Government regulations state:

> The funding agreement for Free Schools includes provisions which require them to have regard to the SEN Code of Practice and to use their best endeavours to meet any special needs of pupils. This mirrors the legislative requirements on maintained schools. If any Free School were to fail to meet its SEN funding agreement obligations, the Secretary of State would have to ensure that those obligations were met. (Department for Education, 2012)

Only time will tell whether the patterns already witnessed are going to be repeated.

This clearly raises questions regarding the education system in England such as what is education for, as well as who is it for? In a policy climate which places ever increasing emphasis on the extrinsic purposes of education such as the need to increase the level of human capital, those who represent a financial burden on the system and have little power to assert their rights are more likely to be vulnerable to the changing priorities of those with the power to make decisions regarding resource allocation.

Chapter summary and comment

In this chapter we have examined the emergence of disability studies, which pioneered the development of new ways of seeing and understanding the nature of disability. In particular, it was responsible for identifying the social construction of disability revealing how those with impairments are disabled by society rather than by specific impairments. Sociology has been a relatively recent contributor to both the academic and policy debate on SEN. Nevertheless, it has provided some useful conceptual and theoretical tools with which to understand and analyse issues relating to disability and SEN.

The insights of disability studies and sociology have undoubtedly had an influence on policy makers and experts such as medical practitioners and psychologists in bringing about a reassessment of their traditional assumptions about disability and the education of those with SEN. With the increasing pressure from the disability rights movement and international organisations such as the UN, we have witnessed a demand for all children to be educated together. However, such rights based approaches to the education of children with SEN are not universally accepted, even within the disabled community, which is made up of a variety of groups each representing their own disabled culture and priorities. In addition, there is a good deal of disagreement as to what an inclusive education system should be. Nevertheless, any model of inclusion is required to fit into a National Curriculum that has been designed with the 'normal' pupil in mind. As long as this is the case, children with SEN are likely to remain disadvantaged, particularly in a policy climate that places an emphasis on human capital and the importance of employability.

References

Ainscow, M., Booth, T. and Dyson, A., with Farrell, P., Frankham, J., Gallannaugh, F., Howes, A. and Smith, R. (2006) *Improving Schools, Developing Inclusion*. London: Routledge.

Armstrong, C.A., Armstrong, D. and Spandagou, I. (2010) *Inclusive Education: International Policy and Practice*. London: Sage.

Ball, S.J., Bowe, R. and Gerwitz, S. (1994) 'Market forces and parental choice', in S. Tomlinson (ed.), *Educational Reform and its Consequences*. London: IPPR/Rivers Oram Press.

Barnes, C. (1998) 'The social model of disability', in T. Shakespeare (ed.), *The Disability Reader: Social Science Perspectives*. London: Continuum.

Bateman, B.D. (1995) 'Who, how and where: Special education's issues in perpetuity', in J. Kauffman and D. Hallahan (eds), *The Illusion of Full Inclusion: A Comprehensive Critique of a Current Special Education Bandwagon*. Austin, TX: ProEd.

Becker, H. (1963) *Outsiders*. New York: The Free Press.

Becker, H. (1967) 'Whose side are we on?' *Social Problems*, 14: 239–47.

Brignell, V. (2010) 'When the disabled were segregated', *New Statesman*. Available at: www.newstatesman.com/society/2010/12/disabled-children-british (accessed 7 Feb 2015).

Brisenden, S. (1998) 'Independent living and the medical model', in T. Shakespeare (ed.), *The Disability Reader: Social Science Perspectives*. London: Continuum.

British Psychological Society (BPS) (2002) *Inclusive Education: A Position Statement*. Leicester: BPS.

Burt, C. (1937) *The Backward Child*. London: University Press.

Christopolos, F. and Renz, P. (1969) 'A critical examination of special education programs', *Journal of Special Education*, 3(4): 371–9.

Coard, B. (1971) *How the West Indian Child is Made Educationally Sub-normal in the British School System*. London: New Beacon Books.

CSIE (Centre for Studies on Inclusive Education) (2002) *The Inclusion Charter*. Available at: www.csie.org.uk/resources/charter.shtml (accessed 7 February 2015).

CSIE (Centre for Studies on Inclusive Education) (2003) *Reasons Against Segregated Schooling*. Bristol: Centre for Studies on Inclusive Education.

Department for Business Innovation and Skills (2009) 'Higher ambitions: The Future of universities in a knowledge economy executive summary'. Available at: http://aces.shu.ac.uk/employability/resources/Higher-Ambitions-Summary.pdf (accessed 14 January 2015).

Department for Education and Employment (1997) *Excellence for All Children: Meeting Special Educational Needs*. London: Department for Education and Employment.

Department for Education and Employment (1998) *Meeting Special Educational Needs: A Programme of Action.* London: DFEE.

Department for Education (2011) 'School exclusion statistics for the academic year 2009 to 2010'. Available at: www.gov.uk/government/news/school-exclusion-statistics-for-the-academic-year-2009-to-2010 (accessed 14 January 2014).

Department for Education (2012) 'Free Schools FAQs – special educational needs'. Available at: www.education.gov.uk/a0075661/free-schools-faqs-special-educational-needs (accessed 14 January 2014).

Department for Education and Science (1978) 'Special educational needs: Report of the Committee of Enquiry into the Education of Handicapped Children and Young People', Cmnd 7212. London: HMSO.

Dunn, L.M. (1968) 'Special education for the mildly retarded – Is much of it justifiable?' *Exceptional Children,* 35: 5–24.

English Federation of Disability Sport (EFDS) (2012) 'Measuring the impact of the Olympic and Paralympic Games on disabled and non-disabled people'. Available at: www.efds.co.uk/assets/0000/5208/Legacy_Questionnaire_Report_20121031FINAL. pdf (accessed 14 January 2015).

Farrell, M. (2010) *Debating Special Education.* London: Routledge.

Ferrara, J.K. (2012) 'Public attitudes towards intellectual disabilities after watching Olympic/Paralympic performance', PhD Thesis, Christ Church University, Canterbury.

Finkelstein, V. (1980) *Attitudes to Disabled People: Issues for Discussion.* New York: World Rehabilitation Fund.

Finkelstein, V. (1998) 'Emancipating Disability Studies', in T. Shakespeare (ed.), *The Disability Reader.* London: Continuum.

Foucault, M. (1973) *The Birth of the Clinic: An Archaeology of Medical Perception.* Tr. A.M. Sheridan. London: Tavistock.

Garner, P. (2009) *Special Educational Needs: The Key Concepts.* London: Routledge.

Gillie, O. (1976) 'Crucial data was faked by eminent psychologist', 24 October, *Sunday Times* (London).

Goffman, E. (1964) *Stigma.* Harmondsworth: Penguin.

Goffman, E. (1968) *Asylums: Essays on the Social Situation of Mental Patients and Other Inmates.* London: Pelican.

Hodkinson, A. and Vickerman, P. (2009) *Key Issues in Special Educational Needs and Inclusion.* London: Sage.

Illich, I. (1976) *Limits to Medicine.* London: Marion Boyars.

IPPR (Institute for Public Policy Research) (1993) *Education: A Different Vision: An Alternative White Paper.* London: IPPR.

Kamin, L.J. (1977) *The Science and Politics of IQ.* Harmondsworth: Penguin.

Laville, S. and Halliday, J. (2013) 'Report reveals Savile assaulted children as young as 10', 11 January, *The Guardian.*

Leyden, G. (1978) 'The process of reconstruction: an overview', in B. Gillham (ed.), *Reconstructing Social Psychology.* London: Croom Helm.

Light, R. (2003) 'Social model or unsociable muddle?', in M. Nind, J. Rix, K. Sheehy and K. Simmons (eds), *Inclusive Education: Diverse Perspectives.* London: David Fulton.

Marsh, I. and Keating, M. (2006) *Sociology: Making Sense of Society*. London: Pearson.

Morris, J. (1991) *Pride Against Prejudice*. London: The Women's Press.

Office for Disability Issues (ODI) (2013) 'Disability facts and figures'. Available at: http://odi.dwp.gov.uk/disability-statistics-and-research/disability-facts-and-figures.php (accessed 14 January 2015).

Oliver, M. (1990) *The Politics of Disablement*. Macmillan: Basingstoke.

Oliver, M. (1993) 'Re-defining disability: A challenge to research', in J. Swain, V. Finkelstein, S. French and M. Oliver (eds), *Disabling Barriers – Enabling Environments*. London: Sage.

Oliver, M. (1996) *Understanding Disability: From Theory to Practice*. Basingstoke: Macmillan.

Osgood, R.L. (2007) *The History of Special Education: A Struggle for Equality in American Public Schools*. London: Praeger.

Rosenthal, R. and Jacobson, L. (1968) *Pygmalion in the Classroom*. New York: Holt, Reinhart, Winston.

Scambler, G. and Hopkins, A. (1986) 'Being epileptic: Coming to terms with stigma', *Sociology of Health and Illness*, 8: 26–44.

Scott, R. (1969) *The Making of Blind Men: A study of adult socialization*. New York: Russell Sage Foundation.

Shakespeare, T., Gillespie-Sells, K. and Davies, D. (1996) *The Sexual Politics of Disability: Untold Desires*. London: Cassell.

Swain, J. and French, S. (2000) 'Towards an affirmative model of disability', *Disability and Society*, 15(4): 569–82.

Taylor, S. (1994) 'Beyond the medical model: The sociology of health and illness', *Sociology Review*, 8(1): 2–6.

Thomas, G. and Vaughan, M. (2004) *Inclusive Education: Readings and Reflections*. Maidenhead: Open University Press

Tomlinson, S. (1982) *A Sociology of Special Education*. London: Routledge and Kegan Paul.

Tomlinson, S. (2005) *Education in a Post Welfare Society*. London: Routledge.

Townsend, P. (1979) *Poverty in the UK: A Survey of Household Resources and Standards of Living*. Harmondsworth: Penguin.

Turner, B.S. (1995) *Medical Power and Social Knowledge*. London: Sage.

UNESCO (1994) *The Salamanca Statement and Framework for Action on Special Needs Education*. Paris: UNESCO.

United Nations (1989) 'United Nations Convention on the Rights of the Child'. Available at: www.unicef.org.uk/Documents/Publication-pdfs/UNCRC_PRESS200910web.pdf (accessed 14 January 2015).

Vaughan, M. (2004) 'Mark Vaughan: Kirsty Arrondelle-early integration', in G. Thomas and M. Vaughan (eds), *Inclusive Education – readings and reflections*. Maidenhead: Open University Press.

Wertheimer, A. (1997) *Inclusive Education: A Framework for Change. National and International Perspectives*. Bristol: CSIE.

Woolfolk, A. (2013) *Educational Psychology* (twelfth edition). London: Pearson.

Wright Mills, C. (1959) *The Sociological Imagination*. New York: Oxford University Press.

CHAPTER 9

THE SOCIAL CONSTRUCTION OF CHILDHOOD

Chapter Aims

This chapter will examine the concept of *the child* against the background of its social, cultural as well as biological context. There will be a focus on the shift in the notion of the child as an incomplete and unformed member of society to one of 'the child' as part of a social group in its own right with its own subject matter – *childhood*. There will also be an examination of the claim that we live in a child-centred society and a consideration of nineteenth-century children's literature as an example of transmission of culture, thus making an impact on the childhood experience. Foucault's (1980) theoretical overview of schooling, based on the 'Panopticon' (Long, 1977), will be used here to challenge the Enlightenment view of education as creating a liberated, rational and autonomous population by presenting the notion of schools as essentially places that act like prisons for children whose actions and behaviour are controlled and monitored very closely by those (adults) in authority.

Key words: childhood, life-cycle, life-course, socialisation, social control, child-centred, panopticism.

Introduction

Every now and again our common-sense beliefs about the world are subject to challenges that question our fundamental assumptions, often leaving our previous certainties in tatters. We can see this in the dramatic changes brought about by industrialisation and urbanisation in Europe during the eighteenth and nineteenth centuries (see Chapter 2) and the civil rights movement in the last century, which led to the increase in political, social and legal recognition for women, oppressed racial groups, those with alternative sexualities and those with impairments. That is not to say that there is a consensus in which everyone agrees on the merits or desirability of such changes or the enhanced status of these different groups. Nevertheless, the legal protection they have acquired and their enhanced civil and political rights afford them recognition as well as protection, which they did not have before. We can see this in the recent change in the law on same sex marriage, which came into force in England in March 2014. Although not everyone agrees with the changes in the law (Squire, 2014; Williams, 2014), with some claiming that it fundamentally ends the traditional notion of marriage, evidence shows (Park et al., 2010) that there is a growing level of tolerance towards same sex marriage in Britain. It could be argued that over the past century there has also been a dramatic change in the way children have been perceived as well as in the notion of *childhood* itself, but accompanied by a similar degree of scepticism from some as to the merits of the rights and benefits children have acquired during this period (Phillips, 1997; Postman, 1982).

The notion of the child

An interest in children as a distinct group is not new. As far back as 380 BCE Plato in the *Republic* wrote about the need for children to be educated according to their abilities and future occupations (Plato, 2007), and Aristotle emphasised the importance of instilling in children a strong sense of moral values, believing that they could not be trusted to think independently (Aristotle, 1985; Verharen, 2002). Indeed, philosophers have long pondered over the nature of 'the child' who, according to James et al. (1998), has in turn been viewed as burdened with the evil of 'original sin' and therefore in need of 'saving'; as an innocent corrupted by society – a view of the child proposed by Rousseau ([1762] 2009) in *Emile*; as a blank slate, such as in Locke's ([1693] 2007) idea of the child born with no categories of understanding or ability to reason and who is therefore infinitely malleable; as a naturally developing being going through specific stages to become a 'normal' adult (Piaget, 1954); and as the unconscious child of Freud (1953) and psychoanalytic theory, who is full of conflicting unconscious drives that must be resolved if the child is to become a well-adjusted adult. All these views of the child are pre-sociological according to James et al. (1998). By this they mean that none of them places the child in her or his social context – society, race, class or culture; however, they are the precursors of the subject of childhood as a distinct field of study.

Early sociological approaches to the study of childhood

Early sociology of childhood was very much based on determinist assumptions that the child is a product of society through the process of socialisation. Institutions such as the school and family are identified as agents of socialisation in which the child acquires the appropriate culture and values. This can be seen most clearly in the work of Talcott Parsons (1961), who identifies the family as the key institution in the process of primary socialisation. Children are rarely looked at as children with a focus primarily on the role of the institution doing the socialising. If children were looked at as a group it was usually in terms of socialisation 'gone wrong', for example, as deviants or criminal gangs. Such an approach has been criticised by Wrong (1961) for providing an 'oversocialised conception of man' by which he means that there was little or no examination of the world from the child's perspective as an active agent in the process of becoming an adult. Although early sociological attempts to deal with children were rather too generalised and determinist, they do mark what James and Prout (1997) describe as a newly emerging *paradigm*, which is beginning to put the child at the centre of childhood research. A paradigm shift refers to a new way of thinking about and conceptualising a particular issue or phenomenon (Kuhn, 1962). In this case it relates to a 'reconstruction' of how we see children and childhood. James and Prout (1997) are careful to stress that, although there is a move towards new ways of thinking about and understanding children, there has not been a complete break with the past in that children are still seen by many as subordinate and in need of adult interpretation.

A shifting paradigm

The period we call childhood is regarded by most of us as a *biological period* linked to the *life-cycle* in which we are born, develop, mature, age and die, bearing in mind, of course, that not everyone will pass through those stages due to premature death. While sociologists are interested in these biological processes and their influences on such issues as body image, self-concept and stereotyping, they would point out that biological age is not the only factor that determines the stages of people's lives. Indeed, each of these stages in the life-cycle is experienced differently around the world and at different times in each society. For example, a person who may be considered 'old and useless' in one society may be accorded high status in another. Hockey and James (1993) give various examples of societies where the signs of ageing such as dementia, grey hair and wrinkles are seen in a positive way. The Sherbro people of Sierra Leone, for instance, view the sometimes incomprehensible 'ramblings' of the elderly as evidence of communication with the dead ancestors of the tribe who are believed to play a key role in the fate of the community. In other words, there is no universally defined old age.

A universal child?

Similarly, there is no single experience of childhood, though the United Nations (UN) has attempted to create one through its Convention on the Rights of the Child (1989). In this declaration, which the UN expects will be adopted by all signatories, there is a definition of the economic, cultural, educational, civil and political rights of children, as well as an outline of the duties and responsibilities of governments and adults for the welfare of children (UNICEF, 2009). Article 12 of the Convention identifies the right of children to be able to express their views and for these views to be taken into consideration when decisions that affect them are made. Reality, however, is very far from this 'minority world' ideal of what childhood should be like. The term minority world refers to the more affluent developed industrial societies such as Western Europe, which, it is alleged by some, are attempting to impose their views and ideas on the majority world, which are the less developed countries of Africa, South East Asia and Latin America (Boyden, 1997). The countries of the majority world may be unable, for economic reasons, to end child labour (Article 32), or may have cultural practices involving children that they are unwilling to give up. Article 19 of the Convention, for example, states that 'any form of discipline involving violence is unacceptable'. Countries such as Britain have refused to ban the use of physical punishment by parents. In October 2008, the British Parliament voted against ending of the right of parents to 'reasonable chastisement' despite the fact that the British government has agreed to comply fully with all the articles of the Convention.

Thinking point 9.1

1. Read the 45 Articles of the United Nations Convention on the Rights of the Child (see reference list below).
2. Do you think that the UN is right in trying to create a universal concept of childhood?
3. What might be the problem with such a concept? For example, Article 1 of the Convention defines a child as anyone under the age of 18.

Social age

It is for these reasons that sociologists such as Ginn and Arber (1993) use the concept of social age, which is how one feels in relation to one's life experiences as part of an age group, rather than one's chronological age. A child soldier in one of the many regional conflicts around the world, for example, will behave in many ways like a person several years his or her senior, but may in some cases be no more than 9 or 10 years old. Views of age-appropriate behaviour are therefore socially constructed rather than based on some objective standard. This is not to say that the experiences of such children are seen as unproblematic, however, the age at which an individual or group can start to drink alcohol, smoke or work for a wage is not based purely on their ability to do such things, but also on cultural practices and traditions, and it is usually adults who decide what children are, or are not, allowed to do. What we also find is that these practices in terms of age change over time and vary from society to society.

To understand these differences in relation to age, sociologists refer to life-course rather than life-cycle. The latter is based on biological or chronological age and is particularly useful to medical practitioners and psychologists who are interested in processes such as language acquisition and puberty, which are relatively fixed in terms of timescale. Social age, on the other hand relates to processes that are more fluid and culturally dependent. This is not to downplay biological factors but to point out that they occur in a social context. In western societies such as Britain today it is common for children to try to look older than they are (Brooks, 2006; Madge, 2006; Postman, 1982). So, although they may not be prepared for adult roles and responsibilities, they may feel the pressure to develop the cultural and social characteristics of one who is. This rush towards adulthood tells us as much about the status of adults in Britain as it does about that of children. Indeed, while childhood and old age occupy positions of subordination and marginality in this country, adulthood represents a position of autonomy and power. However, although it may be the case that childhood and old age occupy positions of subordination to adults, we should bear in mind that adults are neither totally independent of children and the elderly, nor are children and the elderly completely dependent on adults. It is too easy to stereotype each group in this way when in reality each of them contains a diversity of experiences based on factors such as *social class, gender, ethnicity* and *disability*. To take one example, the UK Census of 2001 reveals that there were over 178,000 young carers in Britain, looking after other family members, both adults and children, for a variety of reasons such as mental illness, sickness and old age. The average age of these young carers was 12 years (Barnardo's, 2006).

Life-course, like age is socially constructed in that the ways in which different age groups are perceived varies over time and from society to society.
The factors that shape these perceptions are *social, political, historical, cultural* and *ideological* (Hockey and James, 2003). There has therefore been a
shift away from common-sense assumptions about childhood as primarily a
biological process in which the child is seen as a developing human in the
making, to one in which childhood is seen as much as a social construction
in which children are part of the process of constructing their own meanings
and understanding of the world. In addition, the notion of childhood cannot
be separated from issues of class, gender and ethnicity; there is no universal
experience of being a child.

Modern childhood

One of the defining features of modern childhood is the growth in the right of
children to be educated (Ariès, 1962). Indeed, part of the definition of the
western (minority) concept of childhood is an extended education. This is
derived from the Enlightenment view of education as a means of creating an
informed and rational population, which both liberates the human mind from
ignorance and superstition, and enables individuals to develop their full potential (Usher and Edwards, 1994). However, many post-Enlightenment philosophers
and sociologists (Adorno and Horkheimer, 1972; Foucault, 1970, 1972; Usher
and Edwards, 1994) take a more pessimistic view of the Enlightenment project
and the understanding of school as not only a place that offers education but
as a mechanism of control in the management of large groups of children with
the implementation of discipline strategies and instruction on how to behave.

Panopticism and social control in schools

According to Deacon (2006), who explores Foucault's theoretical overview of
education, schools have evolved as the chief mechanism of socialisation in
childhood, delivering not only a prescribed curriculum but acting as a training
ground for the need to manage growing populations; as such they concentrate
on specific areas including 'the implementation of discipline strategies; an
understanding of the apportionment of time; the management of sexuality; the
manipulation of bodies and the reconceptualisation of childhood' (Deacon,
2006: 181). In this way schools are understood as a disciplinary response to the
rapid changes in society and a rise in population. The reconceptualisation of
childhood is a powerful discourse that marks a shift from the need to protect

(Ariès, 1962) in the family, to the need to control and maintain surveillance in the school (Gore, 1998), including the indirect supervision of parents (Foucault, 1986) and society as a whole. Schools are noted as powerful spaces of state control exercising what Foucault (1980) calls 'epistemological power' – a power to take over the knowledge of individuals from individuals. This is made possible in the understanding of schools as prisons and the notion of confinement itself where surveillance, accumulated knowledge and segregation all ensure that the hidden curriculum of social control is the scaffold around which schooling is structured. Based on this rationale, it is critical to view schools as institutions where relations of power and knowledge connect. The education system is a prime example of government-imposed regimes such as monitoring attendance, testing and segregation by 'race' class and gender and also from adults (Perryman, 2006). Concepts such as social control, the hidden curriculum, class based ideologies, human capital and class based inequality all seem appropriate here as well as the more conventional concepts such as secondary socialisation, training, schools as sites for role allocation and effective social stratification. This is illustrated by Foucault's influential publication *Discipline and Punish: The Birth of the Prison* (1995) in which he confirms 'whenever one is dealing with a multiplicity of individuals on whom a task or a particular form of behaviour must be imposed, the panoptic schema may be used' (1995: 293). In this quote the reference made to the panoptic schema is based on Foucault's social theory of panopticism (1995), which was influenced by the work of the English philosopher and political radical Jeremy Bentham and his nineteenth-century prison reforms. Bentham (1791) argued in *The Panopticon* that the ideal prison would be structured in order to ensure that cells would be open and face a central tower where individuals in the cells do not interact with each other and are constantly confronted by the panoptic tower (pan – all; optic – seeing). The element of wraparound surveillance is located in the idea that individuals cannot see when there is a person in the tower; however, the belief that they could be watched at any moment is the element that secures their confinement. The transmission into a pedagogy of education is swift in that theoretically the 'Panopticon' functions successfully because it requires little actual observation; it is the psychological fear or threat of being observed that causes the observer (be it a prison inmate or a school pupil) to take it upon themselves to control their own behaviour. In the school context, pupils are socialised to internalise this fear by the surveillance gaze of teachers and the language of discipline; the interplay of power constrains and controls their behaviour; they become self-regulating in order to progress and succeed. Central to this ideology is the fact that surveillance is carried out by an invisible source reinforcing the omnipresent notion of school discipline and, ultimately, the removal of this burden from teachers. Based on this vision of schooling, childhood is noted as a time when social codes are embedded and understanding of rewards and sanction, responsibility and conformity (Gallagher, 2011) are transmitted via a powerful schooling culture.

Other postmodern examples of the surveillance gaze include CCTV, credit card use, internet use (Hope, 2005) and even the fact that gyms are designed with walls of mirrors to reinforce the notion that one is being watched and accordingly must amend one's behaviour (put in an energetic workout) in order to comply with societal ideas about the perfect body. The anxiety and distress caused by this form of surveillance is referred to as 'privacy harm' (Calo, 2012), and acknowledges the idea that fear changes behaviour and that schools, in order to be efficient, must operate on the basis of this rationale. To illustrate, Gallagher's (2010) ethnographic research based in a primary school in Scotland reports evidence of 'embodied docility', where surveillance is a feature of everyday life so that behaviour is monitored not just because children can be seen (by a teacher), but because they *might be seen*. This panoptic school ethos is extended to sounds, what Gallagher calls 'sonic surveillance', so that children are socialised to associate quiet behaviour with good work. In a further development, the panoptic school encourages children to become part of the surveillance of each other and also of teachers and adults in the classroom; in this sense the illusion of control is all-consuming as the surveillance gaze is so widely spread between so many willing participants. This final element is perhaps the most worrying in terms of contemporary discourses on child-centred schooling, teaching and learning as the inevitable influence of the panoptic ethos would be very challenging to overcome.

A child-centred society?

In order to examine the claim that we live in a child-centred society it is important to reflect on the legacy of history to consider how and if changes have taken place in our (western) conceptualisation of childhood. Additionally, it is critical to be mindful of the technological age we now live in and how this alone has acted as a catalyst in the erosion of childhood innocence. The historian Philippe Ariès (1962) has argued that childhood, as a separate stage of personal development, did not exist in early medieval times; instead children were depicted in art and literature as 'little adults', accordingly they dressed and worked as adults (Jordanova, 1987). However, the eighteenth century is notable for the change that took place when people began to understand children as inherently different from adults, paying attention to their vulnerability and sense of being impressionable and in need of protection and care from adults in general, very much in line with contemporary discourses on childhood.

A consequence of this shift was the notion of a 'new world of childhood' where adults were able to nurture affection and compassion for the childhood experience as reflected in the development of schools, toys, games and children's literature (Kramnick, 1983). The explosion of industrialisation and the era of expansion in the nineteenth century saw a dramatic and damaging change in how children were viewed: their physical and psychological welfare were not considered when empire building was so pressing. The hard, cold reality is that it was partly child labour in Britain that sustained economic progress during the industrial age (Humphries, 2011), the legacy of which has left an enduring impact.

Reading and viewing suggestion 9.1

The Children Who Built Victorian Britain Part 1

www.youtube.com/watch?v=87eVOpbcoVo

Watch this YouTube clip to provide a context, from the child's perspective, of the work and treatment they were subjected to before progressing onto the academic journal reader below.

Humphries, J. (2012) 'Childhood and child labour in the British industrial revolution', *Economic History Review*, 2: 1–27.

In this journal paper Professor Jane Humphries explores a revisionist history of child labour that takes account of an increase in the relative productivity of children as a result of mechanisation, new divisions of labour and family instability.

Shuttleworth (2010) provides an alternative lens through which to view childhood, using literature and literary texts suggesting that:

> Literary texts played a definitive role, opening up initially the internal spaces of the child mind, suggesting hitherto unsuspected depths of emotions and thought, and then responding to, qualifying, and questioning scientific and medical theories. Literary texts did not simply supply material for medical case studies ... they also helped frame the questions and categories of an emerging scientific field. (Shuttleworth, 2010: 362)

As a consequence, classical children's books not only captured the creative imaginations of children but also offered a compelling narrative supporting varied discourses on childhood. To illustrate, *Peter Pan* (1904) suggested that childhood should last forever, despite obvious dangers, in a blissful state of happiness; *The Chronicles of Narnia* (1950–56) championed the child hero myth alongside a powerful narrative of spirituality, the nature of God and eschatology; *The Hobbit* (1937) captured myth and adventure with an enduring message of seeking inner courage and strength; *The Wind in the Willows* (1908) reflects on the challenges of facing change through loveable animal characters; and finally, *Charlotte's Web* (1952) delivers the message of friendship and how our identity is formed through our relationships.

Children's literature provides a compelling insight into the political and cultural influences of the era and also acts as a vehicle for the transmission of culture to the next generation, therefore, it is important to consider the development of thinking on issues around 'race' and childhood in the context of a discussion of nineteenth-century children's literature; in particular on the rise of the orientalist (Said, 1978) mindset. As the British Empire changed, so did Britain's relationship to it, as noted in the representation of the exotic other in children's literature. As Said confirms 'nineteenth century writers were extraordinarily well aware of the fact of empire' (1978: 14). To illustrate, Lewis Carroll's fantasy classic *Alice in Wonderland* (1865) is an example of this transmission process. Alice, the very representation of Englishness, travels to fantasy lands occupied by unfamiliar beings living by strange rules that are a total contrast to her own social order. In a croquet match with the Queen of Hearts Alice concludes 'I don't think they play at all fairly, and they all quarrel so dreadfully one can't hear oneself speak – and they don't seem to have any rules in particular: at least, if there are, nobody attends to them' (Carroll, [1865] 2004: 97). The characters Alice interacts with are a potent indication of colonial discourse: they are savage, animal like and ugly, whereas Alice has classic features, blonde, white and angelic. This theme is a dominant strand, as Alice explores the unfamiliar 'Wonderland', so Britain navigates her fragile relationship with her colonies (Bivona, 1986) and the only coping mechanism in all this strangeness of new worlds, magical food and drink and interesting characters, is to emphasise her (British) sense of morality and nobility. This is the marker of the colonial ideology, as explored by the postcolonial critic Homi K. Bhabha (1994) in his influential study of culture, where the morals and social codes of the coloniser are imposed on the inferior and uncultured colonised in order to create balance.

In a further example Frances Hodgson Burnett's *The Secret Garden* (1911) tells the story of Mary Lennox, who starts the story as a sickly, ugly child, spoilt and unruly, a product of her environment in India, and ends the story as an English rose living in England having experienced a spectacular naturalisation through her interactions with varied characters and the discovery of a secret garden. Abandoned by her parents, Mary is cared for by natives with whom the way she conducts herself is a parallel to how the political reports (Freeman, 1907) reflect Britain conducts itself in India: 'Indian servants were commanded to do things, not asked. It was not the custom to say "Please" and "Thank you", and Mary had always slapped her Ayah in the face when she was angry.' The transformation of Mary is a central theme in the book; a lengthy process that is dependent on unlearning the corrupt behaviours of the colonies in the course of her travels. This point is reinforced as her transformation and her understanding of Britishness takes place in the garden, decorated only by roses and a robin and symbolic of the heart of England, the British countryside.

To conclude, this discussion of nineteenth-century literature as an example of how ideas about 'race' become part of a culture that is transmitted to children has included classic sources, however, they are by no means the exception, as illustrated by the work of Kutzer (2000). The emerging picture of a popular culture, framed by political and social changes in Britain, which shapes children's understanding of non-white people, is one of extremes, stereotypes and powerful misinformation, as Little (1947) concludes:

> that popular knowledge was pseudo-anthropological, and concerns the 'mental inferiority' of coloured people; the biological 'ill-effects' of racial crossing and a variety of other superstitions. It is in this cultural 'atmosphere' that most children in English society grow up. It is not surprising, therefore, that many of them absorb prejudicial ideas and notions concerning coloured people. (Little, 1947: 151)

Chapter summary

In this chapter the concept of *the child* was explored against the background of its social and biological context including a focus on the shift in the notion of the child as an unformed member of society, to one of the child as part of a social group in its own right with its own subject matter – childhood. Foucault's (1980) theoretical overview of schooling, based on the 'Panopticon' (Long, 1977) was used to unpack the notion of schools as spaces of social control for children whose actions and behaviour are monitored very closely by those (adults) in authority. Finally, the notion that we live in a child-centred society was considered in light of nineteenth-century children's literature as an example of transmission of culture that can make an impact on the childhood experience.

References

Adorno, T. and Horkheimer, M. (1972) *The Dialectic of the Enlightenment*. London: Verso.
Ariès, P. (1962) *Centuries of Childhood*. London: Jonathan Cape.

Aristotle, (1985) *Nicomachean Ethics*. Tr. T. Irwin. Indianapolis, IN: Hackett.

Barnardo's (2006) 'What we do'. Available at: www.barnardos.org.uk/what_we_do/our_projects/young_carers.htm (accessed 15 January 2015).

Bentham, J. (1791) *Panopticon; or, the Inspection-House*. Dublin and London: Printed at the Mews Gate.

Bhabha, H.K. (1994) *The Location of Culture*. New York: Routledge Classics.

Bivona, D. (1986) 'Alice the child-imperialist and the games of wonderland', *Nineteenth-Century Literature*, 41(2): 143.

Boyden, J. (1997) 'Childhood and policymakers: A comparative perspective on the globalisation of childhood', in A. James, and A. Prout (eds), *Constructing and Reconstructing Childhood: Contemporary Issues in the Sociological Study of Childhood*. London: Falmer.

Brooks, L. (2006) *The Story of Childhood: Growing Up in Modern Britain*. London: Bloomsbury Publishing.

Calo, M.R. (2012) 'The boundaries of privacy harm', *Indiana Law Journal*, 86(3): 1131–62.

Carroll, L. [1865] (2004) *Alice's Adventures in Wonderland and Through the Looking Glass and What Alice Found There*. New York: Barnes and Noble Classics.

Deacon, R. (2006) 'Michel Foucault on education: A preliminary theoretical overview', *South African Journal of Education*, 26(2): 177–87.

Foucault, M. (1970) *The Order of Things*. New York: Pantheon.

Foucault, M. (1972) *The Archaeology of Knowledge and the Discourse on Language*. London: Tavistock Publications.

Foucault, M. (1980) *Power/Knowledge: Selected Interviews and Other Writings 1972–1977*. New York: Pantheon.

Foucault, M. (1986) *Discipline and Punish: The Birth of the Prison*. Harmondsworth: Peregrine.

Foucault, M. (1995) *Discipline and Punish: The Birth of the Prison* (2nd Vintage Books). New York: Vintage Books.

Freeman, A.V. (1907) 'The alien question', *Westminster Review*, 167(5): 539.

Freud, S. (1953) *The Standard Edition of the Complete Psychological Works of Sigmund Freud*. London: Hogarth Press.

Gallagher, M. (2010) 'Are schools panoptic?' *Surveillance and Society*, 7(3/4): 262–72.

Gallagher, M. (2011) 'Sound, space and power in a primary school', *Social and Cultural Geography*, 12(1): 47–61.

Ginn, J. and Arber, S. (1993) 'Ageing and Cultural Stereotypes of Older Women', in J. Johnson and R. Slater (eds), *Ageing and Later Life*. London: Sage.

Gore, J. (1998) 'Disciplining bodies: On the continuity of power relations in pedagogy', in T. Popkewitz and M. Brennan (eds), *Foucault's Challenge: Discourse, Knowledge, and Power in Education*. New York: Teachers College.

Hockey, J. and James, A. (1993) *Growing up and Growing Old*. London: Sage.

Hockey, J. and James, A. (2003) *Social Identities across the Life Course*. Basingstoke: Palgrave Macmillan.

Hope, A. (2005) 'Panopticism, play and the resistance of surveillance: Case studies of the observation of student internet use in UK schools', *British Journal of Sociology of Education*, 26(3): 359–73.

Humphries, J. (2011) *Childhood and Child Labour in the British Industrial Revolution: Cambridge Studies in Economic History*. Cambridge: Cambridge University Press.

James, A. and Prout, A. (eds) (1997) *Constructing and Reconstructing Childhood: Contemporary Issues in the Sociological Study of Childhood*. London: Falmer.

James, A., Jenks, C. and Prout, A. (1998) *Theorising Childhood*. Cambridge: Polity Press.

Jordanova, L. (1987) 'Conceptualizing childhood in the eighteenth century: The problem of child labour', *British Journal of Eighteenth-Century Studies*, 10: 189–99.

Kramnick, I. (1983) 'Children's literature and bourgeois ideology: Observations on culture and industrial capitalism in the later eighteenth century', *Studies in Eighteenth-Century Culture*, 12: 11–44.

Kuhn, T.S. (1962) *The Structure of Scientific Revolutions*. Chicago, IL: University of Chicago Press.

Kutzer, M.D. (2000) *Empire's Children: Empire and Imperialism in Classic British Children's Books*. New York, NY: Garland Publishers.

Little, K.L. (1947) *Negroes in Britain: A Study in Race Relations in English Society*. London: Kegan Paul.

Locke, J. [1693] (2007) *Some Thoughts Concerning Education* (Including *Of the Conduct of the Understanding*, Dover Philosophical Classics). Edited by J.W. Adamson. Mineola, NY: Dover Publications.

Long, D. (1977) *Bentham on Liberty: Jeremy Bentham's Idea of Liberty in Relation to his Utilitarianism*. Toronto: University of Toronto Press.

Madge, N. (2006) *Children These Days*. Bristol: Policy Press.

Park, A., Phillips, M., Clery, E. and Curtice, J. (2010) *British Social Attitudes Survey 2010–2011 Exploring Labour's Legacy* – The 27th Report. London: Sage.

Parsons, T. (1961) 'The school class as a social system', in A.H. Halsey, J. Floud and C.A. Anderson (eds), *Education, Economy and Society*. New York: The Free Press.

Perryman, J. (2006) 'Panoptic performativity and school inspection regimes: Disciplinary mechanisms and life under special measures', *Journal of Education Policy*, 21(2): 147–61.

Phillips, M. (1997) *All Must Have Prizes*. London: Little Brown.

Piaget, J. (1954) *The Construction of Reality in the Child*. Tr. M. Cook. New York: Basic Books.

Plato (2007) [circ. 380 BCE] *The Republic*. Penguin Classics (second edition). Tr. Desmond Lee with an Introduction by Melissa Lane. London: Penguin.

Postman, N. (1982) *The Disappearance of Childhood*. New York: Delacorte Press.

Rousseau, J.-J. [1762] (2009) *Emile*. Tr. Barbara Foxley. Las Vegas, NV: IAP.

Said, E. (1978) *Orientalism*. New York: Vintage Books.

Shuttleworth, S. (2010) *The Mind of the Child: Child Development in Literature, Science and Medicine, 1840–1900*. Oxford: Oxford University Press.

Squire, N. (2014) 'Gay marriage a 'Trojan Horse' says Catholic cardinal', 11 November, *Daily Telegraph*. Available at: www.telegraph.co.uk/news/worldnews/europe/vaticancityandholysee/11223136/Gay-marriage-a-Trojan-horse-says-Catholic-cardinal.html (accessed 15 January 2015).

UNICEF (2009) 'A summary of the United Nations Convention on the Rights of the Child'. Available at: www.unicef.org.uk/Documents/Education-Documents/crc_sum mary_leaflet_2009.pdf?epslanguage=en (accessed 15 January 2015).

Usher, R. and Edwards, R. (1994) *Postmodernism and Education: Different Voices, Different Worlds*. London: Routledge.

Verharen, C. (2002) 'Philosophy's role in Afrocentric education', *Journal of Black Studies*, 32(3): 295–321.

Williams, S. (2014) 'Christian couple to take their stance on gay couples to the European Court of Human Rights', 23 March, *Wales Today*. Available at: www.walesonline.co.uk/ news/wales-news/christian-couple-take-stance-gay-6865011 (accessed 15 January 2015).

Wrong, D. (1961) 'The oversocialized conception of man in modern sociology', *American Sociological Review*, 26: 183–93.

CHAPTER 10

EDUCATION POLICY

Chapter Aims

This chapter aims to present an examination of education policy in England since 1945 when the Welfare State was established. It traces the key shifts in policy from a period of post-war consensus between the two main political parties in which equality of opportunity and meritocracy were key elements, and how during the Thatcher period a new set of priorities relating to the economy and efficiency came to dominate education policy and continue to do so.

Key words: policy, Welfare State, meritocracy, equality of opportunity, social mobility, post-war consensus, Great Debate, human capital, extrinsic and intrinsic purposes of education.

Introduction

What soon becomes clear in an examination of education policy in the UK since 1945 is the sheer number of policy documents, curriculum reports, teaching strategies and legislation produced by successive governments. As a consequence, it is extremely difficult to gain a comprehensive knowledge of the field given the quantity of information produced. In October 2013 The Department for Education website listed some 4,510 publications, which included 62 policy guidance documents covering 2011–2013 alone and 42 departmental advice documents for the same period. Clearly, no single book can do justice to this topic and it is even more problematic when covering it in a single chapter. Inevitably there will be a degree of selectivity regarding what is seen as relevant in terms of current policy debates.

A further point of significance is that the Department for Education is one of the biggest spending government departments and has experienced a real terms growth year on year since 1955–1956, reaching a peak of 6.2 per cent of national income between 2009 and 2010 (£90.5 billion) (Chowdry and Sibieta, 2011). Education is now seen by government as a key way of investing in *human capital* as a means of improving the nation's competitive edge in a growing world economy. The level of importance placed by politicians on Britain's international reputation in terms of education performance can be seen in their response to the publication of international data such as the Programme for International Student Attainment (PISA). The results for 2013, for example, which indicated that the performance of England's teenagers in maths, reading and science had stagnated since 2009, were met with a good deal of hand-wringing and accusations as to who should take the blame (PISA, 2013).

If we take account of public opinion, education consistently comes second only to health in the list of the British public's priorities for state spending (Park et al., 2010). By any standard of assessment the education system is a field of extremes of which much is expected by both government and the public.

Thinking point 10.1

1. Identify some of the events, policies, ideas and processes that may have had an impact on the education systems in England, Wales, Scotland or Northern Ireland over the past decade.
2. Are these global, local or national in origin?
3. What has been their impact?

Global processes

It is becoming increasingly apparent that education policy is influenced by global processes and trends, and that the economy is the key priority for education policy making in Britain (Ball, 2008, 2013). For example, in their report *University of the Future,* Ernst and Young (2012) identify the potential future expansion of the emerging economies of the Far East, Latin America and South Asia, and what this means for the global market in education. The report suggests that the British higher education sector is in a strong position to take advantage of the situation, given its high reputation globally. However, it predicts that the existing model of predominantly state-funded higher education with a minority of independent private sector providers is likely to change, with private companies using their commercial expertise and networks to create new and more flexible higher educational products either on their own or in partnership with existing traditional providers. We are, in the opinion of the Ernst and Young report, on the cusp of a new era in education.

Key themes since 1945

In any assessment of post-war education policy a number of key periods can be identified that have thrown up significant developments and fundamental debates. Between 1945 and 1979 a post-war consensus existed amongst the political parties in which welfare policy generally and education in particular was based on a social democratic agenda featuring such concepts as *meritocracy*, *social mobility* and *equality of opportunity*. These terms relate to a belief that education could be used as a means of equalising a very divided society in which the privileged middle and upper classes had almost exclusive access to secondary and higher education. In the words of the eminent English historian R.H. Tawney (1931): 'The hereditary curse of the English Education system is its organisation on the basis of class'.

During the 1970s, however, there was a collapse of this consensus and a growing debate about what the priorities of the education system should be. The New Right was already carrying out a lively debate in the form of a series of articles by right wing thinkers such as Rhodes Boyson (Cox and Boyson, 1975) and Keith Joseph (1975). They were highly critical of the move away from selection in the post-war period and what they saw as the excessive involvement of the state in directing education policy in terms of equality of opportunity, which they saw as an attack on Britain's educational 'crown jewels', the public schools, grammar schools and the traditional academic curriculum. Ironically, it was a Labour Prime Minister, James Callaghan, who publicly opened the debate in 1976 when he suggested that Britain was falling behind other industrial societies because the education system was not providing the skills needed for an increasingly complex global economy. This 'Great Debate' resulted in a new discourse in education policy that has come to dominate the agenda on education ever since.

The dawn of a new era

In 1945 Britain embarked on a new kind of politics and society: one based on a social democratic agenda in which all citizens would be part of a 'New Jerusalem', in other words, a new promised land. Such ideas had been mooted during the nineteenth century as we have seen in Chapter 1. In England and France, for example, there was division on the political left between those who hoped for a democratically elected socialist government and those who suggested that only a proletarian (workers') revolution could overthrow the political and economic elites who refused to share power and wealth created in the new industrial era with the emerging working class. Indeed, Durkheim spent much of his academic life trying to provide an alternative to socialism and revolutionary change. In this instance Britain had come up with its own democratically elected socialist government without the bloodshed that so many in the establishment feared. This was no small feat given the experiences of those countries such as China and Russia that had witnessed the terrible destruction of life and property during their socialist revolutions in the first half of the twentieth century.

The post-war agreement

What the British electorate voted for in 1945, particularly the British working classes who constituted the majority of the population at the time, was a more egalitarian and democratic society, in which the privilege of birth and wealth would no longer determine a person's future. It became known as Labour's social democratic agenda, and was even embraced by the Conservatives during the 1960s and 1970s, hence the term 'political consensus'. This involved a 'cradle to grave' approach to health, education, unemployment and retirement, paid for by general taxation and a system of social insurance into which everyone contributed. Such a system was not based on the principle that one would expect to receive from the Welfare State as much as one put into it. Instead, it was based on the idea that everyone received what they needed and that the fortunate members of society in terms of educational achievement and occupational rewards, that is, the wealthy, would probably put more into the system than they took out. There was also a policy of full employment, which, together with free education from 5 to 15 (later 16), would ensure a highly skilled and educated workforce and the allocation of positions and employment based on merit (Young, 1958). In addition, the state took control and ownership of the key national industries: energy, steel, coal, transport and communications.

This is the programme on which Labour won the 1945 general election and the main reason why Winston Churchill's Conservative Party, which had no alternative to offer the returning soldiers after the war, lost. Labour offered a new and seemingly fairer society and a Welfare State. For those of us who were not alive at the time it is hard to imagine Britain in the immediate aftermath of the Second World War. Not only was there wide-scale destruction caused by bombing, but there was also the huge class divide in education alluded to by Tawney in 1931, the squalor caused by poor housing and the massive health divide that was a product of these poor living conditions and the lack of a proper health service. For the duration of the war there was a Welfare State of sorts in which ordinary people did not have to pay for education or health care, but the end of the war threatened an end to this.

Thinking point 10.2

1. How would you have voted in 1945 if you were an ordinary soldier returning home to your family after the war?
2. Why do you think many of the middle and upper classes might have feared a Labour government?
3. In a Welfare State why should citizens not expect to receive as much if not more from the system than they put into it?

However, despite this popular vote for socialism the programme itself was based on weak foundations. Economically, Britain was very poor after the years of war and when in 1951 the government decided to re-arm and to build the atomic bomb, there was a corresponding reduction in the funding available for the health service, welfare and education reforms. In addition, critics of the new welfare system on the left (Miliband, 1969) claimed that the main levers of government and the media, parliament, the civil service, central government and the judiciary as well as the press remained in the hands of an economic and political elite that, according to Ralph Miliband (1969), was unlikely to countenance the collapse of capitalism in Britain. He suggested that even those politicians from non-elite working class backgrounds who manage to make it into government tend ultimately to be inculcated into the values of the elite and become part of the establishment. In fact, the Labour leadership at the time, Clement Atlee and Hugh Gaitskell who were both the products of the public school and Oxbridge systems, according to Tony Benn (1994), one of the more radical senior Labour politicians from an upper class background, were reluctant to abolish the grammar schools and public schools, which he suggested would have been necessary if there was to be a real change to the education system.

The tripartite system

At that time the ideas of Cyril Burt (see Chapter 8) still had a great deal of influence on official educational thinking and they played a key role in the conclusions of the 1943 Norwood Report, which was responsible for the design of the post-war education system. There was an implicit assumption within the report of the existence of a limited pool of ability in the population and that such talent could be identified at 11 by which age, Burt suggested, children's intelligence is fixed and at which point it would be convenient to divide them. Hence the establishment of a tripartite school system made up of grammar schools for the academically gifted, and secondary moderns and technical high schools for those demonstrating less academic talent. The selection process was administered through the supposedly objective measure of academic ability known as the '11-plus'. Despite the notional parity of esteem between these three types of school, the grammar schools with their academic curriculum were held up as the model against which all state education was to be judged. As we saw in Chapter 1, when philosophers of the time such as R.S. Peters (1966) referred to what education is and what it means to be an 'educated person', they were usually referring to the academic education provided by grammar schools and the kinds of pupils they produced.

A wastage of talent?

In addition to the myth of parity of esteem (Banks, 1955) it soon became evident that grammar schools were better resourced than the other types of school and that recruitment to the grammar schools tended to be from the more affluent groups in society. Evidence such as the Early Leaving Report (Ministry of Education, 1954) showed that working class pupils (Registrar General's Socio Economic Classes 4 and 5) gained only half as many grammar school places as might be expected in terms of their proportion of the population. This would not have been an issue if indeed the selection of children at 11 was based on reliable scientific assumptions and an effective selection system. As we have seen in previous chapters Burt's notion of the heritability of intelligence was highly flawed and made little allowance for late developers. For example, children attending secondary moderns and technical high schools were denied the right to enter for public examinations. When the Certificate of Secondary Education (CSE) was introduced in 1965 it was considered a distinctly second rate qualification for which mainly working class children were entered (Smith and Tomlinson, 1989). Moreover, since access to higher education was becoming increasingly based on public examinations this placed children from more modest backgrounds at an even greater disadvantage. It is no surprise then that the majority of working class children left school as soon as they could at 15. In 1959 the Crowther Report referred to this as a 'wastage of talent' (Ministry of Education, 1959).

The system as it stood was clearly not promoting equality of opportunity and was letting down a generation of young working class pupils. Goldthorpe (1980) demonstrated that although there was a greater amount of social mobility in England for those born between 1938 and 1947 compared with those born between 1908 and 1917, the chances of a boy from a professional middle class family (doctor, lawyer, accountant, teacher) remaining in the class of his parents was four times greater than the chance of a boy from a working class background (unskilled, semi-skilled, skilled manual occupation) reaching the professional classes. The political debate regarding this issue and the growing acknowledgement by politicians of both main parties of the need to educate more young people to a higher level, led to a huge expansion of higher education during the 1960s. What had not been resolved, however, was how to ensure that the potential talents of working class pupils were not wasted but instead had a much fairer chance of being nurtured and developed (Committee on Higher Education, 1963 (Robbins Report)).

English fudge

In the 1960s both Labour and the Conservatives flirted with the idea of a comprehensive system, though generally speaking Conservative politicians were much less enthusiastic, seeing it as a threat to the grammar schools and the public schools. In the end neither party acted with conviction so the result was a traditional English fudge, which resulted in a mixture of comprehensive and tripartite systems. The Labour leadership had always tended to be rather equivocal about creating a comprehensive system of education. Tony Benn (1994) reflects in his diaries that even though *comprehensivisation* had become official Labour policy by the early 1950s Hugh Gaitskell, the Labour leader at the time, still saw selection as the preferred policy for transfer to secondary school. His successor Harold Wilson is alleged to have stated that grammar schools would be abolished 'over my dead body' (Pimlott, 1992: 512), which might explain why in 1965 the Labour government issued circular 10/65 'requesting' local education authorities to submit plans for the implementation of a comprehensive system rather than requiring them to do so. It seemed that the leaders of both main parties were torn between the pressure to create a fairer and more open education system and a desire to retain the traditional education of the past, from which so many of them had benefited.

A 'comprehensive failure'

When the comprehensive system was introduced by Labour during the 1960s it became the focus of those who saw in comprehensive schools all that is bad in the English education system. The writers of the *Black Papers* (Cox and Boyson, 1975) began painting a bleak and highly tendentious picture of schooling in England (Tomlinson, 2005). The tone of these accounts amount to a 'discourse of derision' (Kenway, cited in Ball, 2013: 104), which focuses on extreme and negative images of public service and welfare with the intention of using them to discredit the whole system. In an interview with Stephen Ball (Ball, 2013) in the late 1980s Keith Joseph talks of his unabashed hatred for the state system of education in England, which he, as Secretary of State had been in charge of in the period 1981–1986. These right wing thinkers condemned what they viewed as the falling standards of teaching, declining respect for authority amongst young people, the danger of pupils being indoctrinated by left wing teachers and profligate local authorities led by left wing councils. In addition, there was a warning of the threat to society posed by those intellectually unsuited to higher education gaining access to it through social engineering advocated by those on the left (Cox and Boyson, 1975). Joseph (1974) claimed that this was upsetting the natural order of things; only a small minority of the population was seen as suited to a university education.

These ideas have been reiterated more recently by London Mayor and leading Conservative Boris Johnson when he gave the Margaret Thatcher lecture in 2013 at the Centre for Policy Studies, the organisation set up by Keith Joseph in 1975 to promote neoliberal ideas and policies (Johnson, 2013). In the speech Johnson acclaims the virtues of greed in encouraging competition and wealth, as well as of the market in promoting human progress rather than a reliance on the state to do so. He suggests that because we are all born with a given amount of intelligence and that as only 2 per cent of humanity has an IQ of 130 or above, inequalities of income, wealth and influence are natural and essential, and that it is these more successful individuals who should lead society. Moreover, he speaks of the virtues of charitable giving by the wealthy rather than taxing them to support the poorer and less intelligent members of society, those with an IQ of 85 or below, who, according to Johnson, make up about 16 per cent of the population.

It could be suggested that in Johnson, the classically trained graduate of Eton and Oxford, we can see the modern day incarnation of the nineteenth-century Victorian upper class gentleman who takes the Platonic view of justice (see Chapter 1) as a state in which everyone knows their place and where the privilege of a higher education should be reserved only for the most intelligent, who, also knowing their place, help those less fortunate than themselves through philanthropic giving. To disturb this natural order can only lead to social chaos according to this view (see Table 10.1 below for a summary of neoliberal ideas).

Table 10.1 Left versus Right

Democratic socialism	New Right/neoliberalism
• *State ownership* of the key parts (*commanding heights*) of the economy such as transport, energy (oil, coal, power stations), steel and other key industries (e.g. ship building).	• A challenge to the welfare state.
• The creation of a *fairer society* through a comprehensive welfare system (free health care and education, public housing) as well as equal opportunities for all in education.	• To *reduce public spending* on welfare in order to be able to *cut taxes* and enable businesses to invest their profits, as well as to *reduce the dependency* of the public on benefits.
• High public spending on these services based on the principle of a *progressive system of taxation.*	• To subject public services to *market competition* in order to increase their 'efficiency'.
• To counter the worst of the effects of market capitalism such as cyclical unemployment, low wages and their effects.	• That educational institutions should become more like private businesses responding to the needs of the *market* and their customers through *competition.*
• A system to be won through democratic means.	• To *reduce the power of the trade unions*, which were believed to be *reducing the efficiency* of (British) industry through industrial action and *restrictive practices.*

Viewing suggestion 10.1

Watch Boris Johnson's 2013 Margaret Thatcher Lecture at the Centre for Policy Studies:

www.youtube.com/watch?v=Dzlgrnr1ZB0

Identify the key points he makes that have direct or indirect implications for education policy.

The period of radical student activity during the 1960s and 1970s was evidence enough for those who feared Labour's social democratic programme. One of the first acts of Margaret Thatcher when she became Education Minister in 1970 was to issue Circular 10/70, which effectively suspended Circular 10/65. Thatcher, educated at Kesteven and Grantham Girls' (Grammar) School, and Oxford, was determined to keep the system of selection and grammar schools. Her plans were interrupted, but only temporarily, when in October 1974 Labour won by a narrow margin the second general election of that year.

The breakdown in the consensus

Under the Labour government of 1974–1979 there was another effort to introduce a non-selective secondary education system in the form of the 1976 Education Act. This, however, was the last serious attempt by the party to do so. There had been a shift of focus away from inequality of opportunity and social mobility to one of educational standards, human capital, economic competitiveness and concerns about increasing welfare spending.

This shift of emphasis was already evident as far back as 1957 when the 'One Nation' Conservative Prime Minister Harold Macmillan stated in a speech that the people of Britain 'had never had it so good', referring to the growing post-war prosperity of the nation. One Nation Conservatives were the dominant wing of the Conservative Party at the time. They enabled the post-war consensus to exist by supporting a significant number of Labour policies. Many Conservative politicians such as Harold Macmillan and Edward Heath had grown up in the interwar period and witnessed the terrible effects of the Great Depression that ruined the lives of many. High levels of unemployment and deprivation were still strong in their memories and resulted in their support for the ideas of a mixed economy as a way of softening the harsher effects of free market capitalism. However, as Macmillan had suggested, the country was becoming prosperous and, though still fragile, the economy was creating undreamt of prosperity. Nevertheless, the One Nation position of the Conservative leadership was slowly being challenged by the more radical free market neoliberalism of Keith Joseph and Margaret Thatcher, who viewed the increasing role of the state with growing concern.

The rediscovery of poverty

Some Conservative politicians and political thinkers at the time believed that the Welfare State had done its job and was outgrowing its usefulness. The cost of free universal education, health care and other benefits was, in their opinion, spiralling out of control and stifling individual responsibility. Poverty no longer existed as shown by Rowntree (Rowntree, 1901; Rowntree and Lavers, 1951), whose large-scale surveys on living standards in York since 1901 revealed that poverty had fallen from 33 per cent of the population of that city in 1899 to 18 per cent in 1936 and to only 1.5 per cent in 1950. The conclusion many people drew from this research was that poverty in England had been defeated. So, when in 1965 Abel-Smith and Townsend suggested that 14.2 per cent of the population, including 2.2 million children were living on the margins of poverty in 1960, it was greeted with incredulity by many politicians, especially those on the political right. They suggested that it was preposterous to claim that what Abel-Smith and Townsend had found was anything other than inequality (Moore, 1989). As Rowntree had shown, only a tiny fraction of the population was earning poverty-level wages and the assumption was that the Welfare State would provide a safety net for them.

Educational Priority Areas

While those on the right were inclined to see the poorer educational performance of the working class as resulting from their lower intelligence and inappropriate lifestyles (Cox and Dyson, 1969), those on the moderate left believed it was possible to 'compensate' for the poorer home environments of working class families with more targeted state spending on the poorest areas of the country (Halsey, 1972). In the Labour leadership this position was seen as more palatable than that of the radical left, which advocated a greater degree of income equality. What was becoming evident is that although the Welfare State established in 1945 had alleviated the worst effects of the class inequalities in Britain that had resulted from unequal income distribution, there did not seem to be a significant shift of income from the top earners towards the bottom nor indeed any change in the rate of social mobility upwards from amongst the working class (Goldthorpe, 1980). Atkinson (1983) examined the trends in income distribution between 1948 and 1979 and found that although the top 10 per cent of earners saw a 3.7 per cent fall in their income after income tax from 27.1 per cent of total income in 1948 to 23.4 per cent in 1979, the poorest 30 per cent of the population actually experienced a fall in their share of income after tax from 14.6 per cent to 12.1 per cent during the same period. The main beneficiaries were in fact the middle 60 per cent.

However, rather than address the issue of income inequality, Labour began to place extra resources in parts of the country designated as Educational Priority Areas (EPAs); the assumption being that the reason for the underperformance of working class children was their unfavourable home conditions. The Labour Education Secretary Tony Crosland had adopted the recommendations of the Plowden Report of 1967 (DES, 1967), which suggested that extra resources should be centred on the schools and communities of the poorest parts of the UK in order to help improve the educational environment of the children in these areas.

The lack of any discernible improvement in the educational performance of the children in these EPAs, however, triggered a debate about whether it is appropriate to apply a deficit model to working class families. For those on the right such as Cox and Dyson (1969) the results of the programme were confirmation of the cultural deprivation of the working classes and the inability of such families to effectively socialise their children. Those on the left were very critical of the assumption that the problem lay with the victims of poverty and that working class culture is somehow deficient (Keddie, 1973), or that a small-scale temporary allocation of extra resources could make a real difference to those living in poverty. A.H. Halsey, the sociologist who supervised the EPA programme for Tony Crosland, was critical of the limited funding and lack of long-term strategy. The Plowden Report had recommended that 3,000 schools be involved, but in the end only about 150 benefited from the extra resources. To have had any real impact, he suggested that the policy should have been more sustained and widespread (Halsey, 1972). In addition, he acknowledged that a structural approach would be needed, involving a more equitable distribution of income. However, neither Conservative nor Labour governments were prepared to take such radical measures.

This debate continues today as we can see from the 2013 speech by Boris Johnson, which is essentially a response to the claims of those such as Wilkinson and Pickett (2009), who suggest that it is only in societies that are more equal in terms of income distribution that all members of society do better in terms of a wide range of social measures, such as education, including those at the top of the income scale.

The shift in educational priorities

Both Labour and Conservative governments, however, were beginning to have little time for sociologists and their claim that it was the system which had let 'ordinary kids' down. The political climate was changing and politicians were starting to focus their attention away from issues of inequality and onto wider economic problems. In the 1960s and 1970s Britain seemed to lurch from one economic crisis to another and in comparison to most of its foreign competitors economic growth was poor (Walker, 1987). The Labour government under Callaghan (1976–1979) began to fear that Britain's economic decline was partly due to the lack of emphasis in schools on the vocational skills needed by a competitive modern economy. What Callaghan did in his Ruskin speech of 1976 was to identify some of the key themes that have dominated the education policy agenda ever since. In particular, he identified what he saw as the need for the education system to prepare young people for their role in the economy as well as their place in society. Resorting perhaps to a discourse of derision, he pointed an accusing finger at teachers for, in his view, failing to teach children basic skills of literacy and numeracy and for failing to implement curricula that were fit for purpose. The following year, however, the education Green Paper *Education in Schools* (DES, 1977) reported that there was in fact no evidence of a fall in standards in schools. Callaghan had echoed ideas already articulated by those on the right in forums such as the Centre for Policy Studies, but what was unusual is the fact that they had been voiced by a senior Labour politician. Although Callaghan did have his supporters in the form of his Education Secretary Shirley Williams, those on the left of the party such as Tony Benn and Neil Kinnock were dismayed by what they heard, and these divisions are possibly why the Labour government did very little to act on these ideas during the remainder of its time in office.

The neoliberal revolution

With the election of the Conservatives in 1979 many of the ideas contained in the *Black Papers* were brought to life and there began a period of radical social and economic reform that severely divided the nation. Thatcherism placed great demands on the country, and the legacy of Thatcher's rule is such that when she died in 2013, alongside the mourning of her supporters there was an unsettling level of celebration amongst her detractors.

The Conservative government set about immediately reforming the economy and public sector driven by the conviction that the British public had become too dependent on the Welfare State and that the trade unions, including the teaching unions, had become too powerful. Thatcher's government embarked on a programme to reduce public spending on welfare in order to be able to cut taxes and enable businesses to invest their profits, as well as to reduce what she saw as the dependency of the British public on benefits. In addition, she subjected public services to market competition with the intention of increasing their efficiency. Keith Joseph, who had professed his hatred for state education, was a prime mover in suggesting that educational institutions should become more like private businesses responding to the needs of the market and their customers through competition. This market was supposed to provide choice by increasing the types of schools available enabling parents to choose where to send their children, rather than being allocated a school by their LEA (Ball, 2013).

Although Joseph, as Education Secretary between 1981 and 1986, carried out few actual reforms during this period, he was responsible for much of the architecture that subsequently brought about a quasi-market in education in which market mechanisms would be applied to how schools operated enabling a greater involvement by the private sector in state education. Ball (2013) identifies two periods during the 18 years of Conservative government between 1979 and 1997. The first was a period of cuts to public expenditure and the privatisation of many of the nationally owned industries. This included telecommunications (British Telecom privatised in 1984), transport (the National Bus Company privatised in 1985) and steel production (British Steel Corporation privatised in 1988). In housing there was the mass disposal of council houses during the 1980s under the right to buy scheme. It also involved the deregulation of the trading system of the City of London. In education the 1980 Education Act promoted the role of the private sector through the Assisted Places Scheme, which was intended to provide places for able children from modest backgrounds with state grants to attend private schools. However, as Edwards et al. (1989) found, most of the children who benefited from the scheme were actually from middle class families which had fallen on hard times.

In terms of the government's desire to cut spending on education, it is estimated that between 1981 and 1987, as a proportion of gross domestic product (GDP) this fell from 5.5 per cent to 4.8 per cent (Tomlinson, 2005). Ball's second period from the late 1980s to 1997 was characterised by the introduction of new structures and systems of delivering education, which was to be achieved primarily through the Education Reform Act of 1988. This would effectively take education out of the hands of teachers and local authorities and put it under the control of schools themselves and central government. Local Management of Schools (LMS) was to give schools the freedom to control their budgets, and the National Curriculum enabled the government to control what was taught in schools and to regularly monitor this through a new inspection regime administered by the Office for Standards in Education (Ofsted) that was established in 1992. Ironically, most of these structural and curriculum changes introduced by the Conservatives during this period actually increased central government control of education, which was the very thing that right wing thinkers such as Joseph had been campaigning against in the *Black Papers*.

Tackling the teachers

More clearly in line with the thinking which informed the *Black Papers*, Education Secretaries starting from Keith Joseph in the 1980s to John Patten in the 1990s viewed the teaching profession as the main reason for what was seen as a fall in standards and as being the upholders of an inefficient and outdated state education system. At the same time, however, teaching according to Joseph, had become a politicised profession that was prone to adopt too many progressive methods of teaching. He believed that training in critical disciplines such as philosophy and sociology was unnecessary. He viewed teaching as more of a technical occupation transmitting basic skills and traditional religious, moral and national values rather than as a creative and reflective profession. It would seem that teachers were suspected of being at once both too progressive and too conservative.

In order to deal with this perceived threat Joseph started by reforming teacher training and reducing the role of teachers in curricular matters by abolishing organisations such as the Schools Council in 1982. In 1984 The Council for the Accreditation of Teachers was set up to review teacher training policy and to reduce the independence of universities and other higher education institutions to develop their own teacher training courses. What seems to come across from this position is the traditional Platonic view that philosophy as well as sociology and the other foundation subjects of many education studies programmes today should only be taught to those privileged few who have been chosen to lead the nation and that in the hands of others it could become a dangerous thing.

In 1987 Kenneth Baker, who had replaced Keith Joseph as Education Secretary the year before, abolished teachers' rights to negotiate their pay by passing the Teachers' Pay and Conditions Act. If these reforms were aimed at reducing the influence and power of teachers, then Kenneth Baker began to lay the foundations for what the Ernst and Young report of 2012 describe as a new era of education. The Education Reform Act of 1988 introduced the main mechanisms designed to promote competition between schools through diversity, parental choice, league tables, per capita funding where schools are allocated funds on the basis of recruitment and freedom of access to information about the performance of schools through a Parents' Charter. Putting the power to choose in the hands of parents rather than local authorities was a key strategy in the government's policy of marketisation. This could only be effective if there was a choice not only of school but also the type of school available, hence the establishment of grant maintained (GM) schools, which were financed by central government and run by their governing bodies independently of local education authorities; City Technology Colleges (CTCs), the forerunners of academies, which were sponsored by businesses and which offered a more vocational education; and a variety of faith schools. In principle the choice was there but in practice the evidence shows that the middle class parents have been better able to use and manipulate the system to their advantage (Ball et al., 1996).

The curriculum

The curriculum became segregated through the establishment of an academic National Curriculum, which was based on the traditional hierarchical division of subjects, and a new vocational curriculum, which together effectively revived the academic–vocational divide. The 'new vocationalism' was promoted by what Whiteside et al. (1992) describe as a 'loose alliance' of politicians, trades unionists, business people and civil servants who wanted to make the education system more responsive to the needs of the economy. Under the new National Council for Vocational Qualifications set up in 1986 a system of National Vocational Qualifications (NVQs) was established relating to groups of occupations including construction, health care and childcare, and these were delivered by some schools and further education colleges. These qualifications even provided entry routes to higher education. However, the system suffered from the traditional English prejudice against vocational education, with employers and universities preferring academic over vocational qualifications. Children attending schools with traditional academic curricula such as the public schools and grammar schools were consequently advantaged when it came to university application. Critics on the left such as Dan Finn (1987) saw the new vocationalism as merely a way of keeping young people off the unemployment register and as a source of cheap labour because most of the programmes included on-the-job training for which the trainees usually received no pay. Cohen (1984) went so far as to claim that schemes such as Youth Training actually deskilled the workforce because most employees tended to use youth trainees to do mundane tasks rather than provide proper training.

Testing, testing

It is during this period of Conservative government that testing became an increasing part of the experience of children in English schools. However, it seems that the regular testing and assessment of children was in fact as much about the monitoring and accountability of teachers as the assessment of children. Although the Task Group on Assessment and Testing (TGAT) set up to implement the assessment regime for the National Curriculum recommended that the new standard assessment tasks (SATs) be administered as just one element in a process that should involve teacher assessments and be primarily *formative* in nature, that is, as means of supporting children's learning, the government chose instead to focus more on the *summative* nature of testing, which relates to the summing up of what has been learnt and a level of attainment. Such summative information provides the data for school league tables, which parents now take for granted and which the government uses to identify 'failing' schools. Children's education in England, therefore, is becoming outcome-driven rather than process-led. High stakes testing is the primary means whereby governments measure educational performance of pupils, teachers and schools alongside a system of inspection established in 1992 through Ofsted.

Such an emphasis on summative assessment derived from a narrow range of data has been seen as problematic by some experts in the field (Alexander, 2009).

Because of the pressure put on schools to perform well in formal testing there is a tendency to 'teach to the test' at the expense of a varied and stimulating learning experience. In addition, there are periods of intense pressure put on primary pupils in England who 'are tested more frequently and at an earlier age than in many other countries' (Alexander, 2009: 324). Experts and politicians tend to have very different ideas of what education is for, with the *extrinsic* purposes, favoured by government, taking precedence over the *intrinsic* priority, which is more likely to be advocated by educationalists. The emphasis now seems to be on education as a means to serve the nation and, it could be said, political and economic ends rather than just being a worthwhile thing in itself.

Thinking point 10.3

Philosophers have debated the purpose of education for centuries. This is a fundamental question that results in divided opinion. What are the main views on the purpose of education? Do you think education should serve a particular purpose or purposes?

New Labour 1997–2010

Most comparisons between New Labour and the previous Conservative government suggest that there was a good deal of continuity as well as change (Ball, 2013; Tomlinson, 2005). Although Labour was initially critical of the Conservative government's policies when in opposition, by the mid-1990s under the leadership of Tony Blair, Labour began to adopt the language of neoliberal reform summed up in what seemed to be Blair's favourite word: modernisation. In order to become electable, Labour had to appeal to a growing middle class resulting from the decline of traditional industries such as steel making, coal mining and engineering during the 1970s and 1980s and the subsequent growth in service sector jobs. Labour had, in effect stolen many of the Conservative Party's clothes. From 1997 it seemed like business as usual. There was continuation and indeed an increase in the marketisation of education through further competition, with an added emphasis on making the market work properly (Labour Party, 1992), a greater focus on standards through enhanced performance monitoring, as well as increasing choice of schools through the encouragement of faith communities to set up their own schools and the introduction of academies, which are independent self-governing schools sponsored by faith organisations, business or other voluntary bodies with the right to decide their own policy regarding staffing and which have no obligation to follow the national curriculum.

Social justice

These policies were part of the modernisation agenda followed by Tony Blair and Gordon Brown, who took over as Prime Minister in 2008. However, Blair made the claim that he did not want to 'run a Tory economy with a bit of compassion' (Blair, 1994), claiming that New Labour did not just stand for standards and modernisation but also for social justice, which he suggested that the Conservatives had neglected. Under New Labour there was a clear agenda to enable certain groups who were believed to have been marginalised by 18 years of Conservative rule to have a chance to engage more fully in society through greater educational opportunities. This included those on benefits, the disabled and certain minority ethnic groups.

When Labour came to power in 1997, it commissioned the Macpherson Inquiry into the killing of the Black teenager, Stephen Lawrence, who was murdered by a white racist gang. This is the first time a British government had acknowledged the problem of institutional racism in British public institutions, such as the police and schools, and this led to the passing of the Race Relations (Amendment) Act of 2000, which obliged all public bodies, including schools, to prevent racial discrimination and promote racial equality. In 1998 the government set up the Social Exclusion Unit to deal with the issue of social inequality to tackle such things as the disproportionate number of Black pupils excluded from schools in England. Official estimates showed that during the late 1990s children with special needs and African-Caribbean boys were six times more likely to be excluded than other groups (Denscombe, 1999). Also, through policies such as the New Deal for 18–24 year olds, which provided subsidised employment for the long-term unemployed and the Sure Start Programme, designed to help the parents and young children from poor families through educational, health and other professional support, New Labour invested heavily in some of the poorest and most excluded groups in society. The results of such programmes were mixed (Tomlinson, 2005), but there does seem to have been a commitment to tackle some of the divisions that had widened under the previous Conservative government.

A Third Way

New Labour's education policy needs to be examined in the context of its wider social and economic position, which was greatly influenced by what has come to be known as the Third Way (Giddens, 1998). This was an attempt to steer an alternative path between the old Labour position of high welfare spending and low levels of accountability over such spending, which had made Labour virtually unelectable during the 1980s, and the New Right approach of the Thatcher and Major governments, which tended to ignore the effects on communities of neoliberal economic policies such as the closure of coal pits, the privatisation of industries such as steel or the lack of effective welfare support and training during the high levels of unemployment. However, with the carrot of opportunity New Labour provided to marginalised groups, there were the sticks of responsibility and accountability. Those receiving support and who were deemed to have abused it were expected to take responsibility for their actions or inactivity. For example, parents who failed to ensure that their children attended school regularly faced the prospect of a fine or even imprisonment, and public bodies such as schools that failed to tackle failure were held accountable and faced the prospect of closure and 'a fresh start'.

For New Labour poverty and deprivation were seen as no excuse for failure to improve if the support was available. There was an assumption that it is necessary to make use of all of society's *human capital* and all sectors of the education system. For example, by supporting single parents through training and helping them back to work, it was hoped to harness a large amount of potential labour power in an economy that had been experiencing a shortage of workers. The link between education and the economy became even more clearly defined at this time and Gordon Brown made this one of his key policy focuses. The higher education Green Paper 'Higher ambitions' (Department for Business Innovation and Skills, 2009: 2) sums this up well:

> In a knowledge economy, universities are the most important mechanism we have for generating and preserving, disseminating, and transforming knowledge into wider social and economic benefits.

Although the Green Paper talks about ensuring everyone reaches their full potential in the interest of social justice, the main thrust of the document is to increase Britain's economic competitiveness in the global economy by investing in each individual's economic potential.

However, Labour's policy initiatives relating to education and tackling social injustice exposed it to accusations by the Conservatives of overspending and wasting taxpayers' money thereby causing high levels of national debt which, they claim, cannot be dealt with without huge cuts in public spending. Whether this is a fair assessment of the situation is debatable (Reed, 2012), and there is certainly disagreement as to how the 2010 coalition government have used cuts in public spending as a means of dealing with the economic crisis which started in 2008.

The coalition government

Although Labour lost the election of 2010 against a background of the global financial crisis and accusations of profligacy, there was no clear winner. A coalition was the only alternative to another general election and, as coalitions inevitably mean compromise, the Conservatives managed to charm the Liberal Democrats more than Labour into forming a coalition.

Although it was not a good start for the Liberal Democrats in the new coalition, with the Deputy Prime Minister Nick Clegg reneging on a key manifesto pledge not to increase university tuition fees in 2012, the Liberal Democrats have managed to win some social justice-based policies such as the introduction of the pupil premium, which involved extra funding for schools with children from disadvantaged backgrounds, though this had to be paid for by cuts in funding on schools generally. There was also the announcement in 2013 of free school meals for all infant school children from September 2014. There has been, however, a degree of tension between the two parties over education policy generally, with Michael Gove the Secretary of State for Education dominating the education agenda with his push for academies and the reform of the National Curriculum from September 2014, which places an emphasis on teaching facts and testing basic skills in mathematics and English.

The National Curriculum

The reform of the National Curriculum has been highly controversial, in particular the changes to the teaching and testing of subjects such as history. In essence, what the government has done is focus on the learning of facts in subjects such as history and geography and emphasised the traditional hierarchy of academic over vocational subjects in school performance assessment. BTECs and vocational Diplomas, for example, are no longer designated as being equivalent to GCSEs.

Perhaps one of the most controversial policies has been the challenge to Britain's multicultural approach to education developed under New Labour. This multicultural approach was based not merely on an emphasis on the rights of minority ethnic groups, but also a celebration and recognition of group rights and the contribution such groups have made to the notion of British identity (Modood, 2007; Parekh, 2000). In the classroom this has involved a history curriculum that examines the experience of those cultures which were colonised by Britain and an attempt to understand their experiences of such forms of domination as slavery.

In the wake of the bombings of 7 July 2005, however, government ministers began talking again of the need to promote 'British values', and under the Education and Inspections Act of 2006, schools are required to promote social cohesion through the teaching of British values. This includes teaching the history of British democracy, tolerance and equality. Michael Gove announced a complete review of the history curriculum in 2011, stating that he wanted a return to a more traditional approach. His initial draft was a history curriculum inspired by the work of the eminent historian Niall Ferguson (2002), whose bestselling book *Empire: How Britain Made the Modern World* takes a linear narrative approach and presents a positive perspective in terms of what Britain gave the world: the English language and literature, modern forms of accounting and bureaucracy and free trade. Ferguson acknowledges the darker side of the British Empire, but claims that, on balance, Britain more than makes up for this in terms of its positive contribution to the world, which he refers to as 'anglobalisation'. This British values approach was the guiding principle of this first draft, which was to be delivered in a chronological manner with regular testing of 'facts'. What exactly are the facts is a very contentious point and, as the Parekh Report (Parekh, 2000) states, we should be cautious of accepting one 'official' version of history.

This approach to the curriculum caused much concern amongst many members of ethnic communities who see in it an attempt to exonerate Britain of its historic 'crimes' as well as to silence the voices of their ancestors. In his review of Ferguson's book *Civilisation: The West and the Rest*, published in 2011, Mishra (2011) states that, although Ferguson does not ignore the crimes of the British during the building, consolidation and dismantling of the Empire, what he does is provide a 'robust defence of British motives, which apparently were humanitarian as much as economic' (Mishra, 2011: 10–12). It is this suggestion that Britain's intentions and the consequences of its actions were ultimately benign that critics such as Mishra take issue with. In addition, Gove's first attempt was greeted with a good deal of criticism from professional historians who were concerned at the narrow and prescriptive nature of it and the sheer volume of facts to be learned by young children (Evans, 2013). The new version published in 2013 recognises the need for children to learn more than just facts and also that the facts do not speak for themselves: there is no single interpretation of historical events and they need to be analysed, debated and discussed by children and not just learned by heart. Gove has accepted the need to provide more coverage of the views of ethnic minorities and the contribution of women to the world we live in today (The Historical Association, 2013). However, the final version has been criticised for making only a token gesture to the contribution of non-white ethnic groups to British history, which, it is claimed, can only alienate black, Asian and other ethnic groups who may feel marginalised by such minimal coverage (Edwards, 2013).

Chapter summary

This chapter has examined almost 70 years of education policy since the end of the Second World War. It started in a spirit of optimism with expectations of equality of opportunity and increased social mobility. What we have witnessed is an era of great change and the expansion of education downwards to all classes in society. However, an important question to ask is whether the educational life chances of the less advantaged have improved relative to those of the more affluent members of society, given that the coalition have placed social mobility high on their list of priorities (Cabinet Office, 2012). Longitudinal research (Jefferis et al., 2002) that shows the influence of class on the life chances of 11,000 pupils born in 1958 who were studied in terms of a variety of factors such as health and cognitive development, shows that by age 7 those children who had experienced poverty in their childhood had fallen behind the more affluent children in school tests. This gap in educational attainment between the higher and lower social classes widened with age.

In terms of access to higher education Connor et al. (2001) found that less than one in five young people from the lowest social class go on to higher education. Moreover, despite New Labour's policy on widening participation in higher education, evidence shows that the relative chance of a child from the working class going to university compared to a child from the middle has changed little since the 1950s (Bolton, 2010). As with all such data, however, it is contestable, with writers such as Saunders (2010, 2012) in particular taking issue with the claim that there is little social mobility in Britain. He suggests that this is a myth perpetuated by both Labour and Conservative politicians to promote their own political agendas. Using alternative data sets and sources, such as those of the OECD, Saunders (2012) claims that a different picture is revealed showing much higher levels of mobility. For Saunders (2012: iii) the politicians 'have been resting their arguments on illusory evidence'. This is an important point because what seems to emerge from historical analysis, according to Alexander (2009), is that the research evidence from the past is very rarely properly understood and is subject to political and ideological interpretation.

Politicians are constantly driven by the 'new idea' when in fact, he asserts, we already know a good deal about what constitutes good practice from existing evidence. As we can see there is no clear answer to this question but, given the political system we have, there is little option but to leave it to the politicians to make the decisions in education policy.

References

Abel-Smith, B. and Townsend, P. (1965) *The Poor and the Poorest: A New Analysis of the Ministry of Labour's Family Expenditure Surveys of 1953–54 and 1960*. London: Bell.

Alexander, R. (ed.) (2009) *Children, their World, their Education: Final report and Recommendations of the Cambridge Primary Review*. London: Routledge.

Atkinson, A.B. (1983) *The Economics of Inequality*. Oxford: Oxford University Press.

Ball, S. (2008) *The Education Debate*. Bristol: Policy Press.

Ball, S. (2013) *The Education Debate* (second edition). Bristol: Policy Press.

Ball, S.J., Bowe, R. and Gerwitz, S. (1996) 'School choice, social class and distinction: The realisation of social advantage in education', *Journal of Educational Policy*, 11(1): 89–112.

Banks, O. (1955) *Parity and Prestige in English Secondary Education*. London: Routledge and Kegan Paul.

Benn, A. (1994) *Years of Hope: Diaries, Papers and Letters 1940–1962*. London: Arrow.

Blair, T. (1994) *Socialism*. London: Fabian Society.

Bolton, P. (2010) 'Higher education and social class'. [Online] Available at: www.parliament.uk/briefing-papers/SN00620.pdf (accessed 15 January 2015).

Cabinet Office (2012) 'University challenge: How higher education can advance social mobility'. London: Cabinet Office.

Chowdry, H. and Sibieta, L. (2011) *Trends in Education Spending*. London: Institute for Fiscal Studies.

Cohen, P. (1984) 'Against the new vocationalism', in I. Bates, J. Clarke, P. Cohen, D. Finn, R. Moore and P. Willis (eds), *Schooling for the Dole*. London: Macmillan.

Committee on Higher Education (1963) *Higher Education: report of the committee appointed by the Prime Minister under the Chairmanship of Lord Robbins 1961–1963*, Cmd. 2154. London: HMSO.

Connor, H., Dewson, S., Tyers, C., Eccles, J., Regan, J. and Aston, J. (2001) 'Social class and higher education: Issues affecting decisions on participation by lower social class groups'. London: Department for Education and Employment.

Cox, C.B. and Boyson, R. (eds) (1975) *Black Paper on Education*. London: Critical Review Quarterly.

Cox, C.B. and Dyson, A.E. (eds) (1969) *Black Paper One*. London: Critical Quarterly Society.

Denscombe, M. (1999) *Sociology Update*. Leicester: Olympus Books.

Department for Business Innovation and Skills (2009) *Higher Ambitions: The Future of Universities in a Knowledge Economy – Executive Summary*. [Online] Available at:

http://aces.shu.ac.uk/employability/resources/Higher-Ambitions-Summary.pdf (accessed 20 April 2015).

DES (1967) 'Children and their primary schools: A Report of the Central Advisory Council for Education (The Plowden Report)'. London: HMSO.

DES (1977) 'Education in schools: A consultative document'. London: HMSO.

Edwards, K. (2013) 'Gove's history curriculum needs to teach more equality', 29 April, *The Guardian*. Available at: www.theguardian.com/teacher-network/teacher-blog/2013/apr/29/gove-history-curriculum-more-equality (accessed 15 January 2015).

Edwards, T., Fitz, J. and Whitty, G. (1989) *The State and Private Education: An Evaluation of the Assisted Places Scheme*. London: Falmer.

Ernst and Young (2012) *University of the Future: A Thousand Year Old Industry on the Cusp of Change*. Australia: Ernst and Young.

Evans, R. (2013) 'Michael Gove's history wars', 13 July, *The Guardian*. Available at: www.theguardian.com/books/2013/jul/13/michael-gove-teaching-history-wars (accessed 15 January 2015).

Ferguson, N. (2002) *Empire: How Britain Made the Modern World*. London: Allen Lane.

Ferguson, N. (2011) *Civilisation: The West and the Rest*. London: Penguin.

Finn, D. (1987) *Training Without Jobs*. London: Macmillan.

Giddens, A. (1998) *The Third Way*. Cambridge: Polity Press.

Goldthorpe, J. (1980) *Social Mobility and Social Class Structure in Modern Britain*. Oxford: Clarendon Press.

Halsey, A.H. (1972) 'Educational priority, vol. 1'. London: HMSO.

The Historical Association (2013) 'Poll on the new history curriculum draft proposal'. Available at: www.history.org.uk/resources/secondary_resource_6202_8.html (accessed 15 January 2015).

Jefferis, B.J., Power, C. and Hertzman, C. (2002) 'Birth weight, childhood socioeconomic environment, and cognitive development in the 1958 British birth cohort study', *British Medical Journal*, 10 August, 325: 305.

Johnson, B. (2013) 'Boris Johnson: 3rd Margaret Thatcher Lecture (FULL)'. Available at: www.youtube.com/watch?v=Dzlgrnr1ZB0 (accessed 15 December 2015).

Joseph, K. (1974) 'Speech at Edgbaston ("our human stock is threatened")' Margaret Thatcher Foundation. Available at: www.margaretthatcher.org/document/101830 (accessed 15 January 2015).

Joseph, K. (1975) *Reversing the Trend*. London: Centre for Policy Studies.

Keddie, N. (1973) 'Classroom knowledge', in M.F.D. Young (ed.), *Tinker, Taylor – The Myth of Cultural Deprivation*. Harmondsworth: Penguin.

Labour Party (1992) 'Manifesto', London: Labour Party.

Miliband, R. (1969) *The State in Capitalist Society*. London: Weidenfeld and Nicolson.

Ministry of Education (1954) 'Early Leaving Report. Report of the Central Advisory Council for Education (England)'. London: HMSO.

Ministry of Education (1959) 'Fifteen to Eighteen. Report of the Central Advisory Council for Education (England) (The Crowther Report)'. London: HMSO.

Mishra, P. (2011) 'Watch this man', *London Review of Books*, 33(21). Available at: www.lrb.co.uk/v33/n21/pankaj-mishra/watch-this-man (accessed 15 January 2015).

Modood, T. (2007) *Multiculturalism*. London: Polity.

Moore, J. (1989) 'The end of the line for poverty', lecture delivered by John Moore at the St Stephens Club, 11 May.

Parekh, B. (2000) *The Future of Multi-Ethnic Britain: The Parekh Report*. London: Profile Books.

Park, A., Clery, E. and Curtice, J. (2010) *British Social Attitudes Survey 2010–20 Exploring Labour's Legacy – The 27th Report*. London: Sage.

Peters, R.S. (1966) *Ethics and Education*. London: Allan and Unwin.

Pimlott, B. (1992) *Harold Wilson*. London: Harper Collins.

PISA (2013) *Education at a Glance: OECD Indicators*. Paris: OECD Publishing.

Reed, H. (2012) '"Credit Card Maxed Out?" How UK debt statistics have been misrepresented', *Mis-Measurement of Health and Wealth*, 107. Available at: www.radstats.org.uk/no107/Reed107.pdf (accessed 15 January 2015).

Rowntree, S. (1901) *Poverty: A Study of Town Life*. London: Macmillan.

Rowntree, S. and Lavers, G. (1951) *Poverty and the Welfare State*. London: Longman.

Saunders, P. (2010) *Social Mobility Myths*. London: Civitas.

Saunders, P. (2012) *Social Mobility Delusions: Why So Much of What Politicians Say about Social Mobility in Britain is Wrong, Misleading or Unreliable*. London: Civitas.

Smith, D.J. and Tomlinson, S. (1989). *The school effect: A study of multi-racial comprehensives*. London: Policy Studies Institute.

Tawney, R.H. [1931] (1964) *Equality* (fourth edition). London: George Allen and Unwin.

Tomlinson, S. (2005) *Education in a Post Welfare Society*. London: Routledge.

Walker, D. (1987) 'The first Wilson government, 1964–1970', in P. Hennessy and A. Seldon (eds), *Ruling Performance: British Government from Atlee to Thatcher*. Oxford: Blackwell.

Whiteside, T. (1992) 'The Alliance and the Shaping of the Agenda', in T. Whiteside, A. Sutton and T. Everton (eds), *16–19: Changes in Education and Training*. London: David Fulton.

Wilkinson, R., and Pickett, K. (2009) *The Spirit Level: Why More Equal Societies Almost Always Do Better*. London: Penguin.

Young, M. (1958) *The Rise of the Meritocracy 1870–2033*. Harmondsworth: Penguin.

CHAPTER 11

YOUNG PEOPLE AND PUPIL VOICE

Chapter Aims

In Chapter 9 there was an outline of the emergence of 'the child' as a distinct group worthy of study in its own right, the role of schools and the impact of nineteenth century children's literature as a means of cultural transmission. This chapter examines the changing status of children in England and the ambivalent position they occupy in terms of the way adults treat them and the policies that affect them. The debate relating to whether children have too many rights or whether they need more rights and a greater voice in society is also addressed as is the way in which pupil voice is employed in schools in England.

Key words: child-centred, children's voice, children's rights, new sociology of childhood, moral panics, community of enquiry, pragmatism, structural vulnerability.

Introduction

In its 2007 report on child well-being in rich countries the United Nations Children's Fund (UNICEF) states that:

> The true measure of a nation's standing is how well it attends to its children – their health and safety, their material security, their education and socialization, and their sense of being loved, valued, and included in the families and societies into which they are born. (UNICEF, 2007: 3)

In England we live in an age that is supposed to be more child-centred than ever, where young people have rights and access to extensive welfare and health provision. There is legislation on child protection such as the Disclosure and Barring Service (DBS) checks on people who work with children, there is free compulsory education for children from 4–19 and laws against child labour and exploitation. Young people have acquired rights through the greater involvement of the state in issues of child welfare as well as through the pressure exerted by international organisations such as the UN and there have been, since 2001 for Wales and since 2005 in England, Children's Commissioners who speak on behalf of children. Legislation such as the Children Act of 1989 and the Children Act of 2004 put the *child first* and require adults to consider the views of young people when making any decisions that may affect them. In 1991 Britain ratified the United Nations Convention on the Rights of the Child (CRC), a set of 45 articles laying down rights and minimum standards of welfare for children globally. For the purposes of this chapter the CRC definition of a child as anyone below the age of 18 (Article 1) will be used.

The CRC includes articles relating to the provision of minimum standards in health and care, the right to education and the protection of children from such things as acts of violence, abuse and cruelty. It also contains articles concerning the rights of children to participate in civil and political processes by having the right to be heard (Articles 12, 13 and 14), particularly in relation to decisions made by parents and other authorities that affect them.

And yet if we examine the evidence relating to the treatment of children and their own views about their experiences, it is evident that the reality does not always match the rhetoric (Oakley, 1994). For example, in 2007 UNICEF, the world's leading organisation representing children's welfare and rights, produced the first study on the well-being and happiness of children in the most affluent countries. Britain came bottom of the list of 21 countries on measures of happiness, health, education and poverty. The figures for 2013 show that Britain is doing better but still came 16th out of 29 of the world's richest countries (UNICEF, 2013).

There was a recommendation by the report's authors that governments should make it a priority to consult children regularly on how they feel about their lives. The report acknowledges that there is no clear relationship between the relative wealth of a country and the happiness of its children; however, the existence of child poverty in Britain, the sixth wealthiest country in the world in terms of GDP according to the International Monetary Fund (IMF, 2014), is a clear indication of the rhetoric not matching the reality. GDP refers to the total value of all goods and services produced per person in the country, so by this common measure the UK is a very wealthy country and yet according to UNICEF (2011) figures, 3.5 million British children live below the poverty line. Moreover, despite the British government's legally binding commitment to eliminate child poverty by 2020, it is estimated by the Joseph Rowntree Foundation that in fact one in four families will be living in poverty by that year (Joseph Rowntree Foundation, 2014).

The problem of children

The child as a 'problem' for adult society is one that has been with us since recorded history. Children have been seen as both an asset in terms of representing future adult citizens with the potential skills, talents and labour needed for society to grow and prosper, and also as a potential threat to the stability and moral character of society. We can see this in the dramatic account provided by Plato of the trial and sentencing to death of Socrates in 399 BCE for 'not worshipping the gods the State worshipped but introducing other new divinities, and further that he was guilty of corrupting the young by teaching them accordingly' (Russell, 1945: 85). We can also read of the Spartans' practice of separating their children from their families at age 7 and subjecting them to a rigorous regime of training for their future roles as soldiers who would defend their city state. For leaders of the Spartans such as Lycurgus, the greatest fear was that the young men would become so used to the pleasures of life that they would put themselves before their country (Russell, 1945). Despite the charges against Socrates, who saw it as his mission to encourage young people to challenge authority, fears about the inability of young people to act responsibly meant that even philosophers such as Plato and Aristotle believed that children should not be taught to reason and question things, and recommended a strong moral education. In more modern times we can see the problem of young people manifest itself in moral panics over the hedonistic and rebellious youth cultures of the late twentieth century (Cohen, 1972; Hebdige, 1980) and the regular demands for greater discipline in schools (Gove, 2010; Phillips, 1996).

Childhood in any culture involves the preparation of young people for their future roles in society, but as we have seen in previous chapters the form this takes varies from society to society and it is highly class, race and gender based. This is what has been referred to as the social construction of childhood. The modern western (minority) concept of childhood only came into existence as a global phenomenon in the last century. It started among the upper classes during the Middle Ages (Ariès, 1962) and culminated in the separation of children from the world of adults in the nineteenth century when they were prevented from working in places such as mines and factories. This is not to say that children did not work at all, but that they were becoming more and more separated from and dependent upon adults. Ariès claims that the idea of childhood as we know it in Europe today did not exist in medieval society. In his examination of historical evidence he found that children were treated as miniature adults. From about the age of 4 or 5 they entered the world of adults, dressing like them and doing similar work such as agriculture or practising a craft.

During the fifteenth century, however, the upper classes started to treat their children differently. They began to 'coddle' them (show affection and fuss over them) and dress them in their own special clothes. Also, children were beginning to be seen as 'fragile creatures of God' who needed to be saved through moral and religious guidance. This gave rise to the desire to save their souls by educating them, thereby separating them from the world of adults. Ariès shows the importance of class in this process in that modern childhood starts among the upper classes in western societies, the only social group that could afford the luxury of not sending their children out to work. However, during the eighteenth and nineteenth centuries the increasingly affluent middle classes – merchants, traders and professionals – began to educate their children (mainly boys) in the growing number of public schools. Such schools provided educational grounding for the growing number of jobs requiring prolonged training such as medicine, engineering and science. Girls, of course, had fewer opportunities. These public schools as we have seen in Chapter 5 still play a significant role in England's class divided education system.

The lower classes, however, were unable to pay for such an education and required the income of their working children. With the growth of industrialisation, restrictions on child labour and the expansion of compulsory education, children from the working class were also separated from the world of adults and began to acquire the status of dependent child. Their education, however, was of a very functional nature that focused on a strict moral education and a respect for the existing social order (Boren, 2001). Ariès claims that no other society had developed such a concept of childhood before, however, it would probably be untrue to suggest that other societies lacked a concept of childhood at all (Archard, 1993). What we can say is that other societies have not shown the kind of focus on children and their separation from adults that places an emphasis on childhood as a period of play and extended education as was emerging in Europe (James et al., 1998). The Spartans, for example, did place their children in boarding schools from age 7, but there was no desire to provide them with the opportunity to play as 'a child' in the way we do today.

The child as incomplete

Ariès' research triggered an interest in the study of children as a distinct group in its own right. Although they were already the subject of psychological and educational research (see Chapters 5 and 8) the focus of these professionals was on the *incompleteness of the child* (Mayall, 1994). In other words, they were seen in terms of what they would become rather than what they were. So the discourse on children was one based on concepts of immaturity, deviance, disability, dependence, vulnerability and the need to educate and control them until they become mature adults (Mayall, 1994). There was a particular focus on the *deficits* of the child rather than their competencies such as the ability to make important decisions or to have a valid opinion.

The 'new sociology of childhood', however, has encouraged a focus on the experience of 'being' a child rather than on a period of immaturity and development. This has enabled researchers to examine the world from children's perspectives rather than imposing adult interpretations on it. As Boyden et al. (1998) point out, it is only by examining the experiences and views of children that we can understand them. From such research it is evident that children are not merely passive actors, for although they are situated within particular structures such as the family and the education system, and are restricted by their legal status, they still have the ability to influence and shape these structures (James and Prout, 1997). There is no doubt, for example, that children have a great deal of influence over the markets in leisure, music and food.

This desire to 'listen' to children, rather than just to focus on what adults expect of them, has been quite significant and has had an impact on the way welfare professionals deal with children. For instance, children's claims against adults of abuse are now taken more seriously, whereas before such children would have been dismissed as 'telling tales'. Nevertheless, those advocating greater rights for those under the age of 18 believe that the hands of adults are constantly intervening in the world of the child limiting the autonomy and freedom of children, thus illustrating their subordinate status in relation to adults (Lansdown, 1994; Oakley, 1994). This can be seen in terms of the regular 'moral panics' about children in relation to drugs, sex, morality, crime and education.

Thinking point 11.1

Moral panics

Governments of any hue tend to be guided in their policies, especially those on law and order and crime prevention, by the desire to be re-elected. Few political parties want to look weak on such issues especially when viewed against a background of extreme events such as riots (witness the exemplary sentencing after the 2011 riots in England; Lightowlers and Quirk, 2014), brutal murders and knife crime. Boyden (1997) argues that the view of childhood in societies such as Britain is based on the priorities of western capitalism, which include ensuring the welfare and safety of children but not at the expense of the rich, and a desire to control undisciplined children, a fear created by moral entrepreneurs through moral panics. In other words, according to Boyden, policies relating to children are based on a 'capitalist ideology'.

(Continued)

(Continued)

Lister (2006) adds to this theme by stating that rather than treating children as full citizens deserving support and a happy childhood, British children are viewed as human capital whose future as worker citizens takes precedence over their needs as young people. This can be seen in a variety of policies from regular testing in school to high levels of control through anti-social behaviour orders (ASBOs) and related legislation such as the Anti-Social Behaviour Act (2003), and the Criminal Justice and Immigration Act (2008), which introduced a new range of orders relating to young offenders. Policies relating to the treatment of young people seem to be very ambivalent. For example, Adams (2002) points to the lack of consistency in policy relating to youth justice, suggesting that some policies and legislation, such as the children acts, are based on welfare principles, and on the other hand we have a retributive model that treats young offenders as any other adult offender, using punishment and detention through such laws as the Crime and Disorder Act (1998) and the Anti-Social Behaviour Act (2003).

A moral panic is the arousal of social concern about an issue that has been identified by moral entrepreneurs, such as campaigning journalists or members of religious or child welfare groups, who often enlist the support of the mass media to highlight a concern that may be out of proportion to the threat or danger posed. Such campaigns may focus on a group, which often acts as a scapegoat, taking the blame for specific social problems. These 'moral panics' often make scapegoats out of children for the deficiencies of government policies in dealing with child poverty, youth unemployment or inadequate education and training. In cases of street crime, for example, children are criminalised by the media and the justice system, rather than being treated as victims of their circumstances and government neglect. Boyden (1997) argues that the government's alleged concern for the welfare of children falls short of proposing any radical measures that might actually help poor children who are demonised for their lack of economic resources. She suggests that governments seem more concerned about controlling the poor and protecting the better off, than with the welfare of these children.

Discussion

1. What do you think of the theory that suggests that young people are scapegoats and victims of government policies?
2. Can you think of any examples of such moral panics which involve the identification of young people as 'the problem', but which may have their origins in wider social factors?

(Continued)

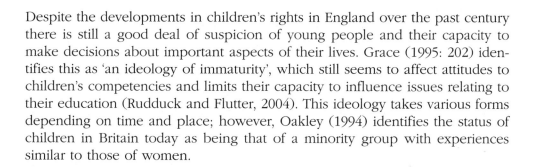

(Continued)

3. It could be suggested that politicians can afford to ignore young people under the age of 18 because they can't vote. Moreover, children have very little say over their education and welfare. Do you think that young people should have more say, such as being able to vote at a younger age?
4. Is there a conflict between the notion that children should be treated as a distinct group, that is, as children, and the idea that children should have more rights?

Despite the developments in children's rights in England over the past century there is still a good deal of suspicion of young people and their capacity to make decisions about important aspects of their lives. Grace (1995: 202) identifies this as 'an ideology of immaturity', which still seems to affect attitudes to children's competencies and limits their capacity to influence issues relating to their education (Rudduck and Flutter, 2004). This ideology takes various forms depending on time and place; however, Oakley (1994) identifies the status of children in Britain today as being that of a minority group with experiences similar to those of women.

Children as a minority group

Oakley (1994) suggests that children as a group share many of the characteristics and lack of status experienced by women within a patriarchal system of power. Because they are both labelled with characteristics and qualities that are believed to be essential to their group, it is seen as justifiable to treat women and children differently to the rest of the adult male population. This 'essentialising' of such difference means that both groups are seen as incapable of making important decisions for themselves. For Oakley, women have been infantilised by patriarchal ideology and, like children, have had little or no power or voice regarding many issues that directly affect their lives. Both children and women have been separated from the wider society through the roles deemed to be appropriate to their 'natural' characteristics and limitations: for women, who are seen primarily as mothers, the home is seen as their sphere, and for children, who are viewed as needing control and socialisation, the school is seen as theirs.

With specific reference to the issue of voice is the notion that due to their childlike qualities, both women and children need others to speak for them or on their behalf. A key difference here, however, is that women have over the past century been able to create a political and social movement with its own language to articulate its experiences and ideas. Children, on the other hand are still located in a legal and social position in which adults 'know better' and are required to speak for them, so despite the rights of children to be consulted and listened to under the various children acts and the CRC, ultimate decisions in relation to health issues, education matters and rights over their bodies are still controlled by adults. In 2008, for example, contrary to Article 19, which states that children should be protected from all forms of violence, the UK parliament, with no attempt to consult children, voted to retain the right of parents in Britain to use 'reasonable chastisement' such as smacking as a means of controlling and punishing them.

On wider issues such as education and health matters, although the CRC requires governments and parents to involve children in decisions affecting them, there is still no legal obligation for the government or parents to do so. For example, children have no right to refuse medical treatment unless they are able to pass a test of their maturity to comprehend the implications of their choices. Policy in Britain, according to Lansdown (1994: 34), is still based on the idea of the 'inherent vulnerability' of children rather than on their rights. This situation was challenged in 2008 by Hannah Jones aged 13 who was suffering from a fatal heart condition and who won the right to refuse lifesaving treatment, despite the threat from her local health authority to take her from the custody of her parents and to enforce the treatment through a court order.

Like Oakley, Lansdown (1994) makes the comparison between children and women, both of whom can be seen as weak and vulnerable status groups that are dependent on men. The effect of this, she claims, is to increase children's 'structural vulnerability', their lack of economic power, political and civil rights. However, with the growth of women's rights over the past century their structural vulnerability has decreased, though not disappeared. Lansdown claims that the CRC has the potential to do the same for children, but there seems to be a lack of political will in Britain. Moreover, there is a strong current of opinion, as epitomised by the New Right, which claims that children should not be given more rights and that they have indeed acquired too many already.

Too many rights?

Phillips (1996) argues that the growth of the rights agenda and child-centred education have led to the collapse of authority in schools and the important distinction between adults and children. This, together with the increasing influence of the media and peer groups, she believes, has also led to the declining importance of parents. She sees children as having rights that they lack the maturity to cope with. Phillips' views echo those of Plato and Aristotle. She suggests that children need to be given more care and discipline, not rights. Child-centred philosophies derived from the teachings of Rousseau and Dewey are seen by Phillips as dangerous because they destroy the distinction between children and adults. Adults such as teachers and parents she argues have been infantilised by bringing them down to the level of children who have in turn been burdened with responsibilities and decisions they are not mature enough to shoulder and should not be expected to carry. For Phillips, child-centred theories and the children's rights movement are destroying childhood in Britain.

A further point which Phillips makes is that child-centred education has harmed poorer children most. Refusing to accept the effects of inequality and poverty on poorer children, Phillips claims that schools and educational experts have been far too prepared to impose lower expectations on poorer children and fewer rules and standards of discipline. This, she claims, has resulted in poor levels of literacy and numeracy amongst children from more deprived backgrounds. For Phillips, as for former Education Secretary Michael Gove, the answer is for there to be less child-centred teaching and more discipline as well as an emphasis on standards (see Chapter 5). However, writers such as Lansdown (1994) argue that children should instead be listened to more, and are also in need of greater protection. This has perhaps been given added impetus in recent years by revelations of child abuse by those in authority (mainly men) in schools, hospitals, care homes and other institutions as well as families. The evidence which suggests that the victims of such abuse were not listened to or taken seriously (Gray and Watt, 2013) seems to lend support to those who advocate more rights and a greater voice for children rather than less.

Giving children a voice in schools

In England there can be no more iconic image of pupil voice and decision making than Summerhill School in Suffolk, which was established by the liberal educator A.S. Neill in the 1920s. In order for children to be themselves and to achieve happiness Neill believed that children should be free from all discipline as well as moral and religious teaching. They should be able to discover and decide for themselves on such issues including whether or not to attend lessons. He had absolute faith in the potential of all children to make the right choices on such matters as he believed that we are born inherently good and therefore, all things being equal and if the child is given complete freedom, there can be no other outcome. The main obstacle to this, for Neill, is the moral and religious ideas imposed on children by adults.

At Summerhill pupils are fully involved in decision making in the school at every level. There are regular weekly meeting during which rules are reviewed and changed on a democratic basis in which each pupil and teacher has one vote. Sanctions for such things as anti-social behaviour, bullying or theft are also dealt with at these weekly meetings. Although Summerhill was criticised by Ofsted in 1999 for its poor academic record and was threatened with closure if it did not bring in reforms related to its policy on non-compulsory lesson attendance – a key principle of the school – it won an educational tribunal held in 2000 that allowed it to maintain its core principles relating to pupil choice. In an inspection in 2011 Ofsted awarded the school an 'outstanding' grade in all areas except that of teaching. Summerhill no longer faces the threat of closure and is able to continue with its key principles relating to pupil voice and choice and, despite the issue of academic standards, research shows that pupils who attended Summerhill tend to feel that their experience has made them feel more confident and better able to deal with adults and those in authority (Bernstein, 1968). Summerhill is a private school, which, unlike state schools, is free from many of the restrictions over its curriculum and organisation and clearly stands out as an exception in terms of the freedoms and rights it affords its pupils. However, it is not the only school that believes in the rights of children to have their say in educational matters which affect them.

Researching pupil voice

Rudduck and Flutter (2004) have conducted extensive research on the use of pupil voice in a variety of schools that employ systems of consultation and pupil participation in decision making. They suggest that evidence collected from across the UK shows that pupils are very capable of engaging in responsible and constructive dialogue with teachers and heads in helping to bring about improvements in their schools. More specifically, Rudduck and Flutter believe that it has enabled pupils to take greater control of their learning and for teachers to be able to adapt their teaching to the specific needs of their pupils. In addition, they point to the changing nature of employment and work practices, which require greater levels of team work, consultation and flexibility, and they suggest that many schools are not adequately preparing their pupils for their future roles (Rudduck and Flutter, 2004). Evidence collected by the *Cambridge Primary Review* (Alexander, 2009) also suggests that there are good pedagogical and civic reasons to seek children's voice in educational matters.

While Rudduck and Flutter make a convincing case for the inclusion of pupil voice in schools through processes of consultation and pupil participation in decision making, they acknowledge that pupils often lack the language and skills to articulate their ideas and needs.

For philosophers such as Verharen (2002), an important way in which children can develop such a vocabulary and skills is through the teaching of philosophy in schools. Focusing primarily on the potentially liberating effects of philosophy teaching on Black children in American schools, Verharen suggests that the methods of philosophical thinking can be used as a means of challenging what he sees as a 'slave mentality', which Black Americans have inherited from their slave ancestors. The general message, however, is that all children need to be able to develop an understanding of fundamental concepts such as justice, fairness and equality in conjunction with the reasoned and logical methods of philosophical enquiry in order to be able effectively to articulate their views and ideas.

In his suggestion that philosophy should be taught to Black children in the USA, Verharen is effectively challenging the beliefs of Aristotle and Plato, who argued that the teaching of philosophy should be restricted to specific age and class groups, as they believed that philosophy is a dangerous thing to teach children and the lower orders such as slaves, workers and soldiers. It is still rare for children to be taught philosophy in state schools in both the USA and Britain, and the subject is certainly not part of the National Curriculum in England. For Verharen this is probably because of assumptions by those in authority regarding children's lack of maturity to deal with philosophical questions and the potential abuse of the knowledge and skills they could acquire. Nevertheless, he claims that philosophy is an essential means for the children in our society to articulate their views and that 'Teaching children philosophy might be the best form of defence against their abuse by authority figures' (Verharen, 2002: 309).

Teaching children philosophy

So what does Verharen mean by teaching philosophy to (Black American) children? He does not mean that we should teach children the kind of philosophy associated with academic philosophy. Instead, he suggests that they should be encouraged to *philosophise*, to think and to act philosophically. This involves being able to theorise and understand abstract concepts that help us study all aspects of human experience, be they natural, spiritual or social. Verharen insists that children are able to philosophise on the basis of their own experience. They may not be able to generalise on the basis of this as Plato and Aristotle claim philosophers should be able to do, but they can reflect on such concepts as beauty, justice, equality, fairness, love, truth and tolerance.

The teaching of philosophy to children has been taken up by a number of scholars and organisations such as P4C (Philosophy for Children), which has been guided by the ideas of Matthew Lipman (2003). The intention is to enable children to think and discuss ideas regarding fundamental concepts such as equality, fairness, justice and tolerance, in ways that are appropriate to their level of understanding, thereby creating a community of enquiry (CoE). Dawid (2006) believes that this will be a means of creating responsible and aware citizens from an early age. These, however, are the very kinds of practices that Plato warned against. Bleazby (2005) also advocates the creation of such communities of enquiry, which she believes should enable children and other groups to create meaning in relation to important issues which affect their lives and that of their community, but she is critical of the fact that Lipman does not include the Deweyian notion of *pragmatism*. By this Bleazby means that for Dewey, who is the principle influence on Lipman, philosophy should be about providing practical solutions to problems or issues in society: pupils should not just have a voice, they should be able to change things for the better. Lipman, however, does not go as far as to propose that children test their ideas in real-life situations and this she believes is a weakness in his approach. Bleazby suggests that philosophy in Deweyian terms should be about changing or transforming society and not just limiting it to the classroom. Such transformations, however, should be pursued in terms of intended consequences: the achievement of justice or the elimination of homelessness in the community. We might add to this the protection of children by giving them a voice.

A growth in the involvement of children

In a review of the literature on the involvement of children in research and their influence on policy and practice in organisations such as schools and youth organisations, Halsey et al. (2006) suggest that there is an increasing commitment by such organisations to seek children's views when considering changes and reforms. In the 26 documents they reviewed they found that children were involved in five main 'impact areas' (Halsey et al., 2006: ii), which included not only areas of service delivery but also policy development and staff recruitment. However, Halsey et al. (2006) found that there is limited information on the impact of children's voice and involvement in policy changes, and recommend that organisations not only involve children more in such consultations but that they also do more to evaluate the impact of any reforms carried out.

Despite the generally positive tone of these documents on the involvement of children and their impact on the areas identified, such as a greater feeling of confidence and self-esteem amongst the pupils, there was also some evidence in a minority of the literature of a sense of disillusionment on the part of children where it was felt that consultations led to little in the way of real change and that the institutions were merely going through the motions.

Chapter summary

Children in England are members of a group whose status has clearly changed over the past two centuries. Though they have gained many more rights than they ever had, they still occupy a position of subordination and ambiguity in terms of the way adults see them and the way they are treated. On the one hand they are defined as a precious and vulnerable group in need of protection and education, as seen in the various welfare rights and legislation protecting them, and yet on the other hand they are viewed with suspicion and concern in terms of their corruptibility and the potential threat they pose to society in terms of their moral, criminal and sexual activities. As we have seen, there is nothing new in this position and it is a possible reason why many of those in authority, politicians, religious leaders and other moral campaigners, are reluctant to give children more rights. This is a position that is becoming more difficult to maintain given the revelations about the behaviour of some of these political, religious and moral leaders towards young people (Gray and Watts, 2013).

In terms of education, young people are the biggest consumers of a service that, in general, provides them with little in the way of choice on issues of where or how they are educated and on matters of testing and assessment. The work of Rudduck and Flutter (2004) suggests that including children in decision making in schools has a positive effect in terms of enabling pupils to take greater control of their learning and helps teachers to identify the needs of individual pupils. However, writers such as Verharen (2002) argue that pupils need to be equipped with the appropriate language and skills to be able to articulate their views and ideas effectively. The work of the P4C movement is an important initiative in this direction but the teaching of philosophical methods and ideas in schools in England is not widely practised. Verharen (2002: 309) claims that 'Children have as much right to this martial art as their parents, perhaps even more, given their relatively defenceless nature'. Others such as Phillips (1996), however, argue that children already have too many rights.

References

Adams, R. (2002) *Social Policy for Social Work*. London: Palgrave.

Alexander, R. (ed.) (2009) *Children, their World, their Education: Final report and Recommendations of the Cambridge Primary Review*. London: Routledge.

Archard, D. (1993) *Children: Rights And Childhood*. London: Routledge.

Ariès, P. (1962) *Centuries of Childhood*. London: Jonathan Cape.

Bernstein, E. (1968) 'Summerhill: A follow-up study of its students', *Journal of Humanistic Psychology*, 8(2): 123–36.

Bleazby, J. (2005) 'Reconstruction in philosophy for children' Inter-disciplinary. net, Second Global Conference, 14 July. Available at: www.inter-disciplinary.net/ at-the-interface/education/creative-engagements-thinking-with-children/project-archives/2nd/#hide (accessed 15 January 2015).

Boren, M.E. (2001) *Student Resistance: A History of the Unruly Subject*. London: Routledge.

Boyden, J. (1997) 'Childhood and policymakers: A comparative perspective on the globalisation of childhood', in A. James and A. Prout (eds), *Constructing and Reconstructing Childhood: Contemporary Issues in the Sociological Study of Childhood*. London: Falmer.

Boyden, J., Ling, B. and Meyers, W. (1998) *What Works for Working Children*. Stockholm: Radda Barnen/UNICEF.

Cohen, S. (1972) *Folk Devils and Moral Panics*. London: MacGibbon and Kee.

Dawid, J. (2006) 'Communities of enquiry with younger children', LT Scotland Early Years and Citizenship Conference, July. Available at:www.docstoc.com/docs/26387812/ Communities-of-Enquiry---Early-Years-Conference-notes (accessed 15 January 2015).

Gove, M. (2010) 'Michael Gove: All pupils will learn our island story', speech given on 5 October. Available at: http://toryspeeches.files.wordpress.com/2013/11/michael-gove-all-pupils-will-learn-our-island-story.pdf (accessed 15 January 2015).

Grace, G. (1995) *School Leadership*. London: Falmer Press.

Gray, D. and Watt, S. (2013) 'Giving victims a voice: Joint report into sexual allegations made against Jimmy Savile', A Joint NSPCC and Metropolitan Police Service Report. Available at: www.nspcc.org.uk/news-and-views/our-news/child-protec tion-news/13-01-11-yewtree-report/yewtree-report-pdf_wdf93652.pdf (accessed 15 January 2015).

Halsey, K., Murfield, J., Harland, J.L. and Lord, P. (2006) *The Voice of Young People: An Engine for Improvement? Scoping the Evidence*. Reading: National Foundation for Educational Research, CfBT.

Hebdige, D. (1980) *Subculture: The Meaning of Style*. London: Methuen.

International Monetary Fund (IMF) (2014) 'Report for selected countries and subjects', World Economic Outlook. Available at: www.imf.org/external/pubs/ft/weo/2014/01/ weodata/weorept.aspx?sy=2013&ey=2019 (accessed 15 January 2015).

James, A. and Prout, A. (1997) (eds) *Constructing and Reconstructing Childhood*. London: Falmer Press.

James, A., Jenks, C. and Prout, A. (1998) *Theorising Childhood*. Cambridge: Polity Press.

Joseph Rowntree Foundation (2014) *Child Poverty Strategy 2014/17 Consultation*. York: JRF.

Lansdown, G. (1994) 'Children's rights', in B. Mayall (ed.), *Children's Childhoods Observed and Experienced*. London: Routledge.

Lightowlers, C. and Quirk, H. (2014) 'The 2011 English "riots": Prosecutorial zeal and judicial abandon', *British Journal of Criminology*, 54(5): 65–85.

Lipman, M. (2003) *Thinking in Education*. Cambridge: Cambridge University Press.

Lister, R. (2006) 'Children (but not women) first: New Labour, child welfare and gender', *Critical Social Policy*, 26(2): 315–35.

Mayall, B. (ed.) (1994) *Children's Childhoods Observed and Experienced*. London: Routledge.

Oakley, A. (1994) 'Women and children first and last: Parallels and differences between children's and women's studies', in B. Mayall (ed.), *Children's Childhoods Observed and Experienced*. London: Routledge.

Phillips, M. (1996) *All Must Have Prizes*. London: Little, Brown and Company.

Rudduck, J. and Flutter, J. (2004) *How to Improve Your School*. London: Continuum.

Russell, B. (1945) *The History of Western Philosophy, And Its Connection with Political and Social Circumstances from the Earliest Times to the Present Day*. New York: Simon and Schuster.

UNICEF (2007) 'Report Card 7: Child poverty in perspective: An overview of child well-being in rich countries', Florence: UNICEF Innocenti Research Centre.

UNICEF (2011) 'Child Poverty in the UK'. London: UNICEF UK. Available at: www.unicef.org.uk/Documents/Publications/Child%20poverty%20in%20the%20UKUNICEF%20UK%20Information%20Sheet.pdf (accessed 15 January 2015).

UNICEF (2013) 'Report Card 11: The well-being of children: How does the UK score?' Florence: UNICEF Innocenti Research Centre.

Verharen, C. (2002) 'Philosophy's role in Afrocentric education', *Journal of Black Studies*, 32(3): 295–321.

CHAPTER 12

TRANSFORMATIONS

Chapter Aims

In this chapter a discussion about what transformation means in the wider context of higher education will take place, including an investigation of economic and cultural transformation which will frame the overall discussion and a consideration of intervention strategies that have set out to facilitate transformation by closing the social gap in educational attainment. Data based on the experiences of students in higher education, a part of a small-scale study, will be applied to the discussion as evidence.

Key words: social capital, widening participation, social justice, meritocracy, intervention.

Introduction

In this chapter a sociological consideration of transformation as a concept and as experienced by students in higher education will be explored. A deeper understanding of how engaging with higher education can so powerfully impact on the lives of the participants to bring about transformation overlaps with many sociological themes including primary socialisation, identity and belonging, and the means by which values are transmitted and internalised.

The higher education journey is a fertile plain for discourses on transformations. The university as a site of the experiential has been the focus of extensive research by the Spanish sociologist Manuel Castells (2001) who presents four central functions of the university. Castells notes that universities have historically played a major role as ideological apparatuses, expressing the ideological struggles present in all societies. Second, they function as an organised and respected domain of hierarchy, another layer of socialisation of dominant elites. Third, the university is a place of knowledge production, thus always valued and a focus of national debate. Fourth, and perhaps most relevant to modern-day understanding, the university is a place where the training of a labour force takes place.

This chapter acknowledges the key forms of transformation in the context of the higher education setting. These include economic transformation (the formation of human capital), social transformation (the mechanisms of mobility by different groups) and cultural transformation (the production and transmission of ideals to a wider societal base). Finally, the chapter will capture first-hand experiences of transformation as shared by students in a small-scale research project based at a post-1992 institute of higher education. This exploration of student voice is central to the notion that transformation is an experience of personal transition from experience to being. The inclusion of case studies of transformation supports the reimagining of the traditionalist role of the university as the alma mater, literally meaning 'nourishing mother', a space where the love of learning can excite, motivate and transform.

Economic transformation

The link between education policy and the needs of the economy has been the preoccupation of many educationalists including Tomlinson (2005) and Ball (2008) who have explored the momentum created by the widening participation agenda that continues to challenge all universities to work towards providing opportunities for non-traditional students to have access to higher education, regardless of their background. As a result, this interventionist strategy has blurred the lines of exclusion and elitism in some of the more prestigious institutes of higher education.

Widening participation in particular has created an opening in higher education for working class people (Reay et al., 2010). Contestably, New Labour's ideas about education – what it does, how it works, whose interests it serves – have fuelled and strengthened the construction of what Ball (2008: 5) describes as the 'inevitable and the necessary' relationship between education policy and the needs of the state and the economy. The social reality of interventions such as widening participation is evident in the vast expansion within higher education post-1997, as New Labour tried to achieve a cohort participation rate of 50 per cent by 2020. As Table 12.1 illustrates, the 1992 Further and Higher Education Act created a provision within the sector primarily to meet the needs of the widening participation agenda, however, as universities are increasingly competitive and survive on healthy and sustained recruitment, this provision has faced stiff competition.

Table 12.1

Key dates of UK policy changes on widening participation in higher education

1919 University Grants Committee formed

1944 Education Act with notion of equality of educational opportunity

1963 Robbins Report on Higher Education

1966 Antony Crosland, Labour Secretary of State, gives speech on a Binary Policy for Higher Education

1970 Thirty Polytechnics created from Local Authority Colleges

1986 Start of Research Assessment Exercise in Universities

1987 White Paper on Higher Education: 'Meeting the challenge'

1988 Education Reform Act

- Created Universities Funding Council (UFC)
- Polytechnic and Colleges Funding Council (PCFC)
- 1992 Further and Higher Education Act
- Created new universities based on former Polytechnics (hence pre-1992 and post-1992 universities) abolishing the binary 'divide'
- Set up Higher Education Funding Councils for the UK nations

1997 Publication of Dearing Report on Higher Education in the Learning Society

1997 Labour government in power, committed to 'education, education, education', accepts a revised version of Dearing

2003 White Paper on 'The future of higher education'

2005 Higher Education Act created Office of Fair Access (OFFA) and post of Access Regulator

2006 Department for Education and Skills (DfES) Paper 'Widening participation in HE: Creating opportunity, releasing potential, achieving excellence'

2010 'Securing a sustainable future for higher education: Browne review'

To illustrate, in 2010 the 1994 Group, which represents 19 of the UK's top research-intensive universities, published a policy briefing on widening participation based on targeted outreach programmes by the Student Experience Policy Group. The National Audit Offices' 2008 report 'Widening Participation in Higher Education' particularly highlighted groups such as those from lower socioeconomic backgrounds, and those living in deprived areas, as being under-represented in UK higher education institutions. Having invested £45 million in 2010 as well as offering a range of scholarships and bursaries, the 1994 Group acknowledge economic disadvantage should not hold talented applicants back from studying at selective universities. Thus, it is apparent that economic trans-formation matters at policy and institute level as well as for the individual.

The coalition's policy document 'Opening doors, breaking barriers: A strategy for social mobility' (Her Majesty's Government, 2011), which sets out to improve social mobility, states that first, a fair society is one where every individual can succeed; second, that social mobility is the principal goal of the government's social policy; third, that there is a long way to go in achieving this goal; and fourth, a lack of social mobility damages individuals and hinders the economic potential of this country. Deputy Prime Minister, Nick Clegg talks of fairness as a fundamental value of the coalition and states that a true test of fairness is the distribution of opportunities for all, in the opening statement of this policy. In relation to higher education the policy clarifies 'Our reforms to higher education funding put new obligations on universities to improve access. In particular, those universities charging over £6,000 will have to attract more students from less affluent backgrounds' (Her Majesty's Government, 2011: 7). However, if we are to acknowledge that social mobility is about breaking the transmission of disadvantage from one generation to the next so that every person has the opportunity to get on in life (regardless of their personal circumstances or social class) then surely access to an elitist experience for a select few is missing the point. The issue of higher education being the space for accelerated social mobility has dominated popular culture, as illustrated by the inclusion of *Educating Rita* as an exemplar from literature later in this discussion, and box office hits such as *Dead Poets Society* (1989), *Good Will Hunting* (1997), *Mona Lisa Smile* (2003) and *The Social Network* (2010). In a further exemplar, the British film adaptation of Laura Wade's play *Posh*, entitled *The Riot Club* (2014), set amongst the privileged elite of the University of Oxford, tells the story of how a distorted sense of values and behaviours are embedded in certain social classes, as played out by members of an exclusive dining club. The links to the infamous Bullingdon Club, the all-male dining club at Oxford whose 'class of '87' included Boris Johnson, David Cameron and George Osborne are transparent and the film is a toxic representation of a society (all male) when the prerequisite for entry is a privileged, elitist schooling background (preferably Eton), where prospective new members are proposed by a current member and then subjected to a club vote and a hefty annual stipend is expected to cover the extravagant drinking and dining meetings. Significantly, the values of such a hyper-elitist setting become problematic when group members interact with different social groups, as illustrated in the conflict with a working class pub landlord and his daughter in this film.

To conclude this discussion on economic transformation it is important to look to empirical data in order to grasp the full extent of the challenges that lie ahead. With this in mind, research conducted by the Higher Education Funding Council for England (HEFCE), an organisation that distributes public money for higher education to universities and colleges in England suggests that children from the most disadvantaged areas are only a third as likely to enter higher education as children from the most advantaged areas (HEFCE, 2010). In a more recent publication, the evidence is more compelling:

> The absolute disparities between advantaged and disadvantaged areas remain large. The entry rate to higher education in the UK for 18 year olds from the most advantaged areas of England is around 47 per cent in the 2013 UCAS cycle, which is still significantly higher than for the most disadvantaged, where the entry rate is around 17 per cent. (HEFCE, 2014: 8)

This evidence presents a picture of social exclusion as the factors that prevent disadvantaged young people entering higher education are so deeply integral to their lives that access is prevented. Moreover, further investigation into the data illustrates that while prior attainment accounts for some of the gaps in access to higher education, it would appear that the research unearths more questions than answers. For example, young people identified as high achievers at GCSE level from a background of social disadvantage (e.g., they are eligible for free school meals (FSM)) are less likely to attend university than their peers (Chowdry, 2010). However, for young people from similar backgrounds who do reach university, the evidence suggests that they often outperform pupils from independent schools with similar prior attainment (Lindley and Machin, 2013). Understanding economic transformation in the context of higher education is a debate that, it would appear, has less to do with social mobility and more to do with individual resilience and identity construction, as explored in the latter part of this chapter, which is based on a small-scale research project with students at a post-1992 institute of higher education.

Assessing interventions

A wide range of interventions by central government, educational settings and charity organisations have taken up the challenge to facilitate transformation for socially disadvantaged groups. In this discussion an assessment of some key interventions is made in terms of policy implications and practical application as a vehicle of economic transformation in education.

The focus on initial teacher training for this first intervention aims to address many of the embedded structures of exclusion and othering in education; reinvesting in a new generation of teachers by applying a business model to the recruitment strategy. The Teach First independent charity was established in 2002 with the intention of training 'exceptional' graduates to work as teachers (and as inspirational leaders) in some of the most disadvantaged and challenging schools in the country, with the support of substantial government financial backing. The publicity materials draw in potential applicants with the strap line 'Change their lives and change yours', and inspires with the ideology of participation in a movement of social change. Following an intensive 2-year training period the leadership aspect of Teach First offers 'ambassadors', equipped with a Master's level qualification, the best networking opportunities to build on classroom experience in the world of business and commerce; and therein lies the major criticism. This is not, in the long term, an intervention designed to reinvigorate and reinvest in the education system, it is a fast track leadership training exercise based in the very schools that need stability and continuity in staffing and resources. The focus on recruiting the highest achieving graduates (who might not necessarily have considered teaching a profession, let alone a vocation) to act as agents of change and as leaders of the next generation is a potent vision, however, as Hutchings et al. (2006) report, a presumed superiority over non-Teach First trainee teachers and the notion that this initiative can be a standalone salvation to the many challenges facing schools are twin causes for concern and scepticism.

Moving on, a raft of similar interventions with a clear mandate to raise the aspirations and thus the educational life chances of disadvantaged groups and concentrating on the primary and secondary sectors include the 'Extra Mile' project (Department for Education, 2010), which was launched in 2008 and provided an enriched curriculum (outdoor learning, educational visits, music and the creative curriculum) in an effort to redress the balance of social and cultural capital deficit for school children in the target schools. The full evaluation report (Chapman et al., 2010) is a celebration of individual success stories; however, the issue of sustainability, selection of school and target pupils as well as funding remain areas for further consideration. The notion that standalone enrichment activities can act as a platform for change making also suggests a deeper lack of understanding of social disadvantage in the lives of young people.

'Excellence in Cities', 'City Challenge' and 'Futureversity' (Futureversity, 2010) are examples of 'area-based' interventions with the aim of enhancing aspiration for families and communities; the last one concentrating on summer school experiences at university. The vision of 'closing the gap' in attainment between pupils in vastly differing socioeconomic groups in initiatives such as the ones mentioned above is dependent on substantial funding, which is unsecured long term and with small gains when it comes to measures linked to indicators of substantive change, according to Kerr and West (2010: 13). Critics including Dyson et al. (2010) argue that the solution to the problem of educational inequality cannot be located in 'bolt on' interventions to a fundamentally unequal education system. To address the causes of social and educational inequality a holistic approach needs to be applied at a local level, taking into account the greatly varying needs of each locality (as well as the talents and resources) in comparison to the deficit discourses and bolt on compensatory models that focus on what communities 'lack'. An American strategy might provide a road plan for progression. A vast array of social intervention programs across the various states have been launched to address issues of illiteracy, gun crime, youth offending and to promote education attainment. A popular African-American proverb has been utilised in the campaign strategy known as 'Each One Reach One' (EORO), where the key mission statement has been adapted into an expansive range of organisations with the unifying mission of each citizen embracing their responsibility to help one other person in a specific category of need. Supported by leading politicians, Hollywood stars and faith organisations, EORO has been successful in empowering local communities to take responsibility for their specific local concerns. By this process, a sense of inclusion and cohesion is incorporated alongside a message of hope and success starting with a grassroots movement of individuals to form collective change making. To illustrate this vision in an educational context, 'Each One Reach One Teach One' is a non-profit organisation created to provide educational and social enrichment programmes for young people with a clear focus on life skills, cultural awareness, diversity training and community engagement. The focus on young people in urban settings and mentoring has employed local skills creatively and on a small scale, thus facilitating continuity and ensuring that cost implications remain small in comparison to indicators of change. This initiative has incorporated creative employment and up-skilling for local communities within a wider strategy of addressing educational failure and anti-social behaviour amongst young people. Perhaps this is the ideal approach, to tackle wide-scale societal challenges through civic engagement embedded in and managed by local communities.

In a final example of interventions to action transformation the Stephen Lawrence Charitable Trust was set up in 1998 by Stephen's parents, Doreen and Neville Lawrence, as a proactive and positive commemoration of their son and his potential. The Trust is dedicated to making an impact on social mobility by supporting young people from London to enjoy the opportunities that were denied to Stephen by his senseless murder. This third sector intervention has attracted significant corporate and private funding in order to work with disadvantaged young people via a school based strategy. They offer practical experience in professional settings so that businesses can benefit from, and are more inclusive of, diverse talent throughout their management structures, encapsulating the vision of the Trust 'that greatness can come from anywhere – Young people, whatever their background, inspired to success because they see people like themselves in senior roles shaping society' (www.stephenlawrence.org.uk). The work of the Trust, alongside similar interventions such as 'Generating Genius' (www.generatinggenius.org.uk), which was founded in 2005 by Tony Sewell with the aim of working with high-achieving students from disadvantaged communities throughout their secondary school careers in order to help them acquire the skills they need to win places at top universities, have a vocation-driven mission to challenge entrenched ideas about young (and in the main Black) people and educational attainment. The sustainable, student-centred and personalised delivery included in the work of Generating Genius means that alumni are recruited as mentors thus feeding their insights and experiences back into the intervention, with case studies and success stories that will gradually replace social exclusion with a social justice, while at the same time supporting diversity in professional settings. Such initiatives, which are founded on tragedy (in the case of the Stephen Lawrence Trust) and distrust of the education system and its treatment of Black boys (in the case of Generating Genius), are criticised as philanthropic and embedded in meritocracy, and are thus unable to really challenge social exclusion in any way. Despite this, they illustrate that small-scale impact-driven interventions need to first ensure ownership by the young people; second, they must be supported by a wider collective; and third, and most critically, they must be sustainable in order to maintain staying power. In addition, the community mentoring element incorporates a mutual learning element with a strong focus on valuing the identity and background of the young people; which, it can be argued, is the missing link in many of the high profile government-driven interventions.

Reading suggestion

The two academic papers noted below explore the many themes discussed in this chapter in the context of research-informed knowledge production.

Wilks, J. and Wilson, K. (2012) 'Going on to uni? Access and participation in university for students from backgrounds of disadvantage', *Journal of Higher Education Policy and Management*, 34(1): 79–90.

This academic paper reports on a research project that investigated the aspirations of primary and secondary school students about access to, and participation in higher education. The research was undertaken at schools in New South Wales – identified as a location of social disadvantage. The report explores financial factors, geographic location, and cultural and social capital in relation to the formation of students' perceptions, choices and decisions about participation in higher education as a step towards self-transformation.

Clegg, S. (2011) 'Cultural capital and agency: Connecting critique and curriculum in higher education', *British Journal of Sociology of Education*, 32(1): 93–108.

This paper investigates some of the contradictions between widening participation and the consolidation of social position in the higher education system. It shows how concepts of social and cultural capital derived from Bourdieu, Coleman and Putnam risk a deficit view of students from less privileged backgrounds. These students are more likely to attend lower status institutions and focus less on professional career making. The paper explores the importance of agency, community and family capital and the resilience of the students encountering the system in which they are disadvantaged.

Cultural transformation

In considering cultural transformation in this part of the chapter, a consideration of how an educational experience can be understood as a transformational part of one's life is explored as well as how values are changed by education, thus bringing about a cultural transformation. In relation to the latter point, the culture of part-time study in higher education is considered as a stepping stone to social mobility and how the university experience itself has undergone a cultural transformation in order to meet the needs of the twenty-first-century student.

To unpack cultural transformation Lewis Gilbert's (1983) cinematic production of Willy Russell's (1980) stage play *Educating Rita* provides a powerful and timeless narrative of self-discovery, or as Foucault (1926–1984) describes 'self-fashioning'. Inspired by Russell's experiences in evening classes, the film shows the experiences of a working class, non-traditional student called 'Rita' who is notable as she dresses, speaks and behaves differently to her middle class counterparts; thereby exposing her working class heritage. However, through a desire to transform her mundane life, Rita abandons her working class identity in order to fit into university habitus. In this context, habitus means a person's predisposition to be affected by something and, when applied in the Bourdieuian context, incorporates a sociological transformation of culture. To use an American expression, this can be understood as Rita attempting to hide her feelings of 'imposter syndrome' (Williams and Cochrane, 2010), a mechanism employed by non-traditional students to fit into academia; literally the feeling of being an imposter in a public space; not belonging, the outsider. Diane Reay (2011), a sociologist who has conducted research on social class and educational attainment, argues that there are multiple and overlapping barriers for working class people in terms of access and engagement in higher education, however, the most significant is the theoretical assumption that students suffered from 'imposter syndrome' and feeling undeserving of their place. Rita experienced all these negative feelings as her attempts to fit in meant that she not only compromised but opted to distance herself (initially) from her working class-ness, marking a psycho-sociological internal conflict between one's social identity and one's undeveloped learner identity. This conflict has an enduring impact and can subsequently affect retention and attainment, leading to possible self-hatred and reinforcing the notion of the imposter in the higher education environment. Through the story of *Educating Rita* the desire to transform is viewed as a motivational factor demonstrating how processes behind class advantage and disadvantage work through the individual. This, it can be argued, is perhaps the most critical stage of cultural transformation termed by Foucault as 'self-fashioning'; essentially this is an act of (self) empowerment and is understood as an act of creative representation or reconstruction to form a new identity from the social environment in question.

Thinking point 12.1

Educating Rita – Act 1

Rita's dress sense changes in the course of Act 1. Initially, she wears 'tarty' dresses, while after summer school she is wearing 'new second hand clothes'. This is Willy Russell's way of showing how she has become more 'middle class' and started becoming a 'proper student', more independent of her working class identity. Rita gives up smoking, this is shown by the quote 'no, ta I've packed it in' after Frank offers her a cigarette. Here, Willy Russell applies a metaphor to symbolise Rita giving up her old working class life and starting a whole new life. This commentary of Act 1 concentrates on the physical changes made by Rita as part of her transformation.

To fully understand Rita's transformation, discuss and investigate the many structural, social and cultural barriers students face when entering higher education. Explore strategies that institutes of higher education can implement to support students facing such barriers.

Understanding the place of part-time study as a stepping stone to social mobility is an important part of the cultural transformation of higher education as an experience for some students. Callendar (2012) reports that a third of all UK undergraduates study part-time – a trend that reflects a cohort of students with relevant and recent work based (life) skills, with a vision for self-improvement and a flexible approach to lifelong learning and with choices, as the sector has changed to meet their needs. While attending university was once the domain of 18 year olds packing up their bedrooms and moving into university halls for their initiation into adulthood, being at university was a life experience in itself. Now a cultural transformation in higher education reflects a mature (over the age of 21) student, often managing several home and family responsibilities, as well as employment, and still making a significant financial and personal investment into their higher education; life carries on while this student (over a longer period of time) completes their higher education.

The White Paper 'Higher education: Students at the heart of the system' (Department for Business, Innovation and Skills, 2011) confirms that part-time study can contribute to a greater extent to the government's wider higher education policy objectives, in that it is more inclusive and attracts a greater diversity of student to higher education, thereby delivering on the all-important social mobility agenda as demonstrated in the personal reflection captured below by a part-time BSc social sciences student now exploring postgraduate options:

though it has been hard, I have enjoyed it … actually, the other day I got some paperwork about a Master's degree and I sort of looked and thought 'do I, don't I?' you know [laughs] … there's a good chance I will … although I keep saying no, I want my life [back] … maybe I'll do my teacher training, and then go back and do the Master's. (Callendar, 2012: 85)

By way of a conclusion, it is apparent that an unintended outcome of the widening participation agenda has been that not only have universities had to take on the changes demanded of them by external funding bodies, but also a cultural transformation from within has facilitated more significant changes that have resulted in a re-conceptualisation of the provision of higher education (Watson, 2008). The historic traditional seat of the elite (Oxford and Cambridge) is now a distinct minority in comparison to the university based in the community and meeting the needs of the community, thus delivering on their corporate social responsibility (Silver, 2007), while at the same time being open minded about how the university operates as in terms of a business model. A dominant theme of the post-war era was equality of opportunity hand in hand with the ideology that education was the social instrument which would help to shape a new vision for a changing society. A two-tier system persisted throughout the 1970s and 1980s, where the foundations were created for a higher education system which was linked to employability and a stronger economic position for the country as a whole. This ultimate goal was met with an increasing demand for a skilled workforce, emphasising employability as opposed to higher education qualifications. New Labour's mantra 'education, education, education' as a principle for addressing social exclusion has meant that in recent years universities have been given a multi-dimensional remit in the development of disadvantaged regions. To illustrate, first, the university is understood as a space for lifelong learning for all learners, embedded in equality and access; second, the university is known for knowledge creation and transfer and cultural and community development, thus creating 'the conditions where innovation thrives' (OECD, 2007: 1); third, the university has a role in serving and shaping the community, in effect a stakeholder in the community and leading the way in international, cultural and economic networks at a local and global level; finally, the role of the university in raising the aspirations of the next generation (through outreach and community-based interventions) is recognised as a valuable long-term investment, which may pay dividends via part-time study – a less economically sound business model, nonetheless a pivotal role in the changing conceptualisation of the university as a space for public good (Calhoun, 2006).

Evidence of transformation

In the process of conducting research for this chapter a small-scale research project was undertaken to explore experiences of access, engagement and progression with 20 third-year undergraduate students attending a post-1992 institute of higher education in London. The purpose of this study was to interject theoretical ideas about transformation with real-life experiences using focus groups and eight unstructured interviews conducted over a 12-month period. The extracts captured in this discussion are all taken from one-to-one interviews. It is important to clarify that contemporary research, which aims to explore an experience of social class, cannot forge ahead without acknowledging the influence of a range of significant factors including how parents' own educational experiences play a role in determining their children's access to higher education; economic and cultural capital; and the intersections of gender, 'race', ethnicity, religion and age, which can be understood as compounding the consequences of class (Reay, 2012). The data captured below reflect how the elements mentioned above not only influence but can direct and even motivate change-making in the process of transformation in higher education. The application of personal experience in the form of the participant's voice is a well-established research tool used for and by academics. To illustrate, Mahony and Zmroczek (1997) have gathered data from leading female academics on their personal stories of social mobility in order to portray the human experience of social mobility in a reflective and analytical manner. This is captured in the words of Reay (1998: 24), who explains: 'My own experience of growing up working class has left vivid memories of my social origins imprinted on my consciousness. However, that consciousness, rooted in working class affiliation, appears increasingly to be a misfit; a sense of self both out of place and out of time.' Similarly, Skeggs (1997) reports a compelling sense of disconnection as she describes her awareness that she does not 'fit' in the social space she now occupies as an academic, stating that she feels like a 'fraud' among academic colleagues. In a further example, Rollock et al. (2011) describe how upwardly mobile Black Caribbeans struggle with a sense of their self-identity, facing the dilemma of abandoning clear markers of culture and heritage such as accent or social activities which are strongly associated with their 'Blackness'. This struggle is part of the process of fitting into white, middle class, male dominated spaces in order to gain acceptance and to facilitate progression within the context of this new space. For South Asian academics (including the author of this chapter) an element of geographical mobility is an additional expectation; the need to live and work in certain locations as a factor of social mobility challenges established and valued cultural networks, which can be understood as an experience of fracturing and dislocation. Therefore, this spatial mobility can mean moving away from cultural support systems built around family, religion and cultural practice leading to a heightened sense of alienation in their new setting as a result of their social mobility.

Case Study 1

Jamie, aged 30, has worked full-time in the catering industry throughout his degree, having left school with no formal qualifications following permanent exclusion. Jamie is the youngest of three (male) siblings, he lives in a shared flat in London and aspires to be a writer.

On early schooling experiences

I was not able to focus on anything when I was younger, always in trouble. I was even called 'trouble', like 'here comes trouble', that's what my brother, my parents, our neighbours would say. I had a lot of energy! It took me too long to calm down and I lost many years wondering why 18 year olds could get into uni and I could not. I did not care about GCSEs and that has been the reason it has taken me so long to get to this stage. It's not easy when you have bills to pay and you are fighting with yourself every day.

On being at university

It's very easy to become lost in this world, part of me is putting on a brave face, a hard face, like I know what I am doing and why I am here. But inside I dread being asked about my opinion or what I have understood, I might get kicked out, someone will realise that I am not that clever to be here. Some of the lecturers see this and try to have a quiet chat to get me to be myself, less of a clown and a popularity seeker. It's embarrassing if I'm honest, that they can see another person and I feel that I have to hide. Not sure still why I am hiding, but it makes me feel safe. Secure.

Case Study 2

Kellie is 24, a single mother and lives at home with her parents and two siblings. As a result of an abusive relationship she was unable to progress in her

A levels. She works part-time as a cleaner and in a pub and aspires to be a primary school teacher.

On early schooling experiences

I would dream about going to uni. Everyone knew it was my dream. I worked hard, but things were not straightforward at school, like failing to get in the top set and not being 'with it', you know, reading slow, can't do homework, not watching the news and stuff and how my mum and dad never had time to come to any parent's meetings. I kept on trying my best and I liked the support from my friends and teachers because they cared about my dream too.

On being at university

Everything changed when I was expecting. I had a shock to my system and I remember that feeling every day, so I drag myself out of my comfy bed and just get on with it. Dad never read a book in his life and asks me what's it all about and we laugh. They are proud of me, but I am doing it for my daughter now. Uni is very emotionally draining for me. I am always behind. They (the lecturers) think we have nothing else to do all day but read and write. I have two parents and a toddler plus two jobs to look after; I make the time. I am not that intelligent but I know about hard work.

Case Study 3

Sam is 21, an only child and works full-time in a garage. He is the full-time carer for his mother; his father left when Sam was 5 years old. Sam is on course to secure a first class honours award. In the course of his studies Sam has auditioned for the *X Factor* and has secured modelling work.

On early schooling experiences

School was tough, always having to take time off to be with my Mum, and friends not really understanding. I got used to being on my own and after a while I liked it. I love learning and this was something, the only thing, I was good at and enjoyed. Teachers said nice things to encourage me; that helped.

On being at university

No one really knows you at uni so you can escape in a lecture and just get on with opening your mind and being a student. I had some happy times, pushing myself to get higher marks, to think carefully about every spare minute and making the best of all this booky stuff. I loved it. I only had one friend at uni, we shared notes, never socialised outside. I prefer private people so we got on. Lecturers pushed me, too. They made a big difference, for some reason they cared about me.

Analysis of the data

There are some common themes to all three case studies including first, the experience of going to study somewhere where they feel they can fit in and have a sense of security, described by Crozier et al. (2008) as cultivating belonging. This is a point of interest, as both Sam and Kellie revealed that they did not seek friendship as part of their higher education experience. Second, the understanding that prior educational experiences effectively excluded some students from access to elite universities cemented the notion that to feel part of an institute would be a factor in retention and engagement. Thirdly, the level of support was a factor, as explored by Purcell et al. (2009), where a lack of understanding of the many other responsibilities and concerns faced by some students constitutes a constant barrier to progression, as Kellie demonstrates: 'They [the lecturers] think we have nothing else to do all day but read and write. I have two parents and a toddler plus two jobs to look after; I make the time.' Finally, the different experiences of 'fitting in' is solidified as a key element in the higher education experience (Reay et al., 2010), which can range from self-exclusion (Sam's experience) to entering the popularity stakes (Jamie's experience). The commonality of the experience that higher education is for some and not others strikes at the heart of the principle of equality, noting that embedded structures are essentially unfair (Dyson et al., 2010) throughout the education system and that the case studies captured in this chapter are *in spite of* and not because of the education they encountered as individuals.

Implicit in the transformation of the case study participants was the educational experiences of their parents and also early schooling, though for very differing reasons. The impact of low teacher expectations and labelling effectively resulted in Jamie's personal struggles for acceptance, evident in research conducted by DCSF, showing that aspects of primary and secondary socialisation become spaces where the seeds of a culture of self-exclusion are planted:

Children living in deprived communities face a cultural barrier which is in many ways a bigger barrier than material poverty. It is the cultural barrier of low aspirations and scepticism about education, the feeling that education is by and for other people, and likely to let one down. (DCSF, 2009: 2)

The overlapping influences of individual aspirations and parental educational experiences are also significant factors in the transformation experiences as explored by Bauman (2005), who argues that aspiration can nurture a positive work ethic and a belief in meritocracy whereby individuals are encouraged to believe that hard work combined with talent will (at some point) lead to economic rewards. Kellie embodies this belief, as her daughter motivates her to 'drag myself out of my comfy bed and just get on with it'. Bauman's work explores how those individuals who do not invest in this positive work ethic are, in effect, a failure in the system; therefore, to avoid this scenario there is a *need* to recontextualise poverty as a primarily cultural problem; he describes this as a poverty of aspiration. Moreover, the origins of this poverty of aspiration are in parental educational experiences reported as 'unmotivated, unambitious and underachieving' (Reay et al., 2010: 24): in effect a 'deficit discourses' (Francis and Hey, 2009) that shines a spotlight on the individual (and their parental influence) and away from societal economic and social inequalities. To illustrate, a limited knowledge of the welfare system and the absence of another adult for support meant that Sam was the sole carer for his mother from an early age, leading to the emotive disclosure 'School was tough, always having to take time'. In a further illustration, Jamie – as a consequence of his own disrupted schooling, labelling and lack of parental support – questioned even his right to be at university. This is despite the fact that he had met the admission requirements and was a final year student. So compelling is his lack of self-confidence in his own ability, as he explains: 'I might get kicked out, someone will realise that I am not that clever to be here', that the staying power of entrenched ideas of working class failure are indeed difficult to unhinge, culminating in a culture of fear (Jackson, 2010) and of failure. The barriers facing working class students, such as social and cultural capital are discussed in Chapter 5 in the context of differing educational experiences; however, it is important to note at this point that student transformation in higher education can be a fragile state, which is subject to careful nurturing and alongside pastoral and welfare support strategies. The case studies captured in this chapter are about students navigating their own academic career trajectories and in doing so they are transforming their lives based on their experiences of higher education and the opportunities and choices that become available to them as a consequence of their higher education.

Chapter summary

In this chapter a discussion about what transformation means in the wider context of higher education frames the discussion of economic and cultural transformation, including an assessment of interventions that have set out to facilitate transformation by closing the social gap in educational attainment. The chapter captured student voice in the inclusion of data based on the experiences of students at a post-1992 institute of higher education, which reflected a myriad of factors impacting on their access and engagement.

References

Ball, S. (2008) *The Education Debate*. Bristol: Policy Press.

Bauman, Z. (2005) *Work, Consumerism and the New Poor* (second edition). Maidenhead: Open University Press.

Calhoun, C. (2006) 'The university and the public good', *Thesis Eleven*, 84: 7–43.

Callendar, C. (2012) 'FutureTrack: Part time higher education students. A report to the Higher Education Careers Services Unit (HECSU)'. London: National Institute of Economic and Social Research.

Castells, M. (2001) 'Universities as dynamic systems of contradictory functions', in J. Muller et al. (eds), *Challenges of globalisation: South African debates with Manuel Castells*. Cape Town: Maskew Miller Longman, 206–23.

Chapman, C., Mongon, D., Muijs, D., William, J., Pampaka, M., Wakefield, D. and Weiner, S. (2010) 'Full evaluation on the Extra Mile'. London: Department for Education. Available at: www.gov.uk/government/uploads/system/uploads/attachment_data/file/181534/DFE-RR133.pdf (accessed 15 January 2015).

Chowdry, H. (2010) 'Widening participation in higher education: Analysis using linked administrative data', Institute for Fiscal Studies Working Paper W10/04. London: Institute for Fiscal Studies.

Crozier, G., Reay, D. and Clayton, J. (2008) 'Different strokes for different folks: Diverse students in diverse institutions', *Research Papers in Education*, 23(2): 167–77.

Department for Business, Innovation and Skills (2011) 'Higher education: Students at the heart of the system', Cm 8122. London: Stationery Office.

Department for Children, Schools and Families Publications (DCSF) (2009) 'The Extra Mile: How schools succeed in raising aspirations in deprived communities'. Nottingham: Department for Children, Schools and Families Publications.

Department for Education (2010) 'The Extra Mile Project'. Available at: www.education.gov.uk/schools/leadership/schoolperformance/pedagogyandpractice/a0058430/the-extra-mile-project (accessed 15 January 2015).

Dyson, A., Goldrick, S., Jones, L. and Kerr, K. (2010) 'Equity in education: Creating a fairer education system'. Manchester: Centre for Equity in Education, University of Manchester.

Francis, B. and Hey, V. (2009) 'Talking back to power: snowballs in hell and the imperative of insisting on structural explanations', *Gender and Education*, 21(2): 225–32.

Futureversity (2010) Annual Report 2009–2010. Available at: http://futureversity.org/content/415/Annual-reports (accessed 15 January 2015).

Her Majesty's Government (2011) 'Opening doors, breaking barriers: A strategy for social mobility'. London: Cabinet Office.

Higher Education Funding Council for England (2014) 'Higher education in England 2014: Key facts'. London: HEFCE.

Higher Education Funding Council for England (2010) 'Trends in young participation for England'. London: HEFCE.

Kerr, K. and West, M. (2010) (eds) 'BERA Insight: Schools and social inequality'. London: BERA.

Lindley, J. and Machin, S. (2013) 'The postgraduate premium: Revisiting trends in social mobility and educational inequalities in Britain and America'. Available at: www.suttontrust.com/wp-content/uploads/2013/02/Postgraduate-Premium-Report.pdf (accessed 15 January 2015).

Hutchings, M., Maylor, U., Mendick, H., Menter, I. and Smart, S. (2006) 'An evaluation of innovative approaches to teacher training on the Teach First programme'. London: Training and Development Agency.

Jackson, C. (2010) 'Fear in education', *Educational Review*, 62(1): 39–52.

Mahony, P. and Zmroczek, C. (1997) *Class Matters: Working Class Women's Perspectives on Social Class*. London: Taylor and Francis.

National Audit Office (2008) *Widening Participation in Higher Education*. London, The Stationery Office.

Organisation for Economic Co-operation and Development (2007) 'Higher education and regions', Policy Brief, September 2007. Paris: OECD.

Purcell, K., Elias, P., Atfield, G., Behle, H. and Ellison, R., with Hughes, C., Livanos, I. and Tzanakou, C. (2009) 'Plans, aspirations and realities: taking stock of higher education and career choices one year on'. Coventry: Higher Education Career Services Unit (HECSU) and Warwick Institute for Employment Research.

Reay, D. (1998) '"Always knowing" and "never being sure": institutional and familial habituses and higher education choice', *Journal of Education Policy*, 13(4), 519–29.

Reay, D. (2011) 'Schooling for democracy: A common school and a common university? A response to "Schooling for democracy"', *Democracy and Education*, 19(1): Article 6.

Reay, D. (2012) 'Researching class in higher education', British Educational Research Association online resource. Available at: www.bera.ac.uk. (accessed 15 January 2015).

Reay, D., Crozier, G. and Clayton, J. (2010) '"Fitting in" and "standing out": working-class students in UK higher education', *British Educational Research Journal*, 32(1): 1–19.

Rollock, N., Gillborn, D., Ball, S. and Vincent, C. (2011) 'Public identities of the Black middle classes: managing race in public spaces', *Sociology*, 45(6): 1078–93.

Silver, H. (2007) 'Higher education and social change: Purpose in pursuit?' *History of Education*, 36(4–5), 535–50.

Skeggs, B. (1997) *Formations of Class and Gender*. London: SAGE.

Tomlinson, S. (2005) *Education in a Post Welfare Society*. London: Routledge.

Watson, D. (2008) 'The university in the modern world: Ten lessons of civic and community engagement', *Education, Citizenship and Social Justice*, 3(1): 43–55.

Williams, R. and Cochrane, A. (2010) 'The role of higher education in social and cultural transformation'. London: Centre for Higher Education Research and Information, The Open University.

INDEX